THE SINO-RUSSIAN CHALLENGE
TO THE WORLD ORDER

THE SINO-RUSSIAN CHALLENGE TO THE WORLD ORDER

NATIONAL IDENTITIES, BILATERAL RELATIONS, AND EAST VERSUS WEST IN THE 2010s

GILBERT ROZMAN

Woodrow Wilson Center Press
WASHINGTON, D.C.

Stanford University Press
STANFORD, CALIFORNIA

EDITORIAL OFFICES
Woodrow Wilson Center Press
Woodrow Wilson International Center for Scholars
One Woodrow Wilson Plaza
1300 Pennsylvania Avenue, NW
Washington, DC 20004-3027
www.wilsoncenter.org

ORDER FROM
Stanford University Press
Chicago Distribution Center
11030 South Langley Avenue
Chicago, IL 60628-3830
Telephone: 800-621-2736; 773-568-1550
www.sup.org

Library of Congress Cataloging-in-Publication Data

Rozman, Gilbert, author.
  The Sino-Russian challenge to the world order : national identities, bilateral
relations, and East versus West in the 2010s / Gilbert Rozman.
      pages cm
Includes bibliographical references and index.
ISBN 978-0-8047-9101-4 (hardback)
  1. Russia (Federation)—Foreign relations—China. 2. China—Foreign relations—
Russia (Federation). 3. Nationalism and communism—Russia (Federation).
4. Nationalism and communism—China. 5. National characteristics, Russian.
6. National characteristics, Chinese. I. Title.
  DK68.7.C5R69 2014
  327.47051—dc23
                                                                    2013050105

Wilson Center

THE WILSON CENTER, chartered by Congress as the official memorial to President Woodrow Wilson, is the nation's key nonpartisan policy forum for tackling global issues through independent research and open dialogue to inform actionable ideas for Congress, the Administration, and the broader policy community.

Conclusions or opinions expressed in Center publications and programs are those of the authors and speakers and do not necessarily reflect the views of the Center staff, fellows, trustees, advisory groups, or any individuals or organizations that provide financial support to the Center.

Please visit us online at www.wilsoncenter.org.

CONTENTS

ACKNOWLEDGMENTS

This is the third and final publication in the book series on national identities and international relations. All three volumes cover China, shedding light on different aspects of its national identity seen from a comparative perspective and on its foreign policy viewed through the lens of national identity gaps. Whereas the earlier books consider China vis-à-vis Japan and South Korea, this book explores similarities and differences between China and Russia. It revisits the once-familiar field of comparative communism and takes a fresh look at the extreme case of a national identity gap driving bilateral relations during the Sino-Soviet split. The final two chapters focus on Sino-Russian relations, turning the identity lens on their post–Cold War partnership while considering the future impact of their identity gap.

Again, I want to express my gratitude to the Princeton Institute of International and Regional Studies and the Mercer Fund of the East Asian Studies Program for supporting the seminars serving the entire project and an exploratory seminar launching this volume. I am especially appreciative to the Woodrow Wilson International Center for Scholars for my residence in 2010–11, when I conducted much of the research, and to Joe Brinley, director of its press, for supporting this endeavor. I continued the research and writing in two final semesters at Princeton, where I had the opportunity to teach a course covering both strategic thought and national identity in Asia, in which many new ideas coalesced. Although the field of sociology has generally moved away from this type of analysis, I have been fortunate to be able to combine sociology and international relations in my courses, cognizant of the fact that national identity has a powerful effect on foreign policy. In finishing this third book, I benefited greatly from comments by two anonymous outside readers, most of all in reworking the balance between transitional and enduring national identity.

Gilbert Rozman
September 2013

THE SINO-RUSSIAN CHALLENGE
TO THE WORLD ORDER

INTRODUCTION:

NATIONAL IDENTITY STUDIES AND COMMUNISM

Two contrasting images of Sino–Russian relations vie for acceptance. On one hand, talk of a looming "de facto alliance" between China and Russia and articles in Chinese and Russian debating the merits of forging a "military alliance" drew close attention in 2013.[1] This is not so surprising if we recognize that striking parallels exist in the ways in which presidents Xi Jinping and Vladimir Putin, both energized with long terms in office ahead of them, were envisioning the resurgence of their countries domestically and internationally. On the other hand, Xi toured Central Asia in September 2013 offering bountiful largesse while calling for a Silk Road Economic Belt, which was at odds with Putin's aggressive push for a Eurasian Union. This clash indicates the importance of Sinocentrism and Russocentrism as rising themes in national identity that pose a threat to bilateral relations. Our challenge is to make sense of the national identities driving these two states closer together for two decades, but also threatening to divide them in the years ahead.

This book has two readily recognizable objectives: to compare China and Russia; and to assess their bilateral relationship. It also has three other objectives that will be clear on further examination: to extend and deepen the framework of national identity studies and its application to national identity gaps between pairs of states; to revive and redirect comparative communist studies beyond the legacy left since traditional communism was replaced; and to clarify and develop an approach to international relations that centers on national identities rather than on national interests. To realize this range of objectives, the book presents a wide-ranging historical comparison and review of bilateral relations, while concentrating on developments since the end of the Cold War, especially on how identity is being reconstructed in the decade of the 2010s and how these parallel efforts are having an impact on Sino-Russian relations.

The leaderships of Hu Jintao, Xi Jinping, and Vladimir Putin have been determined to forge a lasting national identity in support of regime legitimacy, and they have found convenient building blocks in the legacy of communism combined with elements of earlier national identity. What they are constructing, in line with trends visible in the period just after the end of the Cold War and reinforced by conditions present in the 2010s, has substantial domestic appeal, but that does not mean there exists some inherent identity that dictates the destiny of a country. Although the communist legacy leads in one direction, there are different currents of premodern history, of a modernizing society, and of a globalizing world that could coalesce into a contrasting outcome. The concept of national identity signifies something deeply embedded in the way the country has evolved and can lead to sober awareness of the challenges to be faced if it is to be dislodged.

National identity studies are concerned with what makes a country distinct and how it presents itself to showcase its distinctiveness. In two earlier books, I have compared the identities of China, Japan, and South Korea in the context of an East Asian National Identity Syndrome (EANIS) and have scrutinized identity gaps and their impact on bilateral relations between these countries as well as between China and the United States.[2] Missing in these approaches to China is a comparative perspective on communist great powers. Arguably, the most far-reaching attempts ever made to alter national identity were Stalinism and Maoism. Certainly, the most conspicuous case of a national identity gap reshaping international relations was the Sino-Soviet split. In the post–Cold War decades, great uncertainty has shadowed efforts to explain how Chinese and Russian national identities are evolving, with problematic consequences for the international community. By turning to comparisons and assessments of the changing Sino-Russian identity gap, I can apply the frameworks introduced in these prior books and further demonstrate the utility of the national identity perspective.

In January 2012, Chinese president Hu Jintao and Russia's former and future president, Vladimir Putin, reinforced by Russian foreign minister Sergei Lavrov, successively excoriated the United States for its cultural threat to their countries and its supposed plots in countries such as Iran, Syria, and North Korea to provoke discontent, regime change, or revolution in support of "Western values."[3] US ambassadors Michael McFaul in Russia and Gary Locke in China, who arrived with impeccable credentials as advocates of expanded engagement, were vilified in the media of their host nations as retrograde figures who had to be viewed with great suspicion. On Channel One just days after his arrival in Moscow, McFaul was accused of fomenting revolution, while, by contrast, Lavrov trumpeted Sino-Russian ties as "the highest in the history of our bilateral relationship."[4] The overlapping assault on US national identity and praise for shared values between China and Russia are no coincidence. As Xi Jinping made the "China Dream" his centerpiece and Putin whipped up further resentment of the West, Sino-Russian relations continued to draw closer. This can be well understood by analyzing the national identity legacy of traditional communism and its impact on the Sino-Russian national identity gap and the course of bilateral relations.

Was communism a fleeting influence in the long history of China and Russia? After all, twenty-five years after the collapse of the socialist bloc, its ideology of class struggle, world revolution, and autarchic development antithetical to market integration into a global economy is but a distant memory to most. Eastern European states, once subsumed by communism, have shed this legacy in a manner in keeping with assumptions of an alien intrusion having a passing effect. Yet this book reasons that in the heartlands of Stalinism and Maoism, communism is capable of entangling itself not just like some sort of vine wrapped around the trunk of the established civilization but deep within the trunk itself, reshaping the existing civilization and shooting out branches even as elements of the earlier ideology dried up, fell down, and seemingly left the branches bare and ready for fresh foliage.

Understanding how communism has shaped the continued evolution of national identity in both China and Russia and also how their identities have become entwined in bilateral relations that are affecting joint efforts to reshape international relations is the challenge at hand.

Highlighting this pairing, however, is not the same as arguing that because these two countries were once traditional communist states and are now inclined to authoritarianism, they must be close in national identity. Similarities in the legacy of communism shape their identities, but there are far-reaching differences in other aspects of their identities that are noted in the pages that follow and were extensively covered for China in the two books noted above.

Parallel developments in national identity also leave unclear prospects for bilateral relations. The current upsurge in Chinese national identity—which is associated with narrow notions of the China Dream, tightening censorship over international identity themes, and Xi's push for Silk Road regionalism—puts in jeopardy the Eurasian Union, which Putin keeps aggressively pursuing with hopes of solidifying Russia's own civilizational sphere. This juxtaposition sows the seeds of a widening identity gap, but below I delineate counterbalancing forces and the reality that the main driving forces for intensified identity still draw these states closer.

A FRAMEWORK FOR ANALYZING NATIONAL IDENTITIES

In the previous two volumes, I applied a six-dimensional framework and then estimated national identity gaps in dyadic relations. This volume applies the same framework, scrutinizing Sino-Soviet and Sino-Russian relations through the prism of a national identity gap. Also, it introduces the notion of a national identity transition to assess the abrupt shift from one approach to identity to another. The transition of the 1980s to the 2010s offers a time frame sufficient to evaluate the extension of the communist legacy, but a subsequent transition may lead in a different direction.

National identity is many things. It is a view contrasting an idealized version of what exists in one's own country with what is usually a stereotyped image of the outside world, especially countries deemed most significant for their differences. It is a narrative driven by a portion of the political elite, seeking media affirmation and academic consensus, and succeeding in this endeavor when leaders give their firm support and combine censorship with personnel policies to shape the outcome. If it is often hard to determine if new policy directions refocus identity rhetoric or vice versa, there generally is a close association between national identity and policy.

Three objections to this manner of determining national identity may well be voiced. First, in these countries of considerable censorship and top-down control of rhetoric about identity themes, some may argue that the current narrative should be treated skeptically. After all, it is manipulated to shape public opinion. Critics deny any national identity validity to the top-down, self-serving framework of the ruling elite, as if in the wake of communist identity there is no lasting legacy.[5] But all signs point to the power of this dominant narrative even if it is often embraced skeptically, especially by portions of the urban, intellectual community. Second, some assume an alternative view of national identity among those whose views are less visible, but specifying an alternative with a widespread following and a serious chance of gaining dominance is difficult to do, given the sparse evidence on its behalf. One finds a vague appeal to the people, not the state, and to the future, not the past.[6] Finally, in writing about the present there is a danger of extrapolating it, as if the endpoint of history has arrived, particularly because adjustments in national identity have reinforced trends from recent historical eras. The question of whether a new transition in identity will be discernable is addressed briefly in chapter 5.

The framework applied in this book covers ideology; history; a combination of political, economic, and cultural identity; an indicator of identity for how a state is organized internally; identity centered on international relations; and a measure of the intensity of identity. National identity is treated as a composite of all six of these dimensions, which cover the gambit of what is claimed to be superior about one's country. The evidence for what constitutes national identity comes from a wide array of both official statements and publications, ranging from newspapers to academic tracts. In sources that shed light on the six dimensions, we find evidence about the existing national identity. It is constructed from above by leaders keen on shaping opinion by means of media control and concerted construction of a supportive narrative. It is manipulated for a purpose, is reconstructed over time, and may be removed from the aspirations of the most educated citizens—but it often exerts a powerful impact.

The starting point for treating China and Russia together is an understanding that these countries, which perceived themselves as the true center of communism and considered it their messianic mission to inculcate this ideology unwaveringly at home and spread it incessantly abroad, have persistently sought to transform their national identities. Comparing the two behemoths of communism, we seek to discern the legacy of the communist era and its connection to their current identities, distinguishing the six separate dimensions of identity.

THE COMMUNIST IMPRINT IN RUSSIA AND CHINA

Communism is, arguably, the most powerful transformative agent of national identity ever to spread through the world—but not in the manner that its founders claimed. Because identities at all levels are interconnected, communism's assault on every level of identity and failure to sustain its ideal of a classless, international identity results in national identities growing more intense and unbalanced. The hypertrophied state, as the exclusive object of esteem (along with the Communist Party, whose leadership is considered to be reflected by the state), gives leaders extraordinary power to manipulate individual attitudes and aspirations. Yet this does not occur in a vacuum, because national identity consists of many dimensions that may conflict, while various levels of identity manage to regain some force and require timely adjustments to overall identity. Stubborn resistance to urgently needed changes means that however powerful the impact of communism, it repeatedly finds that its control of the national identity narrative is incomplete. The history of China and Russia following the Cold War is one of vigorous efforts to reconstruct national identity, capitalizing on the legacy of communism while at the same time coping with complex new forces. Sowing the seeds of its own transformation, communism stresses national identity in ways that are unsustainable but indelible in the two great powers it has spawned. National identity will inevitably keep changing, but its nucleus and trajectory must be understood if we are to gain a solid grasp of what lies ahead.

Russian national identity faced thirty-six years of reshaping by Vladimir Lenin and Josef Stalin and—despite the interludes of Nikita Khrushchev and Mikhail Gorbachev—the deep imprint of Leonid Brezhnev. Although Boris Yeltsin strove to identify some clear "Russian idea," it was Vladimir Putin who synthesized what was left of the communist identity with revived elements of precommunist identity and new features reflecting the international environment. Although history does not stop with Putin, as others can draw on the past differently, the Putin synthesis is not going to be easy to dislodge. That more than half of Russian respondents view Brezhnev, Lenin, and Stalin in a positive manner, in contrast to the fewer than one-quarter who feel that way about either Gorbachev or Yeltsin, is testimony to Putin's synthesis of national identity.[7]

Chinese national identity faced a challenge inspired by the same Marxist-Leninist ideology, as Mao Zedong set the agenda to steer identity on a new path. Under Hu Jintao and Xi Jinping, positive thinking about Mao, the history of the Communist Party, and ideology in general are making a comeback, as seen in the Communist Party Central Committee's document "Concerning the Situation in the Ideological Sphere," which was issued in May 2013. Chinese leaders are blaming the collapse of the Soviet Union on "political ill-discipline and ideological laxity" and are charging that the theories advocated by the West pose a similar danger to China, even as they are boosting support on the left with ideology and are initiating new economic reforms with broader appeal.[8]

China and Russia have in common histories as great powers that regarded themselves as the centers of a civilization, as communist powers that claimed to be the leading force in spreading this revolutionary doctrine around the world, and as states that starting in the 1990s struggled with the challenge of reconstructing national identity in the wake of serious challenges to its outdated nature in a globalizing world. More than China, Russia found its reconstruction in doubt. Earlier than Russia, and with a more deliberate strategy, China settled on a new configuration of national identity with clarifications about troubled elements of its past. By the end of the 2000s, the identity of each country had been reconstructed, not without further contestation, but in a manner indicative of further staying power, based on elite continuity. In the mid-2010s, Putin and Xi are showing determination to intensify these identities.

A reform outlook is not inconceivable, given the histories of China and Russia. First, the heritage of China should be recognized as both reform and imperial Confucianism.[9] The latter strain was intensified during the Yuan, Ming, and Qing dynasties. After a contested interlude, communism reinforced elements of the imperial Confucian identity, undercutting the already-weakened reform identity, despite support for it from international influences. Given the communist legacy, a renewal of contestation in the 1980s was unlikely to tip the balance to reform; but this does not mean, as traditional communism recedes, that modernization and globalization will not result in a second transition with a different balance. Similarly, the heritage of Russia is widely recognized to be both Westernization and Slavophilism. Communism again skewed the balance, leaving reform forces in a stronger position than in China but still disadvantaged in the struggle, primarily within the political elite, starting in the 1980s. As Putin attempts to shift the balance further in the direction of the communist legacy mixed with Slavophilism, he risks accelerating a second transition, bringing other elements of Russia's tradition to the fore. This book's aim is to explain how the traditional communist legacy prevailed in the first post–Cold War transition and its impact on Sino-Russian relations. It is not meant to suggest that the resultant national identity will persist as the destiny of these states.

National identity also fails to be destiny in another respect. It is constructed to shape policy debates and mobilize the public, often with the intention of obstructing compromise, pragmatism, and more reform-oriented interpretations of identity. In China and Russia, it became a tool in the hands of the mainstream in the leadership to turn the country away from feared integration into the international community led by the United States, apart from agreed-on economic cooperation. This endeavor works best when the state has the resources to keep many people focused on materialism and to reward the political elite generously, stifling divisions. Other circumstances are likely to lead to more questioning and more divisions at the top. If pragmatism becomes more imperative, then identity assumptions will be doubted. In this process, a new transition away from the prevailing syndrome may begin. Yet, for the immediate future, the existing identity syndrome with its various ramifications must preoccupy us.

THE CHRONOLOGICAL COVERAGE—PLAN OF THE BOOK

When observers focus on national identities in China and Russia, they point to precommunist forces that had regained popularity by the 2010s—respectively, a Confucian, Sinocentric view; and a tsarist, Russocentric view. These worldviews are consequential, but it is misleading to concentrate on them to the exclusion of deeply engrained thinking in the twentieth century, which has only been sporadically and, usually, superficially challenged following its heyday. Through a review of how identities have evolved in each state, chapter 1 clarifies the linkages between the precommunist era and the years when communism took shape and reached an extreme as Stalinism and Maoism.

After assessing the shared legacy of communism as it grew more adamant in its claims, in chapter 2 I turn to the periods of reduced radicalism and lowered intensity, symbolized by the leadership of Mikhail Gorbachev and Deng Xiaoping. Although coverage of Russia puts Khrushchev and Brezhnev into the narrative, there is no doubting that the decisive figures in transforming national identity after Stalin and Mao were the two leaders best known as reformers. A comparative approach again highlights what is similar and different from the perspective of national identity transformation. Condensing into one decade what Russia experienced over three decades and then accel-erated in just a six-year whirlwind of changes, China reached the post–Cold War period with its national identity in a parallel state of transformation to Russia's in shedding the Soviet Union, which has often been overlooked when attention centers on contrasts.

Chapters 3 and 4 follow a similar track in evaluating national iden-tity in Russia and China since the 1990s. The appeal of Gorbachev and Deng to foreign audiences was not just that each changed the course of his nation's domestic system and foreign policy but also that both raised expectations that the worldview that had long been closely associated with communism would be expunged. Replacing an image of two systems locked in mortal combat with whiffs of a single international community working together to solve problems and achieve prosperity, they altered the identity thrust of their country and opened the way to numerous changes. However, it proved unjusti-fied to assume that they had set in motion an unstoppable process of moving away from the national identities long closely associated with communism. In China, the notion of "one world" was only narrowly tolerated, and in Russia it was the theme of one leadership group that resonated poorly with successive leaders.

Slogans proposed by Deng and Gorbachev prioritized stability, devel-opment, cooperation, and pragmatism. The optimism that their impact would be irreversible stemmed from three sources: (1) the assump-tion that communism is nothing more than an ideology imposed from above rather than part of a worldview deeply embedded in popular thinking, and especially in the mindset of the elite; (2) the expectation that universal values would be spread without serious encumbrance given the spread of capitalism and the relaxation of certain coercive controls and censorship; and (3) the theory predicting convergence in modernization or globalization, as countries draw closer together in structure and thinking. Missing from this hopeful anticipation was a grasp of the identities that were embedded in communism and are capable of surviving leadership that was wavering for a time, along with later downswings and upswings in optimism. In the aftermath of the two reform leaders, chapters 3 and 4 show how national identity was reconstructed, especially under Vladimir Putin and both Hu Jintao and Xi Jinping, as they gave new content to trends that had begun earlier.

In October 2011, the Chinese Communist Party devoted a plenary session to strengthening cultural security, explaining that culture is increasingly important to comprehensive national power. Identifying the state as the unit of cultural identity and national unity as critical to competitiveness, the session was concerned about threats from the Internet to the state's narrative on culture and its promulgation of "socialist core values," calling for greater cultural management.[10] In 2012, following his reelection, Putin reasserted national identity themes that had lapsed somewhat under Dmitry Medvedev's tenure as president. The top-down agenda for national identity was reaffirmed. As leaders eligible to stay in power until the 2020s established their power in 2012, the identity legacy was clearly reaffirmed as a matter of life or death for a civilization that was reportedly subjected to propaganda attacks seeking to force an alien system of values on it and was fully obliged to compete fiercely for cultural self-awareness.[11] As Xi Jinping solidified his hold on power, he placed even more weight on identity. In May 2013, a secret directive called the "seven-nos" policy instructed teachers to not mention sensitive identity themes, including universal values, the historic errors of the Communist Party, and civil society.[12] The screws were tightening on identity heresy.

The bravado of both Chinese and Russians was intensifying as Xi and Putin consolidated their leadership positions. In March 2013, Putin called for a "canonical version of our history for the sake of national unity."[13] At the same time, the tone in China, which in early 2011 had seemed to warn against hubris, shifted to assertions that an era of "self-confidence" had dawned, touting the superiority of the Chinese model, politically and culturally as well as economically, and the fading of the West as a model.[14] As both press for an intensification of, or spike in, national identity, at least for now they have set aside grievances toward each other in favor of the parallel targeting of others.

Coupled with assessments of the legacy through the periods of Deng and Gorbachev in chapter 2 and then separate coverage of the post–Cold War era in each country in chapters 3 and 4, chapter 1 launches the comparative analysis of national identity that culminates in what chapter 5 labels the Communist Great Power (Transition 1) National Identity Syndrome, or CGP (T1) NIS, a complementary notion to the EANIS. With the label "CGP," I isolate the communist great powers, of which there were only two. The study of China and Russia starts from a recognition that we need a specific label to separate them, with their attendant claims to be the center of the movement from other states under Communist Party rule. The label "NIS," as in the case of the EANIS, serves as shorthand for a national identity syndrome, a distinctive pattern of identity found through comparative analysis. Finally, by using the label "T1," I make clear that in the first transition, lasting so far for about one generation, the communist legacy has had an impact that we should examine, regardless of what may happen in a second transition, which could be called T2. This book does not take us into T2; it is a study of the impact of the legacy on T1.

THE IMPACT OF IDENTITIES ON INTERNATIONAL RELATIONS

On the basis of a review of Chinese and Russian sources, I argue that national identity in the two states is heavily indebted to the legacy of communism and serves the following purposes: (1) It draws China and Russia close together and, even as national interests increasingly diverge, remains a force for partnership; (2) it puts emphasis on the US and Western threat to the civilizations of these states, making cooperation with the international community difficult; and (3) it empowers states such as North Korea, which benefit from favorable interpretations of their conflicts with the United States and the urgency of transforming the existing international system. This book begins with comparisons and proceeds to the external impact of the two national identities.

Drawing on an image of Deng Xiaoping, the pragmatist, or Vladimir Putin, the realist, observers long stressed a lack of ideology in foreign policy decision-making in the two states. If national interests after the Cold War had been determinative, would Sino-Russian relations have followed the same trajectory? This question is raised in chapter 7, which treats the Sino-Russian relationship after the Cold War from an identity perspective. Before that, chapter 6 looks to the legacy of the Sino-Soviet split and the impact of identities on the troubled pace of normalization during the critical 1980s. Whether in the 1950s alliance, the split over two decades, the ups and downs of the 1980s, or the special relationship developed since the Cold War, national identities play a critical role. The future of the relationship depends no less on their evolution.

The Sino-Soviet national identity gap was much smaller than had been thought from the 1960s to the 1980s. An obsession with the ideological dimension in the two states obscured identity in other dimensions. In the 1990s, when many thought that the gap between China, following its repression of the Tiananmen Square demonstrators, and Russia, energized by Boris Yeltsin's resistance to the attempted putsch, had been widening sharply, in accord with the communism-versus-democracy dichotomy, the leaders of the two states discovered that it was actually quite narrow. The Sino-Russian strategic partnership of 1996 revealed a meeting of the minds with far-ranging implications. Despite some disagreement on particular policies, this shared understanding is not challenged.

Sino-Russian relations, arguably, are strengthened to the extent that their national identity gap narrows, which occurs if a common threat to legitimacy intensifies. This happened in the mid-1990s, with US triumphalism; in 1999, with the humanitarian use of NATO in ousting President Slobodan Milošević of Serbia after months of bombing to protect the people of Kosovo from his depredations, enabling their independence; and in 2011, with the Arab Spring and the NATO-led, UN Security Council–authorized intervention in Libya—which was used, to China and Russia's dismay, to bring about Muammar Qaddafi's overthrow. In the years 2012–13, joint opposition to US pressure on the Syrian regime, mired in a civil war, reinforced a sense of shared thinking, as did accusations, however far from the truth, about why pressure was being applied to Iran and North Korea. Over these years, there has been no countervailing force, widening their identity gap. Although the conclusions offered in chapter 7 do not suggest a shared sense of identity ahead or a revival of a common ideology, a narrow identity gap at a time when other national identity gaps are widening suits closer bilateral relations.

COMMUNISM'S IMPACT ON THE SIX DIMENSIONS OF NATIONAL IDENTITY

The conventional framework for interpreting communist identity is simplistic. Contrasting totalitarianism as the essence of prior communist identity with democracy as the end point of transformation proves inadequate. Using a six-dimensional analysis allows for consideration of diverse elements linked to a nation's identity. Democracy may be part of national identity, but to appreciate the shift away from totalitarianism requires a broad understanding of the dimensions of identity that shape its prospects. An observation based on the two prior books in this series is that it is unrealistic to expect to change one dimension of identity without a consideration of how other dimensions are being changed. Not only democracy but also political changes in general proceed in the context of an overall identity shift, which occurs in stages.

Each of the six dimensions—ideological, temporal, sectoral, vertical, horizontal, and intensity—acquires distinctive meaning under the impact of communism, with ideology in the forefront. Communism also raises the intensity of national identity and imposes its framework on narratives about the past (temporal identity), the main sectors of life (economic, political, and cultural), the domestic order (vertical identity), and the international order (horizontal identity). Why does it exert such a strong impact? The ideological dimension is obviously affected because this is the front line of its obsession with substituting its claims to omniscience. In place of conservative or progressive ideologies with past appeal, it insists on the universal validity of the gospel according to Marx, Lenin, Stalin, Mao, or the current leadership—subject to the new views of the present leaders. The temporal dimension is another preoccupation of communist leaders because they claim unilinear evolution from feudalism to capitalism to socialism and finally communism, fending off doubt with elaborate explanations of how transitions from one stage to another must occur. History is an obsession in Marx' social class analysis, and remains a preoccupation. Treating the sectoral dimension, communists stress the superiority of democratic centralism, a command economy, or proletarian class consciousness, no matter how those concepts may be shifting over time. The political and economic systems are deemed superior, as is their cultural impact. Nothing is more central to party boosters than claims to a unique vertical dimension based on the top-down organization of society in opposition to the supposedly class-based society in capitalist states. As for the horizontal dimension, they divide the world into irreconcilable blocs, although at some points allowing for peaceful coexistence. Communists are keen to arouse high intensity around national identity, countering both apathy and disbelief by insisting that party members and the masses take a fervent emotional stance in favor of the prescribed identity in all its dimensions. All dimensions have a unique profile.

The degree of vulnerability of the old national identity and the prospects for a new identity are subjects for comparative analysis. In the case of the ideological or temporal dimensions, the transition from old to new depends on new evaluations of the founding fathers Lenin and Stalin in the case of Russia (heir to the Soviet Union) and Mao in the case of China. To seriously question the role of the tyrannical figure whose presence towers over the nation's communist history is to steer matters toward a sharp break with the old identity. On the vertical or horizontal dimension, similar significance holds for the evaluation of the United States and its model order. To accept it on national identity terms for the purposes of convergence and mutual trust is to turn fundamentally from the old identity. Holding the line against tendencies to rethink these critical elements of the previous identity depends on finding different elements that can be reinforced while simultaneously reconstructing identity with additional themes that substitute for those losing credibility during the transition.

Communist regimes see existential threats both at home and abroad. Given their prism of class struggle, they perceive the development of civil society as proof of the emergence of a social class challenge to the preferred amalgam of state officials and "revolutionary classes." Yet, even after talk of class conflict fades, the notion of civil society's resistance to the state monopoly on identity again becomes anathema. Also, based on their critique of the United States and its allies, successor regimes regard the spread of what many now call "soft power" from the West as subversive of their own power. The danger is not limited to discussions of human rights, democracy, or other themes that point to current comparisons; also vital to communist notions of legitimacy is a historical worldview in opposition to the periodization prevalent in the West, applauding the Enlightenment and the rise of individualism buttressed by institutions that support checks and balances. Although the ideological confrontation of socialism and capitalism is no longer a focus, the impression of ideological conflict is not gone. In China, this was true in the late 1980s, becoming fixed after China stood condemned for its June 4, 1989, brutality at Tiananmen Square. And in Russia, this was happening starting in the mid-1990s and seized the spotlight from the time of the "color revolutions" in 2004.

As conceived by Karl Marx, communist ideology attacks the nation-state as an anachronism, forecasting the withering away of the state and the replacement of a national identity with an international one. However, in dialectical reinterpretation, Lenin proclaimed the dictatorial state with enhanced power to be the force that would end the era of "nationalism" in favor of a new era of internationalism. This sleight of hand came with fierce criticism against an ethnic nationalism that might constrain dictatorial claims and a "bourgeois nationalism" that operates abroad to resist the expansion of the communist movement under one state's supposed internationalist leadership. In the vanguard of an amorphous proletariat whose interests it claimed to express, the Communist Party dictatorship redefined the state it controlled as the embodiment of everything virtuous, even if it needed purges from time to time to prevent both class enemies and unwelcome notions of national identity from infiltrating its narrative.

Communism in its original intent poses a frontal assault on national identity, blaming it for false consciousness and replacing it with social class identity below and proletarian internationalism above. Yet it is also a sweeping attack on multiple collective identities and global humanist identities that removes virtually all existing barriers to an inflated national identity. Instead of finding self-esteem through other collectives or individualism, persons living under communist rule are, to the extent possible, stripped of alternatives and, as class struggle fades before the glorification of the state, are socialized to judge their own worth through the lens of state success.[15] The "new Soviet man" and the "anti-revisionist" child of Maoism are supposed to be selfless, removing the capitalist stain of individualism, and are devoted to the collective good, as encapsulated in whatever leaders decide is the national quest. Stalin elected to drop class struggle by explaining that the Soviet Union was already socialist and tolerated some role for collective identities, given the requirements of the Great Patriotic War and the all-consuming five-year plans. Nikita Khrushchev and Leonid Brezhnev had ambivalent views of limited collective identities—in Khrushchev's case by allowing more openness of discussion while pressing to reach communism quickly by suppressing religious and other identities, among other barriers, and in Brezhnev's case by acquiescing to their existence while intensifying didactic upbringing to overcome them. Mao had a harsher view of these identities, but his continued invocation of class struggle as a tool in the fight for greater control over the state and his rejection of China's history of state identity left more uncertainty about the deeper meaning of national identity.

Communism reorients national identity through insistence on an inexorable march toward utopia that proceeds only by an uncompromising struggle against class enemies at home and imperialist states abroad. It looks with anathema on the idea of convergence to find common ground with irredeemable, capitalist, imperialist states.[16] Despite a growing middle class and more complex society, it has no room for freedoms that would empower critics of the communist dictatorship instead of harassing them as dissidents or counterrevolutionaries. Asserting the inevitability of its international cause, it nonetheless glorifies the state at the expense of groups and identities that potentially could limit its reach. In these ways, a dichotomous, socialist realist prism demonizes the "other" as without merits while beautifying the communist state as unblemished at its core. No possibility is left for convergence: Capitalism means exploitation, imperialism, and rampant anticommunism.[17]

Communism claims to put a type of internationalism first, while condemning past rulers and their worldviews in the harshest terms. The process of dismantling communism introduces a clear discontinuity, as both China and the Soviet Union in the late 1980s disavowed much of the worldview of Mao and Stalin. In the case of Mao, his vulnerability included splitting communist identity from its past Confucian identity, failing to find a synthesis such as Stalin had achieved. The spiritual crisis arising in China seemed to far exceed that in the Soviet Union. In the 1990s, however, Russia struggled to synthesize tsarist and communist elements of identity far more than China did for Confucian and communist traits. Three factors serve to explain this contrast. First, the nature of the two countries' identities regarding the West and humiliation differed in ways that made synthesis easier in China. Second, Chinese leaders were far more adept at constructing a suitable national identity for the political elite and others, in part by learning the lessons of the Soviet/Russian experience. Finally, circumstances gave China a huge edge, independent of the past national identity and how it is consciously reconstructed. The comparisons given in the chapters that make up part I of this volume add detail on how China's identity synthesis gained an edge, despite later vulnerability.

There are at least five reasons why communism's impact on national identity might be expected to be enduring. First, its sweeping eradication of other, potential rival identities leaves a vacuum even if the approved state identity unwinds, losing its monopoly for at least a time. Second, the intensely inculcated national identity is all-encompassing, so that discrediting portions of it, however fundamental, does not extend to many other aspects, which can gain traction and also bring back with them the seemingly discredited elements. Third, communist national identity had evolved to embrace a chronology of precommunist history amenable to the postcommunist search for identity, leaving a symbiosis that owes much to the communist legacy. A fourth reason for communism's continued impact is the degree to which it forged an impression of significant others as enemies that cannot readily be expunged. Fifth and finally, this impact depends on a mixture of the sectoral identities—cultural, economic, and political—that may, during a time of pessimism and uncertainty, appear to serve the aim of negating the old national identity but will inevitably have a different effect as the nation's prospects change. For all these reasons, we have reason to look for continuities with the period after traditional communism has been dismantled, and we do so not as an inductive exercise but as an empirical, comparative undertaking.

Efforts to construct an unchallenged national identity from the top down do not mean that there is no basis for contesting it. Under Stalin and Mao, open disagreement was too dangerous. Under Khrushchev, Gorbachev, and Deng, certain differences were aired, revealing contested dimensions of national identity. Attempts to impose more uniformity under Jiang, Hu, Xi, and Putin (after more contestation under Yeltsin) do not mean that a clashing identity is not held by a sizable part of the urban, educated population. Yet it is rare for this to be formulated clearly and fully in an atmosphere skewed to favor the hegemonic identity. Speculating on how distinctive this rival identity may be or under what circumstances it might challenge today's top-down identity strains the limits of the existing evidence, but I attempt to do so in chapter 5.

Ever since 1986, divergence within the political elite in Moscow has exceeded that in Beijing. Advocates of universal values and of Russia's place in a community of shared heritage dating back to the Enlightenment, if not earlier, continue to serve in leadership positions and to express their views more openly in the media than do their Chinese counterparts. Signs of revitalized resistance to Putin starting in late 2011 after Medvedev's rhetoric offered some hope to those with these views were evidence that the opposition could quickly galvanize around a different notion of national identity. China's repressive apparatus has taken steps to prevent parallel developments, despite rare hints from certain leaders of a similar desire. It seems possible in both states for now to keep marginalizing alternative identity discourse, but slowing economic growth and rising social discontent may mean clashes ahead.

THE LEGACY OF DEMONIZATION OF THE UNITED STATES

The essence of communist national identity has generally been that the biggest threat comes from the anticommunism propagated by the United States and other Western states, whose view of democracy and human rights is intended to undermine the present order. The legitimacy of a tyrannical, corrupt system is premised on demonization of the West. Although reforms at times call for learning in specific areas from the West and regularizing politics to remove arbitrary tyranny, they are reversed when elite legitimacy is threatened. The end justifies the means if national identity is at stake. A humanitarian external use of force is anathema because it could serve as a precedent for domestic questioning of the existing order.

In the forefront of Chinese and Soviet worries about the other state is the fact that it will succumb to the West, joining its civilizational community and strategic alliance. This fear was greatest in the USSR in 1979–81 and in China in 1990–92. In the 1980s, the USSR hesitantly overcame it, and by 1993 China was confident this would not occur. In 1996, they had agreed to join together as a minority in the contemporary world. This was proof of a turning point that appears to be difficult to reverse. Although many writings explained the ideological sources of the Sino-Soviet schism, the national identity perspective opens the way to investigate their strong rapprochement. This includes assessing their treatment of the United States as a target of enmity.

Operating from an inadequate paradigm, optimists anticipated democratic transformation centered in Moscow and Beijing for the 1990s. Accepting Gorbachev as the spokesperson of change, many saw Russia becoming a "normal society" by joining a shared international civilization in which freedom and democracy would become the goals at home and the driving forces in international relations. Before June 4, 1989, many had expected China to become a "normal society" in a similar manner, and after June 4 they simply adjusted the timetable rather than the outcome. Yet this outlook did not take into account the impact of the two nations' traditional and communist national identities and the easily aroused antipathy to joining a community that had so long been demonized. Views of the United States moderated for a time, but as soon as circumstances permitted, with "democratic values" also being targeted, they worsened.

Chinese and Russian publications and official pronouncements repeatedly charge that the United States is not just pursuing its national interests but that it also keeps being consumed with messianic goals driven by its national identity. The problem is not occasional policies of misguided leaders but the fundamental orientation of the political elite, supported by the population. Moreover, this is not a problem limited to one powerful state. It is an orientation shared by a broad spectrum of Western and allied states, with the United States as the nexus. Beyond a clash of strategic approaches is a clash of civilizations. Beyond competition for regional leadership are incompatible views of the international system. Making accusations of this sort is not just a misreading of the US scene. It is also a mirror image, reflecting one's own views on identity gaps.

The international community was blindsided by Russia's reversion to anti-Western hostility, evident in the vitriolic rhetoric of Putin during his second term as president in the years 2004–8, and by China's antagonistic tone toward Western civilization in 2010–13, which went far beyond the critical rhetoric during Hu Jintao's earlier years as leader starting in 2002. The demonization of the West, represented by the United States, is an essentialist critique not of divergent national interests or complicated problems that were being incorrectly addressed but of fundamentally dangerous ambitions in a civilization with which compromise could not be reached. In 2013, Xi Jinping's "China Dream" and Putin's obsession with the threat from the West intensified this critique.

The obvious conclusion is that for both states, but especially China, the post–Cold War era is best characterized as a struggle between two civilizations: theirs and the West. This thinking echoes communist thought, as developed by Stalin and Mao, and is also a fusion of a traditional imperial worldview centered on a unique civilization and an orthodox communist ideology obsessed with its struggle with capitalism as it reflected a different civilization. Although both Russia and China keep insisting that they are only responding to provocations due to the persistent US Cold War mentality and no longer allow ideology to shape their foreign policies, it is they who view the recent divergence through the lens of incompatible civilizations.

On one dimension after another of national identity, the Chinese and Russian leaderships have reasserted hostility toward the United States in terms familiar to those raised on Cold War rhetoric. Their concerns have not centered on national interests or US hard power, despite frequent reference to these matters. Instead, narrowing the gap in hard power appears aimed at preventing damage from US soft power. On the vertical dimension of national identity, class struggle had long since ceased to be a concern in the Soviet Union and was quickly forgotten in China at the end of the 1970s. Rather, hierarchically organized state power represented the communist means of monopolizing control; and in the new era, after various controls had been relaxed, civil society again loomed as a serious threat. Similarly, on the chronological dimension, after censorship had been loosened, confusion increased over what parts of the officially approved historical records were correct, prompting leaders to put further emphasis on themes that would reinforce regime legitimacy, including a more positive spin on the dark spots in communist history. Demonizing the United States has become essential to bolstering the horizontal dimension of national identity, while insistence that ideology is driving the United States is at the core of the criticism.

Communism, in essence, is a rejection of full-scale reform, and thus entails a clash of systems that only can be settled by victory for one. Convergence is anathema. Although class struggle was long in the forefront, vigilance against both domestic reformers and foreign advocates of convergence is more fundamental. From this perspective, as in China's late imperial history and much of Russia's imperial history, ideas are seen as a battleground. To preserve "civilization" requires reinforcing a set of ideas and preventing the spread of clashing ones. In the case of China, those were demeaned as "barbarian." In Russian history, they were admired as Western but were also considered dangerous. Revolutionary victories in 1917 and 1949 were not so much against capitalism, as ideology prescribed, but against the mounting threats to the existing civilization that had not been adequately addressed over previous decades and appeared to be growing more serious. The United States symbolized the renewed threat in the late twentieth century, as many old assumptions faded and a globalized world loomed. Widening identity gaps serve to keep this threat under more control.

THE COMPARATIVE PERSPECTIVE ON COMMUNIST NATIONAL IDENTITY

After two decades of searching for what separates the "Russian idea" from the Soviet worldview, observers have good reason to turn the question around by searching for what unites these two outlooks. Similarly, after long focusing on how China's transition from the Deng era was leading identity away from its communist legacy, the question that should be of growing interest is how the legacy is reviving. This is an open invitation to compare legacies as well as to compare their survival.

China and Russia are bound together by national identity. Ironically, when they appeared to have similar orthodox community identities, this did not facilitate bilateral relations. From 1956 to 1978, they construed the ideological dimension of their identity—each claiming to be the rightful heir to Marx, Lenin, and Stalin—in a manner that drove them into a vitriolic rivalry. In contrast, after communism had been denied a recognized place in Russian identity, they were able to discover an affinity of identities with the vertical dimension in the forefront. Instead of a growing awareness of the differences in national interests driving the two apart in recent years, the pull of national identity affinity is drawing them closer. This is the opposite of how intensification of precommunist identities was expected to affect relations and obliges us to look more closely at the legacy of the prior communist identities.

Communism makes national identity a fetish, minimizing national interests as a theme inviting compromise. Although Soviet leaders beginning with Khrushchev and his "peaceful coexistence," and Chinese leaders since Mao countenanced a breakthrough with the United States in 1971, have acknowledged national interests, the legacy of putting identity in the forefront has been readily revived. Ironically, at the same time as it celebrates materialism, communism has made ideology the engine of social change and prioritized culture to the extent that it has gained growing salience since ideology was downgraded. Lenin and Mao both saw revolution as a far-reaching purge of culture, wiping away "false consciousness." Yet, in striving to replace "bourgeois" culture with "proletarian" culture, the leaders of the two countries drew heavily on what they had criticized as "feudal" culture, raising some authoritarian ideals to a new extreme while subordinating citizens, despite showy pretense, in a reinvigorated manner.

Through criticisms of Maoist deviations from socialism, Soviet writers had new scope to explore culture as an autonomous force in politics and social policy. F. M. Burlatskii was one of the leaders in this endeavor, which gathered steam starting in 1970.[18] His interest in *dukhovnaia kul'tura* (the autonomy of the superstructure), was often couched in criticisms of China, even as it was intended as a breakthrough in explaining the course of Soviet history. In the 1980s, Chinese authors likewise saw culture as a powerful determinant of China's history under socialism as well as that of the Soviet Union. Another thread common to Chinese and Russian writings was an upsurge in analyses of culture as a determinant in other countries. Turning away from previous objections to culture as an explanatory variable, leaders joined in strategizing how to manipulate it to boost legitimacy in trying times. They called for changing the consciousness of the people through ideological mobilization by the Communist Party, and increasingly also by changing the content of ideology and looking beyond ideology for understanding, which leads to an awareness of national identity.[19]

National identity conveniently maintains what is deemed essential from the worldview of communism, with or without the label. It restores the dichotomy between communism and what is seen as a Western worldview. In place of class struggle and economic blocs, civilizational differences rise to the forefront. In 2008, the culture theme drew close attention in the shadow of China's cultural jubilation at the Beijing Olympics, and the momentum was not relaxed by 2011, when the Communist Party made culture its theme for the annual plenary meeting, or afterward. The run-up to the Sochi Olympics was similarly characterized by intensification of national identity, after the backlash in 2011 against Medvedev's rhetoric downplaying the cultural gap with the West served to signal Putin's reassertion of national identity. This has revived the role of the sectoral dimension in an obsessive push to raise the intensity of national identity for the public.

Communist states are obsessed with inculcating national identity, including ideology. Realizing that weakness made expression of this identity inadvisable for a time, leaders determined in the 2010s that, at last, they could openly speak their minds. Having retained power, the Chinese Communist Party preserved much better than Russia the apparatus for coordinating and inculcating national identity. In comparison, it had more clarity about premodern identity, a less complicated sense of anti-imperialist humiliation, more continuity with traditional communist identity, and a more elaborate orchestration of new identity construction. In line with the Confucian "rectification of names" and traditional communist *tifa* (set phrases chosen to further ideological and identity objectives), China's censorship apparatus conveys a sustained narrative unrivaled in Russia. Although serious academics in both countries write in a manner that avoids much of this narrative, they rarely challenge it directly. Backed at times by leaders supportive of more modernization and international cooperation, these experts convey information that may, at times, be potentially subversive of the national identity rhetoric but that falls short of presenting a choice. There is no serious identity debate, just leadership fervent regarding its top-down construction.

On all six dimensions of national identity, the overlap between China and Russia is considerable. On the ideological dimension, the early 1990s' impression of an unbridgeable contrast between China's desperation to salvage communism and Russia's rejection of its communist legacy proved shortsighted. To the extent that Russia has reconstructed an ideology, it too has many markings of socialism, with post–Cold War characteristics and "anti-imperialism." Above all, both states are preoccupied with what they regard as the ideological threat from the West, depicted as if it is just a variant of imperialism. On the temporal dimension, the main forces shaping identity in the two countries are in agreement on the importance of taking pride in the era of traditional communism, no matter what shortcomings have, at times, been acknowledged. Where past leaders—Mao and Khrushchev/Brezhnev—drove them apart, the need to find merit in these leaders, as in Lenin and Stalin, is paradoxically drawing the two states closer. On the vertical dimension, each is obsessed with strengthening the state at the macro level and with some sort of state-party amalgam, to the exclusion of the intermediate level of civil society, ethnic and religious identities, or identities encouraged by international nongovernmental organizations (NGOs). Because both states regard this dimension of national identity as under threat by the United States, they seek close partnership in resistance, putting the horizontal dimension into play.

Communism is an all-encompassing movement targeted at revolutionary change in national identity. It was inspired by a manifesto consumed with deconstructing the existing identity from two directions: (1) substituting "internationalism" insistent on solidarity across state boundaries; and (2) eradicating the internal pillars of national identity, whether ethnic, religious, or civil society. Calling for the "withering away of the state," the classics of Marxism denigrate the intellectual foundation of the rise of "nationalism" from the sixteenth to nineteenth centuries. Yet the putative "proletarian internationalist" identity proposed as a substitute is little more than an abstraction with no hope of realization. Filling this void, Leninism, Stalinism, or Maoism reconceptualized what in fact became the basis of national identity under Communist Party control. In the preoccupation with establishing revolutionary parties and later building a socialist state, they proceeded to reconstruct national identity as one of the most powerful tools to achieve their ends. The resulting shared national identity syndrome is distinctive. Contrary to Marxism, it constricts internationalism except as a contrived extension of one's own country's assertive national identity. Attempts to eradicate the old internal pillars of national identity lead to the glorification of a party-state leviathan that exaggerates the very features of identity that classical Marxism had criticized. A new type of national identity thus has been born, with enduring consequences for the two powers as traditional communist states and, more recently, when they turned to reforms.

Not only must traditional communism be dismantled for sustained reform; the national identity it spawned must be reconstructed. Success in this endeavor is not a function of how close the proposed identity ideals are to universal values but of how vulnerable the prior national identity, in all its dimensions, is to challenges from the new environment; what conditions prevail for establishing a new identity; and what is the viability of a strategy selected for reconstructing national identity. As challenges to the current regimes mount, criticism of assertive national identity is bound to grow. Observers should avoid the mistakes of the 1980s and 1990s of seeing the transition simplistically without grasping shifts in many dimensions.

Ironically, overlapping national identities centered on communist ideology left open the gap that drove Moscow and Beijing apart for a quarter century. The chance of another bout of gap widening should not be dismissed—if two developments occur. First, if the domestic divide inside Russia comes to a head, it could expose the danger in supporting an assertive China, leading to new polarization and undermining multipolarity requiring balance among various poles, notably in the Asia-Pacific region. A sharp setback in Russian economic development and marginalization could spur reconsideration by many Russians; after all, few feel close to China. Second, if China's leaders were to grow confident enough to allow more of their recent bluster to center on Russia, the backlash could be considerable. There remains great sensitivity to charges against past Russian humiliation of China and infringements against the Russian "sphere of influence." The odds against either of these developments in the near term are high because of Putin's thinking and that of the elite he has assembled around him and of the Chinese track record over more than two decades of hypersensitivity to Russia. With China guided by a national identity that is widening the gap with the United States as much as possible on all dimensions, and with Russia blurring the lines between joining in demonizing the United States and claiming to support multipolarity, as leaders fear civil society's challenges to regime legitimacy, the Sino-Russian identity gap is likely to remain much narrower and less obtrusive than the two nations' gaps with the United States. However, an overconfident China pressing for a Silk Road along Russia's southern border and showing displeasure over Russian diplomacy with Japan and Vietnam could be less cautious than before, while stirring narrow, intense identity thinking in Russia. Narrowing the identity gap will prove difficult to sustain.

The transition from traditional communist national identity has reached a crossroads in the 2010s. In the 1990s and 2000s, Russians could take comfort that they were guided by multipolarity, while the Chinese stuck with a low-key approach that did not appear contradictory. Critiques of US arrogance in pressing versions of globalization as an identity resonated with various audiences. After the global financial crisis, the decision of China's leaders to be more assertive in policies and identity altered the situation. Medvedev acknowledged the reality with a softer approach to identity; however, Putin decided to campaign and govern by doubling down on sustaining the communist legacy, blurring the line between multipolarity and new signs of polarization. This may be further contested, both by increased discontent over Russia's failed model of modernization and by Russia's marginalization, in part due to China's lack of restraint.

Clarification of China's assault on "Western ideas" came in the April 2013 Document No. 9's list of "seven perils." The vertical dimension is represented by the perils of "Western constitutional democracy," media independence, and civic participation. The sectoral dimension is covered by perils from both universal values of human rights and promarket neoliberalism. On the temporal dimension, readers learn of the threat of nihilist criticisms of the Communist Party's past. Together, these perils along with attacks directed at socialism with Chinese characteristics constitute what are deemed to be threats on the ideological dimension. They clearly represent a divide, seen as unbridgeable in scale, on the horizontal dimension between China and the West. In issuing this secret document, leaders further ratcheted up China's intensity dimension.[20]

REFLECTIONS ON NATIONAL IDENTITY COVERAGE IN THREE BOOKS

Certain conclusions pertain to all three books in this series, as reflected in a series of questions about national identity. Is it something deeply rooted in a country's history and carried forward in its culture, or an artificial creation of today's ruling elite? Current narratives would have people believe only the former, going to great length to draw these connections. However, what is more apparent is the effort by the political elite to force a connection, even when it is tenuous. The more intense the national identity rhetoric, the more contrived the claims about supposed connections to the past. Censorship facilitates this linkage, making the case more monolithic, but it also occurs in states with democratic traditions. Roots exist, but they are one-sidedly nurtured.

How serious are growing national identity gaps? In the Internet era, they arouse passions beyond what may have happened earlier, leaving a flammable environment, which limits options for pragmatic diplomacy and opens the door to demagogic manipulation. Given fear of a loss of power, leadership groups are tempted to create a distraction and claim the mandate of an aroused population. These gaps are indeed serious, and they appear to be growing more so in the backlash to globalization and in the hypersensitive atmosphere of online mutual incitement.

How do national identity gaps widen? Are ongoing interactions between states at fault, or could it be that civilizational premises carry the seeds of deepening clashes? National identity narratives suggest such seeds, but the reality often is that political elites latch onto symbols that serve to demonize the other nation for purposes both of rallying domestic opinion and of gaining an edge in foreign policy. One side is usually much more responsible for widening the gap, although some on the other side may provide a pretext or an affront that is hard to ignore.

What can be done to narrow national identity gaps? The nation less guilty of widening the gap can yield to the temptation of a downward spiral, but it is likely to be more productive by calming emotions at home, intensifying public diplomacy, and using multiple channels to inform the public on the other side, especially by reaching more pragmatic groups there. This, however, could easily fail, as leadership in the country driving the gap wider persists for its own reasons.

What should we make of an apparently narrow national identity gap that is not supported by evidence of cultural closeness or trust, as in the case of current Sino-Russian relations? This case suggests the need to look closely for signs of further transition (T2) before long from the current transitional identity (T1). National identities have predictive value; but over time, contending forces can vie to reconstruct them and structural conditions can lend support to that.

To what extent is national identity deterministic, a reflection of a country's unavoidable destiny? The arguments in this book seeking to explain the impact of national identity up to the 2010s are not justifications for Putin and Xi to stay the course of intensifying narratives of victimization and civilizational superiority. The communist legacy has had a sustained effect for a generation and it endures, but leaders can abuse it and lose touch with the next transition in national identity, which would ordinarily move further away from this legacy. Extremism in the name of national identity distorts transitions that would otherwise be likely to take place.

PART I

CHINESE AND RUSSIAN NATIONAL IDENTITIES

CHAPTER 1

THE PRECOMMUNIST LEGACY AND THE
IMPACT OF STALINISM AND MAOISM

The decade of the 1990s saw the return of history, which communist identity had tried to erase in the march to socialism and which Western thought had minimized in the call for democracy and free markets. Replacing one universal model of national identity with another, now encompassed in a vision of globalization, proved elusive. But this did not mean that the way was now open for civilizations suppressed by the communist regimes to advance at will, displacing what had been embedded through many decades of unmitigated social engineering. As Russian leaders groped for the essence of their history—the Russian idea—and Chinese leaders authorized debate on the legacy of their premodern past—the Confucian tradition—expectations that communist identity would be overwhelmed proved incorrect. It is necessary to look back to these precommunist identities, assessing how they had been transformed in the frantic construction of a new identity culminating with Stalinism and Maoism, to grasp the challenge of reincorporating them.

Communist revolutions pledge to negate the past. Constructing socialism is equated with tearing down capitalism and also what remains of "feudalism," structurally and, no less, ideationally. To the extent that past national identity is acknowledged, it is dismissed as no more than the class consciousness of a small elite, which must be uprooted along with the false consciousness foisted on others. Those who sustain the pillars of this mindset—religion, ethnic nationalism, and cultural ideals handed down through generations—must be punished, or at least thoroughly reeducated. Vladimir Lenin started this process with War Communism. In the New Economic Policy, Soviet leaders did not permit much letup, and Josef Stalin carried it further, establishing the standards for what came to be understood as socialism. Mao went much further in eradicating the cultural heritage of his country, as he castigated those with class backgrounds deemed susceptible, those who expressed ideas out of step with the often-changing Communist Party line, and those not on his side of factional battles. Given the modern means of control at the disposal of these leaders, they surpassed past efforts to sweep away national identities and replace them with a strikingly different, if wildly mislabeled, outlook on identity.

What makes the transformation of national identity in China and Russia from premodern times to the heyday of communist orthodoxy exceptional? The answer is likely to be found in four characteristics of identity transformation. First, the earlier national identity was unusually immune to both gradual reconstruction and displacement, setting the stage for a prolonged, disruptive process. Second is a great degree of resentment, building over a long period, at the failure to realize reforms that addressed the mounting anxiety. Third, the communist hiatus with the past opened a gap in national identity with few parallels. Fourth and finally, Stalinism and Maoism, with their radical purges and ideological campaigns, both exacerbated such extreme discontinuities. There is no doubting that modernization and the diffusion of culture from the West served everywhere to transform civilizational and national identities, but there is reason to conclude that these four characteristics combined to exert a rare impact. Earlier identities proved tenacious, even though they long had been understood to be outdated and inadequate. Frustration mounted without real satisfaction from timely identity changes. A shift of unprecedented intensity caused wrenching discontinuity. Finally, megalomaniacs went further in exacerbating these disruptive forces, leaving their nations in a state of both exhaustion and confusion.

NATIONAL IDENTITIES IN THE NINETEENTH CENTURY

Well before the West made a strong impact on China or even Russia, identity was twisted toward more rigid authoritarianism. This took a decisive turn in China, narrowing Confucianism's focus, under the impact of conquest dynasties and also the founder of the indigenous Ming Dynasty. No longer would elite Confucianism in pursuit of national salvation be a promising venture. A venerable civilization still had a "vital cultural tradition that gave it unity, strength, and resilience," but cultural confidence could hardly compensate for poor governance, compounding an identity shift driven by alien defensiveness or social upstart anxiety toward scholarly ideals.[1]

In Russia, the Mongol occupation left a deeper imprint than in its briefer rule over China long after Confucian identity had been solidified, contributing to the Orthodox Church's rise as essentially an offshoot of state authority. As state requirements for service were tightened during the Muscovy period, they went well beyond China's ideal of voluntary state service to intense requirements for local elite service. The result in Russia was an ideological state for an elite torn between service and foreign ideals entering from the West, in contrast to a Chinese elite with no such ambivalent ties to the outside, while balancing both national and local Confucian identity.[2]

To find a divide in late imperial Chinese national identity, one must look for the impact of the Mongols, the peasant-based Ming, and the Manchus, all of which raised the emphasis on the state at the expense of intermediate identities and closed the door to the outside with more inward-looking Sinocentrism. The corresponding divide in Russian national identity is also linked to an awareness of tightening control over intermediate levels, as marked by Ivan IV's Oprichnina period (1565–72), when terror was applied to make the tsar's power absolute, and also by Peter I's authoritarian approach to Westernization. In contrast to China, Russia had more variation from tsar to tsar; more impact from the outside world through Westernization, as in the world of the arts, which was considered superior in many ways; and more ambivalence about civilizational identity. Richard Pipes traces factors contributing to a uniquely powerful form of Russian autocracy, recognizing historical examples when autocratic power fell into some jeopardy but stressing that it was later reinforced.[3]

By the time of the Ming Dynasty, Confucianism had become a pact between the emperor and the scholar-officials, whereby they both became prisoners of a fixed outlook on civilizational identity. Loyalty to civilization trumped loyalty to dynasty, although it put more restrictions on reform than on arbitrary authoritarianism. Compared with Russia, there was room for religious diversity in daily life and for localism. Yet the reformers were blocked from transforming the national identity or establishing a city or regional identity that could challenge it. Law was denied any role in contesting identity.[4]

Confucian China and tsarist Russia grew paranoid about the threat of ideas deemed heterodox to orthodox beliefs. Tsars feared that the Enlightenment would spread anger against their narrow authoritarian order based on serfdom. Emperors—especially the Manchus, who were suspect for their barbarian origins—scrutinized writings to ensure that they did not conceal hidden messages questioning the legitimacy of the dynasty. These preoccupations, resulting in exile or death sentences, exposed the extreme alertness to ideas that could inspire rebellion. They reflect the immersion of China's literati and Russia's intelligentsia in the world of ideas, often confronting regimes intent on shaping their worldview in support of authoritarian power. China went much further in banning writings with suspect ideas while striving through education, examinations, and the diffusion of didactic messages to manage national thinking about politics, history, and culture. Managing ideas was deemed essential to maintaining the state's authority. Russia was inconsistent in censorship, and thus was more vulnerable to Western thought.

Confucian orthodoxy had become the equivalent of an ideology, proclaimed the exclusive worldview of all who aspired to belong to the elite, inculcated without tolerance for heterodox interpretations once accepted, and rigidly imposed with attention to fine details and elaborate ritual reinforcement.[5] If tsarist ideology did not enjoy comparable support, as intellectuals gravitated to the thinking then popular elsewhere in Europe, defensiveness contrasted to China's confidence. Despite this discrepancy, ideology grew more rigid in both states: the Russians sought to widen the identity gap with the increasingly advanced West, which was threatening to their identity; and the Manchus hardened their outlook on Confucianism as dynastic decline became apparent. Ideologies were squeezing out reform propensities. Although in the 1860s reform thought gained some ground in both states, it was later constrained.

The reign of Nicholas I and the pre–Opium War Qing Dynasty rule epitomized the way national identity was understood before the weight of foreign pressure grew to the point that fierce resistance proved fruitless. In Russia, traditional thought gained new life, reformulated as Slavophilism versus Western thought, penetrating with great force but also arousing more strident resistance. In China, Sinocentric thought rooted in Confucianism was affirmed by Manchu rulers in order to control the country. Until the 1900s, these traditional views repelled other ways of thinking, even as they were facing increasing challenges from rebellious forces and also Western thought.

Over time, Chinese identity themes acquired a more extreme character. The Manchus made men wear braids as a sign of submission.[6] Confucianism became even more closely associated with the submission of women, as in foot-binding. Imperial examination responses had to be written as formulaic eight-part essays, stultifying intellectual creativity. Imperial Confucianism grew more ritualized, as reform Confucianism was more suppressed. Although Russian identity was tempered by Western identity, as a badge of education and culture, Chinese identity was narrowed when education and culture, under the impact of a conquest dynasty as well as earlier trends, were redefined from above.

China's historic conceit centers on its superiority as a civilized state. This concept is predicated not just on confidence in a shared moral advantage at the level of the family, community, and individual, but also on an idealized representation of the dynasty in control of the state as governing through moral authority. The state is the caretaker of the civilizational identity of the Chinese people; it is entrusted to sustain cultural life at an elevated level and is destined to be judged by histories written in succeeding dynasties with an eye to how it performed a well-established set of functions. Thus, the dynasty embodies the state's identity and anticipates being evaluated for administration related to the maintenance of peace and civil order, the unification of territory, the support of economic well-being, and the application of rewards and punishments in furtherance of what is understood to be a just society. In late imperial China, claims that the dynasty's identity met the highest standards generally were disconnected from reality, buttressed by tight censorship, and immune to official remonstrating based on independent Confucian standards of benevolent rule. Loyalty took priority over honest feedback, and self-congratulations took precedence over objective analysis of how well the dynasty actually conformed to the recognized criteria of state identity.

Belief in the distinctiveness of their language became a major element in the national identities of China and Russia. Unlike the written forms of Japanese and Korean, there was no shift to an accompanying phonetic script in China, and words from Western languages were rendered in characters that reduced awareness of their external origins. The language became a focus of cultural identity. In Russia, Alexander Pushkin's poetry and other literary developments raised the notion that translations could not do justice to thoughts and ideas that originated in the Russian language. China's language seemed so far removed from outside culture and so filled with meaning through its pictographic presentation that a policy to revise it, as in the shift from classical to vernacular Chinese in writing, played a large role in identity debates. Tight control over language, used even as allegory, occurred in the Qing Dynasty and resumed later, especially under communist rule.

National identity is an indicator of confidence that takes different forms. Confidence in Chinese civilization, rather than in a particular dynasty, was a sign of assurance of China's comprehensive merits compared with those of others, of the elite's wholehearted support for such merits, and of expectations that the more the masses learned the more eagerly they would share this confidence in their civilization. Dynastic confidence under the Qing, as under some other conquest dynasties, was less assured, acquiring an even more defensive character in the second half of the nineteenth century. As national identity struggled with the mixed legacy of civilizational and dynastic identity, this tension between deep-seated assurance and immediate doubts was growing larger.

The shock for Chinese national identity was severe and prolonged. Regarding their nation as chosen, close to heaven, and civilized beyond comparison, the Chinese were traumatized as all elements of their national identity were disrupted. Whether or not the humiliation was attributed to imperialism, it was an inevitable blow to a civilization steeped in its past glory confronting irrefutable, universalistic claims.[7] China's cultural and political identities were slow to accept the standards of the West. They remained a source of extreme pride until finally becoming matters of embarrassment. The gaps were much wider, and as they finally narrowed through self-criticism, the case for some drastic adjustment became imperative. This did not mean, however, that the heritage of pride and distinctiveness would not survive.

Russian national identity did not have either the longevity or the ideology to make a clear distinction between civilization and dynasty. Confidence was narrower and much more defensive. It rested on more supernatural grounds, in the face of the harsh reality of elite infatuation with a rival civilization; preference for mass beliefs based on faith and ignorance; and by the second half of the nineteenth century, clear indications of inferiority according to almost any objective measure. An intensification of ideology occurred inconsistently against the backdrop of reforms that revealed a loss of confidence. There was a defiant tone to efforts to reassert an identity that had little hope for survival without dynastic continuity, which was in great doubt.

Russia's vertical identity owes a lot to Ivan IV, who established the "Russian Tradition" with his push for unlimited power; Peter I, who made the state sacred; and Josef Stalin, who turned the state into a Leviathan, atomizing the people and making society no more than the "state's fodder."[8] Other leaders attempted great state transformations that challenged this vertical identity, causing disruptions without succeeding in the goal of forging a new equilibrium, and thus provoking a backlash, in the 1880s in the aftermath of Alexander II's reforms and in the 1990s after the Gorbachev-Yeltsin reforms. Robert Legvold observes values opposed to "Europe's values": attachment "to community over the individual, to spirituality over materialism, to cooperation over competition, to tradition over 'liberal modernism,' and to Orthodox Christianity over Catholicism and Protestantism."[9]

The process of Russia's integration with the West was interrupted by the Mongols, the Oprichnina period, Peter I's duality in balancing Europeanization, and the nineteenth-century initiatives to widen the gap in identities. The tsars found a powerful ally in the Orthodox Church, if at times they had to rein it in. Proclaiming itself to be the "Third Rome" after the fall of Byzantium, Russia defined itself in opposition to the West, helping the tsars maintain power in the face of a civilization superior in many respects. Communal religion claiming the mantle of otherworldly truth failed to serve as much of a check on power because it accepted the authority of the tsar in a nearly unqualified manner, parallel to China's situation of no priestly authority in the path of unlimited political aggrandizement. James Billington describes how social conservatism gathered steam after the war against Napoleon, as religion expanded its reach and Asia drew new interest in the backlash against the West. He writes that it was "fateful that the high tide of anti-Enlightenment feeling should occur at the very time when Russia was becoming conscious of its national power and identity."[10] Not only was Napoleon equated with revolution; he was associated with rationalism, in contrast to Russian identity.

Billington also depicts Russian national identity as geographically, historically, and culturally unique. With the largest land mass and harshest climate and also many unprotected borders, Russia had a special sense of vulnerability. Assigning nearly unlimited power to a godlike ruler, who was legitimized by the Orthodox Church or later the Communist Party, Russian identity has little to say about state institutions or checks and balances. Lacking a broad cultural identity until the nineteenth century, Russians began an intense intellectual debate that has yet to be resolved, while their sense of victimization limited trust in the outside.[11] Billington traces through decades how tsars and literary figures defined national identity—religiosity trumped roots of democracy in the search for a unifying vision, including "naive idealization of past events and heroes" and a "strong sense of cultural distinctiveness."[12] Stalin fixed on

new versions of old symbols in forging a "quasi-religious cult of ven-
eration for an allegedly infallible political leader," extolling the *partiinost'*
(sacrificial party spirit) while boosting Russocentrism through a narrative of "a perpetual victim of external invasions and internal betrayals."[13]
Weathering Khrushchev's thaw and Brezhnev's aspirations to renew
communist ideology with a stronger dose of Russian cultural identity, the
Stalinist synthesis had enduring impact even in the 1990s and beyond.[14]

Russian identity shifted from who is more genuinely Christian, to
who has a superior culture, to who has a superior system for modernization. Lacking self-esteem, Russians kept looking for an identity to
affirm their advantage in a strongly felt competition with not one state
in Europe but the combined civilization of the continent. Russia was
in Europe, but it was not satisfied with a peripheral status by identifying heavily with Europe. Catherine II and Alexander I came closer to
accepting shared European identity, but this did not last. Finally, communist identity made the case for superiority, albeit one that eventually
appeared hopelessly contrived.

Russia's historic pride was more grounded in distinctiveness than
in claims to superiority. As Russian national identity took shape in the
shadow of European Enlightenment and then modernization, inferiority in countless respects could not be disguised. Other countries did not
look to it as a beacon of civilization. Yet the Russian state—associated
with reverence for the tsar as a unique exemplar of just authority, and for
the Orthodox Church—became the one source of identity, which was
seen as giving Russia entitlement to stand among the European powers.
Defensive about images of the backwardness of the Russian state associated with its dependence on serfdom, unchecked autocracy, and resistance to the modern currents found across much of Europe, Russia clung
to an identity sharply differentiated from other states. The special quality
of *gosudarstvennost'* (the power of the state) became its enduring symbol.

Russia perceived itself as under pressure from the West, no longer interpreted as one form of Christianity versus another but as Enlightenment
versus backwardness for serfdom and absolutism. Although some tsars
sought a middle way with support for a kind of Russian enlightenment,
others responded assertively, widening the divide by playing up the

religious difference, claiming positive qualities from the Russian form of autocracy, and attributing superiority to Russian nationality and religion. This was encapsulated in the views of Slavophiles, who instead of regarding Russia as backward depicted a unique pathway to the future of a state leading the masses. Fyodor Dostoevskii was a leading voice in resisting Western identity, championing the "Russian idea" and claiming a unique form of Christianity and historic destiny. Refusing to cede humanism to the West, he joined in trumpeting communitarianism as more advanced than the individualist tendencies spreading there. The cleavage between the elite and masses in Russia left the Enlightenment impact narrow, raising the potential for utopianism to bridge the gap or xenophobia to contain the contagion. The foundation for class struggle was set well before 1917, and communism was to repackage the notion of the evil West and the messianic mission of Russia.[15]

The Chinese and Russian identity dilemmas in the late nineteenth century appeared different, but there were some important similarities. Both had civilizational claims that resisted borrowing heavily from Western identity. Of course, Russia's elites were steeped in Western identity, speaking French, regarding their contributions to the arts as comparable to the best of those made by the countries in the West, and associating in dealings with the rest of the world alongside the European powers. Yet tsarist defenders and Russian Orthodox priests remained deeply opposed to convergence and reform that would presumably have led in that direction. The long delay in abolishing serfdom, the staunch resistance to a nonclerical education that would raise abysmally low literacy rates, and the powerful appeal of Slavophile thought kept the West at bay. In proximity, Russia kept aloof from Western identity, despite waves of reform, much as China at a distance did over the seven decades following its defeat in the Opium War. To be sure, a rival identity steeped in Western thought also had a broad following.

The temporal dimension provides a sharp contrast, but not a decisive one. The Chinese could look back with few qualifications to a history of preeminence. Although the only thing that seemed to matter was the failure to give rise to modernization, this memory remained. Russia could recall becoming the "Third Rome," standing for a separate religious and political tradition, while also finding success under Peter I through state-centered reforms distinct from development elsewhere in Europe. In the late nineteenth or early twentieth century, it was difficult for Russians to take much comfort from these recollections, but the identity consequences would matter in the 2000s.

On the sectoral dimension, China was more distinctive. For Russia, too, this was foremost in widening the gap with the West. Cultural and political identity drew new attention, as Pushkin stood in the forefront in the expression of high culture at a standard recognized in the West. In ballet, symphonic music, and opera, distinctive Russian achievements were a source of pride. Modernist pioneers put Russia at the world's cultural forefront in the early twentieth century. But officials were ambivalent regarding whether their cultural products narrowed the identity gap by putting them at the leading edge of the West or widened the gap by demonstrating Russia's uniqueness.

Confucianism is obsessed with this-worldly matters, in contrast to Eastern Orthodoxy, which is otherworldly. The former led to mass education, the latter to mass illiteracy. Yet both became closely linked to state legitimacy, the former setting forth standards for state performance and the latter putting loyalty to the tsar above other principles. Despite Mencius' Mandate of Heaven, Confucian thought prioritized loyalty to the emperor except in the most extreme circumstances. It did not identify another source of authority, just as Russia's religious hierarchy was not granted any independent authority. Communism built on these traditions, which at times opened the door to intellectual debate but were shadowed by images of narrow censorship.

China had a bureaucratic government with widely understood symbols of a single national entity. So did Russia. Elites in both states were committed to public service. Both populations had a strong sense of the unique cultural character of their nation. If in the case of China, the cultural gap was aimed at "barbarians" who were way behind their country, in Russia it centered on enlightened Europeans who were well ahead of it, although in Asia many peoples were deemed to be far behind. The Russians long perceived an outside source of civilization as important for borrowing; the Chinese did not. Even in borrowing

Buddhism, China paid little heed to its foreign origins, just as Russia had lost interest in the external origins of Christianity. The examination system and the study leading up to it forged China's connection of cultural and political identity.

China had a well-established hierarchy of identities, with state and family at the center, limiting the scope for civil society and individualism as alternatives. The universe was closely linked to the ruler (the son of heaven), while Han ethnic identity was left undifferentiated from state-sponsored civilization. Russia's hierarchy, from tsar to the table of ranks for the hereditary aristocracy to serfs and state peasants in closed communities backed by religious identity, fell into flux with the rise of the intelligentsia and the end of serfdom. Until new hierarchies were imposed through communism, resting heavily on one dictator reliant on class struggle, the decay of the old hierarchies confused national identity as it complicated the restoration of order.

Obsessed with state-society relations and the ideals of a well-ordered society, Chinese political thought put more limits on the ruler. It was positive about human nature, leaving no room for the sort of disrespect for the people that made serfdom possible. It had elaborate ideas about ritual propriety, benevolent rule, righteous behavior, and moral obligations before the people. There was no parallel in Russia. The identity implications are more trusting of bottom-up forces, but not as limits to many of the big, top-down claims of vertical and horizontal identity. Bottom-up aims lurked in China as alternate ideals, as did Western-inspired reform ideals in Russia.

The Russians debated whether their state was backward compared with the West or was following a unique trajectory of development. Aware that they were falling behind, people were inclined to turn to the state to catch up.[16] This further widened the country's distance from the West. As in China, service to the state had become the route to elite mobility, and elite mediation in controlling rural communities furthered this objective. Although the mechanisms of service and of representing local communities differed in the two countries, Slavophile idealism about this hierarchical order came to parallel Confucian idealism. It was more fiercely contested, but it fought back.

Chinese native-place identities trumped national identity in ways not found in Russia. There were native-place associations and gazetteers as well as groups of migrants with monopoly control over certain occupations. This complicated a shift in the century before 1949 to national as opposed to dynastic identity. Confucianism centered on the family, and it operated at the community level without a central hierarchy, in contrast to Russian Orthodoxy, with its tight-knit communities under central control.

Russia had possibilities for identity change that aroused uncertainty. The reign of Alexander II, sandwiched between the identity-intensifying eras of Nicholas I and Alexander III, is best noted for far-reaching reforms. Narrowing the gap with European modernization, especially through the abolition of serfdom, the reformist tsar loosened centralization as *zemstva* (local government) reform came to symbolize the rise of civil society. Yet the serfs were constrained by communal obligations, legal reform did not advance smoothly, and more autonomy to nationalities on the periphery of the empire and to an intelligentsia growing more radical aroused a backlash. Alexander II could not break the hold of his predecessor's troika of orthodoxy, autocracy, and nationalism, centering on claims to a separate civilization. Increasingly, secularism and the spread of democracy in Europe, along with revolutionary movements, drove Russians to widen the identity gap by glorifying their own history and claiming superiority.[17]

Aspirations for equality with the West rested on China's cultural identity, but that had to be connected to political identity. This process was delayed by the Qing Dynasty's success in holding onto power and by the tenacity of past identity.[18] Consciousness of exceptional cultural continuity was rooted in history; the preeminence of one path of social mobility, and the intense socialization of the great many who aspired to it, delayed the arrival of elite challengers who could have made the case for a shift in national identity. Reliance on rites over law meant that identity overshadowed interests. Without a notion of sin or a personalized God, and with a history that was assumed to be cyclical, it was difficult to make the case for an abrupt transformation. The trauma of identity transformation was more acute in China, given its cohesive identity at odds on all dimensions with what would follow. This trauma left a tremendous vacuum but also a residual confidence in cultural national identity, which would prove itself to be resilient in the years after Mao.

Russia and China linked the state and the people in one identity. Russians did this by positing a direct bond between the tsar, the embodiment of the state, and the people. China made this linkage by inculcating Confucianism, assuming that the more "civilized" the populace, the more loyal it would be. It was not easy in either setting to refocus identity away from the paramount leader. One difference in the paternalistic role of the state was that Chinese civilization was above the emperor, while Russian civilization was not above the tsar, freeing the tsar to try reforms or tighten control. However, these Russian and Chinese identities left their people vulnerable. Crediting the state with driving moral behavior, they supported autocracy with few identity checks. Russia's acceptance of its identity in Europe left some room for outside opinions shaped by the choppily advancing humanism in the West to have an influence. The Confucian state's links to society also paved the way for criticism. After all, history was a mirror on the present, keeping ideals alive and keeping the focus on linking identities at different levels of society. Even if this framework repeatedly lent itself to abuse at the top and rituals for their own sake with only a veneer of ideals, this heritage was not erased.

NATIONAL IDENTITIES IN THE TRANSITION TO COMMUNIST RULE

The precommunist transition left Russian and Chinese national identities in desperate retreat. Western identities were gaining ground, but not fast enough to fill the void. Seeing the prosperity or power of the West, Russia's elites grew increasingly embarrassed by their country's backwardness. Its ideology was the object of scorn in the context of European humanist values and representative government. Claims to economic identity and political identity were laughable, while Russians grasped for cultural pride as their sole sectoral identity recourse. The notion that the tsarist order warranted praise stumbled when faced with the images of backward masses and disgruntled intelligentsia, giving rise to a radicalism premised on populist leaps forward, whereby communalism brings rapid progress. Russia was fading as a great power, lacking the glory of empire building or any appeal to other states. To find an identity shortcut, utopian solutions were all that seemed possible.

Sinocentrism was shaken by China's marginalization over a century. There was no longer a sense of respect for China's superior civilization. The tribute system (a hierarchical order in East Asia) collapsed. States insisted on China's acceptance of international law and mores, while the Chinese felt humiliated by their impact. Ethnic minority groups on China's periphery found support in other countries, casting doubt on Han superiority close at home. Searching for a new combination of state, territorial, and cultural identity, the Chinese paid lip service to the Western-centric world order they had joined, but they bridled under feelings of injustice that were exacerbated by Japan's growing role as the prime villain and the imperialist aggressor, whose actions epitomized this order's unfairness. Being obliged to accept the superiority of the West or even Japan, because they represented ideals long associated with civilization, the Chinese felt the humiliation more in cultural terms than in military or economic ones. Premodern identities had put culture (including religion) in the lead. The West posed a challenge through its ability to discredit cultural identity for important segments of the local population. Communism offered a political identity that challenged Western identity and also promised that cultural and newly important economic superiority was within reach.

The intrusiveness of Western powers and later Japan resulted in a duality in China that differed from Russia, where tsarist authority remained formidable. With the treaty port system and modern cities (led by Shanghai) emerging under foreign protection, while the old order resisted reform, modernity was not well blended with tradition. The rise of merchant communities with international linkages came with an awareness that the Chinese state was failing. The idea of modern national identity rallied the Chinese against the old order, as it rallied Russians against tsarism.

China's delayed reforms and rejection of Western civilization contrasted with Japan's response in the nineteenth century. Assuming civilizational superiority, the Chinese felt humiliation greater than had the Russians, where images of being the chief laggard in Europe were keenly felt. The Manchus and the scholar-officials serving them failed to countenance reforms much more than in Russia, where intermittent reforms were conducted. As seen during the Boxer Rebellion, the resulting frustration led to xenophobia. Even when reforms finally came, political disputes interfered, as the backlash grew against Confucian culture, notably the May Fourth Movement in the 1910s. If this movement appeared to be the rejection of China's previous identity in favor of the West, symbolized by science and democracy, it quickly combined with anti-imperialism, rejecting many elements of the West. This led both to a search for some deep national essence (*guocui*) and for a strong state, which called capitalist development into question.[19] Delay in reforms capable of ameliorating resentment in both states left growing doubt about the adaptability of existing national identity. Both the Chinese and the Russians were inclined to associate failure with a weak state.

The identity divide between the elite and the masses widened sharply. For Russia, it had long been very wide, reflecting a split between the academic and cultural world stars celebrated since the time of Catherine II and the illiterate serfs, whose horizons narrowly centered on community churches. For China, it widened sharply with the reforms that brought knowledge from the modernized world to a select few. In both countries, movements to bridge the gap stalled, leading to growing radicalization.

Astrid Tuminez argues that Russian national humiliation has been the trigger for the arousal of aggressive forms of what I label national identity. She cites pan-Slavism in 1856–78, after Russia's defeat in the Crimean War; great power nationalism in 1905–14, in the aftermath of Russia's defeat in the Russo-Japanese War; and a backlash after the collapse of the Soviet Union, picking up steam in the 1990s. Such reactions draw on Russian pride in greatness associated with empire and imperial rulers. In turn, Tuminez finds, society was sacrificed to the interests of state security and aggrandizement and Russification failed to serve nation building—yet in cases of aggressive reactions to humiliation, as ideas resonated with public opinion, Russian leaders reimposed control to preserve their autonomy (if war had not led to the erosion of governance).[20]

The Chinese were slower to awaken to their civilizational turnabout. In place of a quasi-ideology of superiority in an environment where no other civilization had any appeal, they lost faith in their own tradition under the humiliation of being pressed to embrace another. Chinese economic and political identities were in tatters, while cultural identity was under siege despite its deep roots. Loss of unity and of the established order solidified by Confucian bureaucratic administration left confidence in vertical identity in shambles. After centuries of being a "middle kingdom" dependent on no other state, China had lost its centrality as the advanced civilization and model. These shocking turnabouts aroused strong emotions in search of radical answers for reconstructing identity, not by copying the West but by leapfrogging it, as the Soviet model did.

The broad concept of Tianxia (All under Heaven) presumed a universal cultural identity, which was not sustainable after the arrival of the Western powers. Ethnic identities spread in the anti-Manchu mood at the end of the Qing era and over the following decades. Yet, countering *minzu* (ethnic nationalist) thinking was the resurgent ideal of *datong*, which envisioned a great community achieving prosperity together. For Han Chinese, this ideal resonated more than narrow ethnocentrism. Assuming the political assimilation of minorities or their marginalization at the periphery, the Han Chinese briefly entertained anti-Manchu feelings, which had been rather suppressed after the Manchus chose to rule through Confucianism and a largely Han imperial bureaucracy, but they sought a renewal of pride in a shared Chinese civilization (*Zhonghua minzu*) again to be held in the highest esteem. In the new world order, it was also essential to forge a strong state (*guojia*).

The Pan-Slavists, communists, Eurasianists, and multipolarity champions all have rejected Russian integration into an international community centered in the West. Horizontal national identity requires a pronounced gap with the states seen as leading the West and the cultivation of partners hostile to them. Without horizontal identity as a bulwark, vertical national identity appeared vulnerable. The two could not be readily separated. They were encapsulated together as parallel abstractions—*gosudarstvennost'* (again, the power of the state) and *der-zhavnost'* (putting one's role as a great power on a pedestal)—themes as comfortable for Vladimir Putin as for Nicholas I. The decisive break occurred in 1917, when Lenin gained power, followed by Stalin.

Russia had phenomenal success in expanding its territory from the sixteenth to the nineteenth centuries. This buttressed the idea that the messianism of holy Russia serves a noble calling. Communism rekindled such thoughts on the basis of a new wave of efforts to expand Russia's reach. China had also expanded its territorial reach, as the test of territorial control was being added to that of unification in evaluating the success of a dynasty. Loss of territory from the 1890s to the 1940s left an indelible stain of humiliation, also providing a rallying cry for leaders with messianic aspirations.

Russia was the embarrassing outlier in Europe, criticized for serfdom and autocracy. China went from pride as the center of civilization to humiliation as the embodiment of Asian backwardness. Both experienced backlashes from those resentful of the sense of superiority in the West. For the Russians, there was resentment that they were seen as outside the West and having missed a vital part of the Enlightenment, rather than as a legitimate, eastern branch of Western civilization. The Chinese resisted arrogant claims of the eternal superiority of Western culture, sometimes associated with the religious pretensions of God's chosen people. Long on the defensive, first the Russians and then the Chinese found that communism turned the tables, enabling them to claim superiority; but this required extreme distortions about reality at home and abroad.

COMMUNIST IDENTITY BEFORE STALINISM AND MAOISM

Karl Marx turns history into impersonal forces, strips it of any morality as "false consciousness," and makes utopian claims about a shared community that ignores national interests and paves the way for identity claims to reign uncontested. Given the failure to understand how national identity evolves and a revolutionary process could influence it, Marxism, with its misleading arguments about substructure and superstructure and social classes and their thinking, leads the way to Stalinism and Maoism. Misunderstanding identity, it leaves room for the ends to justify the means.

Marx defined communism in sharp contrast to capitalism. Lenin did not allow the great discrepancy between Russian reality and communist ideals to stand in the way of strong contrasts, although when he approved the New Economic Policy, the ideas of the War Communism period were overshadowed. Stalin forged the identity that has come to be associated with socialism. On all dimensions, the Soviet Union starting early in the 1930s had settled on what would, despite some minor adjustments after Stalin's death, be the crux of its socialist identity until the late 1980s. This, in turn, would become the basis for Chinese socialist identity through the Maoist period.

Marx developed the idea of communism as a system of belief or identity that centered on the withering away of the state. Struggling for class consciousness against the "false consciousness" of national identity, the people would forge new types of associations and shared identities. Lenin carried the argument of internationalism further, pronouncing anti-imperialism the revolutionary banner in resistance to "nationalism." Yet a closer look at the views of successors to the leadership of the communist movement and its aftermath in Russia and China points to a newly intense awareness of national identity as the outcome of communism and, indeed, in the face of emergent challenges, its means of salvation. Along with terror, Stalin found it critical to boosting legitimacy or popular support. Even more so, Mao put a national identity gloss on his terror tactics. These dictators fervently transformed identity rhetoric.

Lenin put identity in the forefront of the communist cause by emphasizing the spread of "revolutionary consciousness" through a vanguard at first committed to overthrowing the existing regime and then to constructing a socialist society under party tutelage. To foster a corps of devoted believers and educate a mass of willing followers, cultural revolution became a high priority.[21] As divisions in the political elite led to purges and as demands on the populace intensified, socialization into a new identity fell short of what was demanded, resulting in more widespread terror than Lenin had anticipated. The focus on class enemies widened into terror against those with different ideas and to "thought reform" on an unprecedented scale. Mao went even further than Stalin in forging a "statist society" and expanding the "community of the faithful" by eliminating ideas that could conflict with his own.

Communism replaced Confucianism and tsarism with abstract claims to both universality and world leadership. Concrete claims centered on state identity, which revived critical aspects of earlier identity in both countries. One critical difference was the presence of the Soviet Union as both the external source of the ideology as far as China was concerned and the ongoing claimant to authority in defining the standards of national identity. As long as China's leadership accepted the Soviet-led, international communist movement, they were constrained to accept its monolithic criteria for setting these standards. This proved intolerable. At "liberation," Mao coupled his "nationalistic" message about China rising up with a distinctive appeal on behalf of its "people's democratic dictatorship." In the transition to socialism in the first half of the 1950s, this distinctiveness was in danger of being lost. Only by rushing the pace could Mao insist that China was completing the catch-up phase and reclaiming the right to set the standards. The origins of the Sino-Soviet split can be traced to insistence on China's identity without sacrificing claims to universality.

In contrast to academics, who discern multiple causes for divergent interests, and to diplomats, who strive to narrow differences in national interests, the believers in a supposedly pure national identity are prone to approach divisions as the outcome of clashing identities, ruling out compromise. The communists carried this differentiation to an extreme, dividing social classes, foreign nations, and adherents to particular ideas as either with us or against us. Although Marxism-Leninism and Maoism also claimed that social structure accounts for causality, communist power holders made ideas the focus, feigning flimsy connections to social structure. Defining the national identity precisely and raising it to a high intensity, they sought to forestall any type of challenge at home and to draw a very sharp line with external national identities. Threats to peace came from a refusal to narrow the identity gap on a one-sided basis by the other country. Threats to stability and progress came from a refusal to accede to the full spectrum of national identity claims, however changeable, from above. If cynical manipulation by leaders lowered the credibility of these claims, the charade of total adherence continued in a setting of ideological indoctrination or censorship.

Historical identities weigh cultural distinctiveness heavily. This was the case in both Russia and China, although China's universalist identity as if nation mattered little was a sharp contrast with Russia's national focus in competition with nearby states. Chinese identity was more threatened by subversive effects of the transition to modernity, reacting with a culturally rooted identity more intense in its extremes, some manifested in the transitional decades and others peaking with Mao's fervent identity claims in the 1960s.[22] Cultural narrowness muddied the communist ideal, but imposing communism on each country had a similarly transformative effect, as the old order was eradicated in most respects and a new model was harshly built.

THE IMPACT OF STALINISM AND MAOISM

Communist identity borrowed from tsarist Russia more than from imperial China. In both states, "harmony" based on terror and the inculcation of beliefs was grafted onto a modernizing society to the exclusion of individualism, pluralism, or an acceptance of the West as a model and partner.[23] Stalin left a stronger identity legacy, even if his place in it was fragile; Mao's approach to identity was harder to sustain, but his place was more secure. Both spared no effort to reeducate people.

David Brandenberger analyzes how ideology was popularized in the Soviet Union starting in the mid-1930s through the rehabilitation of tsarist heroes and Russocentric imagery, reaching a mass audience through a carefully controlled process of identity formation. Given low rates of literacy and a focus on narrow local identities, Russians had long trailed other nations in disseminating national identity. Their focus was the tsar and the Orthodox Church, but it took communist methods after the Revolution and notably after the shift away from utopianism or vague internationalism and toward glorification of the state to widely implant national identity. Political education plus the spread of popular films promoted mass culture. World War II gave a big boost to this endeavor, linking the glories of Russian history to the great victory of the Soviet Union.[24] Yet there were at least three challenges confronted with limited success in the late 1940s, when Zhdanovshchina, a campaign against heterodox thought, made targets of cosmopolitanism (ideas from the West), non-Russian minority identities, and civil society identity. First, pride in Russian historical culture carried the seeds of respect for the culture shared with the West. Second, privileging the Russian people marginalized other nationalities, which had found openings in the earlier phase of "internationalization," and left unresolved the balance between Russian tradition and Soviet socialism. Third, the tension between class struggle and civil society kept growing, with no resolution in Stalin's simplistic response to identity.

Despite Mao's insistence on independence from Stalin's model of revolution, he came to power accepting the ideological authority of the Soviet Union. This was assumed to bring socialist modernization, and little awareness was shown of how it would clash with Chinese or even Chinese Communist Party traditions. In the years 1956–58, attacks spread against dogmatically following a rigidly centralized model, as Mao sought a more radical interpretation in response to Khrushchev's reformist outlook.[25] Soviet ideology was seen to fall short in transforming identity, while Mao was confident that China could do better in reeducating intellectuals and others.

The transition from "internationalist" to Chinese identity, drawing heavily on history, was more complicated. When ideological fervor was waning in the second decade after the revolution, Mao responded differently, long pursuing Cultural Revolution centering on socialist utopianism and denigrating Chinese history. Yet he was less successful than Stalin in inculcating sustainable beliefs, notably among the disaffected educated population and officials. Once utopianism was abandoned in

1978, China would have the edge, left freer from ideological ortho-doxy. Also, its revolution is steeped in heroic struggle against imperial-ism, laying a foundation for Sinocentrism, which lacks Russocentrism's ambivalence about the West. Stalin's alliance with the United States in World War II, like Mao's virtual alliance with it starting in 1972, did not mean that either country reduced the national identity gap substantially.

Stalin established a national identity more in keeping with the past Russian identity. Indeed, many have suggested that the Russification of Marxism had occurred. Mao resisted the Sinification of Marxism, leav-ing more of a vacuum for successors in need of reconstructing national identity. But two centuries of Russian reform trends to 1917 proved that an alternative strain of identity has viability, while Mao's role in reviving Sinocentrism qualifies any single-minded conclusion of dis-continuity. Both leaders left a legacy that would be contested and could combine anew with the past.

Under Stalin and Mao, grandiose claims permeated all dimensions of identity. Ideology was treated as an authoritative blueprint, giving the nations who commanded it unquestioned superiority. History mattered only from the time of the revolution, after which the inexorable march to socialism and communism left others behind. Claims to sectoral identity rested on insistence that the dictatorship of the proletariat, pro-letarian culture, and centralized planning confer huge advantages. The vertical dimension centered on assumptions about equality, collectivity, and the devotion of the masses. As for horizontal identity, workers of the world were waiting to join in proletarian internationalism, leading to a new world order. Even if national identity would supposedly fade away, leaders heralded its intensity as evidence of success.

Stalin and Mao imposed a doctrinaire approach to ideology as the driving force in addressing all questions. By the last years of their total-itarian rule, they had narrowed the scope of ideological discussions, demanding conformity to their own omnipresent judgments as to what is politically correct. Although each leader insisted that his views were universal on behalf of a system of belief that was valid everywhere, the ideology became a part of Soviet and Chinese national identity, attrib-uting to one state the status of the vanguard in the spread of a model of transformation to all corners of the globe. Compared with noncommunist states, ideology was placed on a higher pedestal, endowed with sacrosanct qualities as if handed down by a godlike figure with omniscient abilities. It was unchecked unless opposition arose within the Communist Party, which was programmed to concur on the priority of ideology.

The transformation of identity was made easier after each revolution by class struggle. Inculcating an artificial class identity undermined existing identities and opened the way for the Communist Party to refocus loyalties, often on abstractions and collectives manipulated by the state. Social disorientation served this purpose. The notion of the dictatorship of the proletariat or the mass line helped to atomize the population, leaving many helpless to resist the inculcation of new identities.[26]

Stalin in the late 1920s and Mao in the late 1950s and again in the early 1960s found that identity remained a barrier to their grand designs to remake society. Kulaks (supposedly affluent farmers) and Nepmen (private traders and small business owners under the New Economic Policy) were then targeted in a ruthless fashion in the Soviet Union, but Mao went further in targeting even the educated and bureaucratic elites. They both had ways of narrowing the gap between Red and expert, but Stalin's coercive methods allowed more room for experts to keep their distance from the identity pressure. For Mao, "proletarian nature" was about attitudes, although class persisted as a factor, more than in Stalin's later decades. "Single-minded hatred of the enemy" was expected, along with devotion to the thought of Mao Zedong.[27] For Stalin, he was virtually the sole source of truth, reshaping the social sciences to fit his beliefs.[28] For both leaders, twisting the truth in shaping identities could proceed with no limits.

Mao was obsessed with correct thought in ways that had no parallel, as Stalin relied more heavily on terror. In China, the goal of reforming "thought" (*sixiang*) permeated frequent campaigns, demanding that individuals who were not directly targeted denounce others, "speak bitterness," and undergo psychological conversion.[29] This left a more disruptive legacy than that left by Stalin in his more targeted campaigns.

In contrast to Beijing's discomfort at subsuming national identity under the universal claims of another state, Moscow grew arrogant with superpower identity as it competed with the United States and anticipated victory. China's communist identity changed abruptly at the end of the 1950s. Mao set his country on a twenty-year course of revolutionary hubris, claiming to lead the international movement, competing with the Soviet Union to define orthodox communism as opposed to a deviant version, and supporting radicalism, as in North Korea. This put pressure on the Soviets to reject their sprouts of moderation and to limit "peaceful coexistence."

Campaigns to achieve socialist reeducation persisted through the Stalin and Mao eras, only to be replaced by other forms of "upbringing" with more subtlety in orchestrating national identity construction. Lacking control over institutions and often means to implement their proposals, the broad spectrum of intelligentsia, first in Russia and then in China, became more fixated on their struggle over ideas than over policies. The most politically correct method to challenge orthodoxy was to appeal to reform strains of socialist thought. Intense inculcation of ideology kept the focus on debating alternative concepts that could turn the party-state in a different direction. The classic Soviet home scene was of people sitting around the table deep in a discussion of abstract ideas. In China, the Cultural Revolution is remembered as a decade of small group "study" sessions, thought reform, or sessions of criticism and self-criticism. Under pressure to transform their thinking in accord with the official orthodoxy, people struggled with ideas in a way few others around the world did.

As Graeme Gill explains the situation, the Soviet goal was a sweeping reconstruction of the identity of their country through a rejection of their own past and the existing world community. Putting ideology in the forefront to guide all dimensions of identity, this gave rise to what Gill calls a "metanarrative" consistent with the ideology and filled with myths that simplistically linked the regime and the people. All appeared under Stalin and were reinforced by Mao with adjustments for China's own experience. In sanctifying the Bolshevik Revolution, the building of socialism, and the communist leadership, the myths glorified national identity. And in demonizing the supposed internal and external opposition, they widened identity gaps. Another myth made victory in World War II a sacrosanct phenomenon not subject to reexamination.[30]

The impact of the 1940s remains important. When doubts over the legacy of Stalin and Mao's rules were widespread in the 1990s, long-distorted claims about the personal role of these leaders in saving a civilization were reasserted. These claims had an impact on temporal identity, glorifying not only achievements that might be seen as peripheral to socialism but also the value of communist rule, which was linked to the enduring struggle against imperialism. In this way, it also served horizontal identity, widening the gap in China with Japan and the United States, whose role in defeating Japan was relegated to the sidelines, and in Russia with the United States, whose performance in World War II is still treated ambivalently. The 1940s link socialist and presocialist identities at the expense of shared identity with the United States and with many other countries.

China put more stress on the party than on the state. Although World War II and the powerful Red Army gave a boost to Soviet state identity, Mao's slogan "the party commands the gun," followed by attacks on bureaucrats and experts in favor of "Reds," kept the party above the state. Moreover, Mao's campaign style deprived the Chinese of other identities apart from class and locality, in contrast to the diversity of identities sustained in the Soviet Union and given new life after Stalin's death.

Stephen Kotkin explains Stalinism as a civilization, rejecting arguments that it was a throwback to Russia's past. Revolutionary idealism in its world-historical mission and an intense desire to build a mighty state are two features he observes. More than an ideology, Kotkin says, "The revolution constantly announced itself as being about values, behavior, and beliefs. This cultural dimension is critical." Rather than great Russian nationalism being a rejection of socialism, he sees it as part of a shift from building socialism to defending socialism.[31] Similarly, China's transition to great Han nationalism meant forging a civilization steeped in Maoism, reinforcing socialism, and leaving a legacy that would endure beyond a single leader's conceits.

Communism presents a worldview pretentious in its national identity claims. If we set aside the ideals articulated by Karl Marx and others in the decades before the Bolshevik Revolution, then we are dealing with one regime or another bent on preserving its power through contrasting the identity of one country and the global movement it represents with the alleged identity of the leading capitalist countries. The result is an extreme rendering of national identity distinctiveness and of the gap with the identities of rivals. The identity gap appears as an extreme dichotomy—good versus evil, progress versus retrogression, scientific adherence to orthodox prescriptions versus revisionism or hostile rejection. Identity is put on a pedestal. It drives policy. It is the test of judgments about loyalty versus subversion. All opposing forces are lumped into a single force—anti-Soviet or anti-Chinese, antisocialist, and anti–Communist Party. With this logic, Lin Biao in the mid-1970s was pro-Confucius to China's leaders, and Deng Xiaoping at the beginning of the 1980s was pro-imperialist to the Soviet leaders, who, following this way of thinking, insisted that "any distortion of socialism" leads to a cruel fate.[32]

On the vertical dimension, ethnic minorities were kept under tight control as Stalin and then Mao radicalized socialism with identity claims about eliminating the backwardness of these peoples. Yet, Russification and the disparagement of all forms of tradition during China's Cultural Revolution exposed the extreme nature of this homogeneity.[33] It would be relaxed in the 1980s and 1990s, more so in Russia, but would never be fully displaced.

The Soviets feigned success in suppressing ethnic nationalism while, unwittingly, in the Brezhnev era titular minorities in the republics reinvigorated their identity. Assimilation policies worked poorly. Despite evidence that minority culture had been eviscerated and religion had been severely suppressed, a pretense of support for ethnic diversity helped to breathe new life into these forces as Soviet identity grew stale.[34]

Chinese and Russians expressed their alienation in the overthrow of the Qing Dynasty, the May Fourth Movement, the 1905 Revolution, and the 1917 Revolution. Yet, in the vacuum left by weakening central government and identity confusion, the way was cleared for ethnic identities to pose a serious challenge. Russia was much more vulner-able. Separation of nations that had been part of the Russian Empire, along with the victory of the Bolsheviks in the civil war, kept this chal-lenge under control; but totalitarianism came only with the purges, class warfare, and cultural revolution in the years of the First Five-Year Plan and collectivization. Great effort was made to replace existing culture. Mao went much further than Stalin. He was more distrustful of intel-lectuals, or at least was less willing to rely on terror to keep them in check. After creating a sense of siege, identity could be refocused on the authority of one man.

The Russian intelligentsia did a better job of preserving a separate identity. They had more alternative identities available, having been given leeway starting in the 1930s to take pride in traditional Russian cultural identity and having from the time of the thaw in the 1950s had relative freedom to become acquainted with the trends in Western culture. The force of cultural debates in Russia appeared to be matched in the late 1980s, but "culture fever" was blocked starting with the Tiananmen Square repression on June 4, 1989, and was never allowed to regain momentum. Those Chinese who were disposed to carry this forward found many outlets of individual expression, ranging from going abroad to going into business.

Hadley Cantril explained that communism is a purposeful strategy of a small elite to change the identity of the peoples under its control. Eliminating any sphere of privacy, subordinating the individual to the collective, and defining all collective identities as part of a rigid hierar-chy, the Communist Party demands not only total loyalty but also an abandonment of other allegiances with potentially divisive effects.[35]

A heavy burden is placed on ideological work and upbringing to ensure these results and to reduce the weight of coercion, which was not spared by either Stalin or Mao. Such ambitious aspirations drove what were called "vestiges" underground. Terror could be expanded, thought reform intensified, campaigns to frighten people added, but atomizing individuals from old connections and herding them into artificial new groupings did not leave a secure foundation for the desired identity goals. Stalin was more compromising than Mao on middle-class and careerist values that could stand in the way of totalitarianism.[36] After failed attempts, Mao did much less to transform the structural conditions of life, such as the spread of urban living and of wage labor, which would work against earlier identities.[37] Stalin was more accepting of experts who were not "Red," as Mao's campaign methods left more of an identity shambles.

In China, as in the Soviet Union three decades earlier, identity formation following the consolidation of power meant a very sharp differentiation of past and present. History was reconstructed through a prism of class conflict. Cultural and economic identity meant the sharpest possible condemnation of capitalism, accompanied by firm insistence that an entirely new identity was being built. Yet even this was not enough. From the end of the 1920s in the Soviet Union and the end of the 1950s in China, both domestic and foreign enemies appeared even more dangerous, as the notion of international communism lost meaning, except as a vehicle for exporting what one center of communism had decided. With more simplification and intensified purges, identity was brought to its peak intensity in a hysterical atmosphere and through a cult of personality focused on one infallible leader. In the following period, class was losing ground to nation, as seen in the Soviet appeal in the war to Russian nationalism.[38] Similarly, Mao's rapprochement with the United States was linked to this outcome, although as in the case of Stalin, ideology was soon reasserted.

The Chinese rapprochement with the United States at a time of radical socialism was more far-reaching than its Soviet counterpart thirty years earlier. In both cases, the abrupt change was for limited great power balancing in conditions of war or fear of war. The intent was to confine the impact narrowly, expecting to widen the divide before long. Stalin succeeded in this strategy, benefiting from lend-lease, keeping the US presence to a minimum, and seizing the opportunity of victory in World War II to reinvigorate radical mobilization, a demonization of the United States through the anticosmopolitan campaign, and a glorification of communist identity. Mao and the Gang of Four also tried in the years 1973–76 to keep the identity gap wide, but with a faulty strategy, spending more energy attacking Soviet revisionism than

Western capitalism, and blaming the Soviets more than the West for imperialism. Meanwhile, they faced another gap of increasing salience, because Taiwan, Japan, and other areas of dynamic Asia were having success linked to Confucian culture. Despite harsh condemnation of this tradition, it was giving rise to an alternative identity, making room for society. Russia had no alternative identity from its past associated with economic incentives. It saw reform through a polarized lens of socialism versus capitalism (acceding to the West), not socialism versus East Asian modernization, capitalist or not.

The seeds of the Sino-Soviet rift were sown in the strengthening after the end of Russia's brief cultural revolution in 1928–31 of *kulturnost'*, as approval was given to a new elite to aspire to the high culture shared with the West and well embedded during the tsarist era in the old elite.[39] This refocused the Soviet Union on the West, opening the door for Khrushchev's "thaw." Mao's Cultural Revolution opposed such a linkage, drawing a firmer line against the West, with further identity consequences.

The great purge and the Cultural Revolution, although later repudiated, were important in imprinting communist identity in a manner that was difficult to dislodge. If the cult of personality proved unsustainable, that did not mean that the intimidation of those with other viewpoints and an eradication of symbols would not have enduring effects. Briefly, the backlash under Khrushchev and Deng seemed sweeping. Yet the backtracking that followed was evidence of the lasting legacy of Stalinism and Maoism.

"Stalin established the 'otherness' of the Soviet experience, its exceptionalism and independence from strictures that governed other societies," Jeffrey Brooks observes. Noting this impact, Brooks argues that Stalin got many people to establish a bond with Stalin himself and left a public culture with no room for alternatives.[40] Mao did the same. Following the charismatic rule of these leaders, public culture changed substantially, but Putin was able to reestablish a lesser bond and the Chinese refocused the bond on Communist Party rule. Over time, their individual legacies weakened; yet elements of both stood right in the path of globalization.

Stalin and Mao retained generally positive images for their achievements on the horizontal dimension, resisting external enemies and "saving" their countries. They also received considerable credit for the vertical dimension, forging a powerful and united country able to defend itself and to exert influence. They were credited with overcoming backwardness, too. Regardless of the merits of these conclusions, those who sought to concentrate on the terrible crimes and great losses caused by these megalomaniacs were unable to convince the political elite or even the broad public. In the periods 1956–62 in the Soviet Union and 1978–81 in China, charges against them were more tolerated, but that ended abruptly in formulaic, minimal criticism.

The national identities constructed by Stalin and Mao proved unsustainable, but that does not mean that they were erasable. Their ideologies were at odds with national interests at the time of their deaths. Each country required closer relations with the United States, a peaceful environment for refocusing on modernization, and relaxation of totalitarianism in order to create incentives for the populace. Yet these changes had to be put in the context of an altered national identity. That meant not only reassessing Stalin and Mao but also reevaluating the identity they left behind. Go too far, and all of communism, built on an extraordinary record of lies, would lose validity. Say too little, and identity adjustments would fail to meet pressing needs.

The legacy of Stalin and Mao, the leaders who forged the communist systems, was far-reaching for national identity. De-Stalinization, despite talk of its humanistic thrust in the Khrushchev period and of a single world economy in the Deng era, left key elements of national identity largely intact. Putin and Hu Jintao did not suddenly reverse course. They rose to power after years of anti-Americanism and restoration of elements of identity that had lost traction or been obscured. Despite much talk of the "children of the Twentieth Party Congress" and both the victims of the Cultural Revolution and the beneficiaries of the "reform and open door," power remained in the hands of the heirs of zealots and their accomplices in purges that decimated old elites, traumatizing their offspring and others who may have revived their mantle.

CONCLUSION

Mao equated himself with Qin Shi Hwang, a villainous emperor in the historiography of China. Stalin is identified with Ivan the Terrible, who was also extreme in his conduct. Each leader took communism to an extreme, while invoking similarities with the most extreme leaders of the past. National identity was understood to be continuous in Russia, despite persistent Soviet claims to be following in the tradition of the Decembrists and others who opposed tsarist rule. In contrast, Mao's more comprehensive rejection of China's political tradition was a sign of the greater lack of fit between past and present. Mao was more extreme in trying to erase China's past identity, aware that it would be irreconcilable with his agenda. The tenacity of Russia's Westernizers was a persistent concern of leaders in all periods, giving them cause to affirm rival Russian tradition.

Chinese and Russian traditions differ sharply on some dimensions but not on others. Both had strong, comprehensive ideologies, reinforced by leaders (despite some Russian exceptions) reluctant to acknowledge changing forces in the eighteenth and nineteenth centuries. Seeing the past as successful in resisting outside civilizations, leaders were constrained in how open they would be to outside forces that would remove such resistance. They had a strong sense of both political and cultural identity. One difference was the greater Russian pessimism regarding human nature and the capacity to realize an ideal order, in contrast to the repeated appeal to "*datong*" (Great Harmony) in China. When running into trouble in socialist construction (1921, 1956, 1985), the Soviet Union flirted with convergence with the West, despite difficulty in sustaining it. In China, trouble evoked utopianism in 1958 and 1965. Although, starting in 1978, it seemed to be following the Soviet "thaw" strategy and eschewed utopianism, certain ideals trumped convergence.[41] Seen in later chapters, China is more distant from the West.

Maoism and Stalinism left similar legacies of totalitarianism, a command economy without market forces, and an atomized and mobilized population little prepared for organizing to assume responsibility. There were also common features in their national identities. Ideological obsessions trumped everything else, and history was seen through a very rigid formula of good and evil that glorified the present; while economic and cultural identity claims may have seemed artificial, political identity claims were at their apex, and the vertical dimension was in its most extreme form, as was the horizontal divide, demonizing much of the world and privileging a global hierarchy of communist states under one's own leadership; and identity intensity was at a feverish pitch. However, dismantling the old identity and constructing a new one posed somewhat different problems in China and Russia. A survey of each of the six dimensions in chapter 2 points to differences with consequences for the transition. The periods 1953–56 in the Soviet Union and 1976–78 in China were starting points of reconstruction, whose subsequent main figures, Deng and Gorbachev, are the main subjects of the next comparisons.

CHAPTER 2

THE COMMUNIST LEGACY AND THE IMPACT OF DENG AND GORBACHEV

The process of building socialism and communism is conceived as forging a comprehensive national identity, with ideology in the lead, that entails subsuming everyone's consciousness to the point that other identities (e.g., ethnicity, religion, class) would fade away. Josef Stalin compromised in letting Russian historical and cultural identity regain a role, while Mao Zedong redoubled the focus on class identity as he allowed room for Sinocentrism tied to reunification. Yet, in the wake of a relentless onslaught on alternative identities with no reprieve in Stalin's and Mao's final years, new leadership recognized the need to relax the stranglehold over identity, abandoning totalitarianism. This could have been seen as a step in the dismantling of communism, but that idea was ruled out of bounds until it started to get a hearing at the end of the 1980s with opposite results in the two countries. This process—which was set in motion in 1956 and 1978 by Khrushchev's de-Stalinization speech and Deng Xiaoping's "reform and open door" policies, respectively—did not proceed smoothly. Communism's legacy was tenacious; there was no alternative acceptable to the elite that it had nurtured in place of the old elite it had decimated. After communism shifted from vague internationalism to a state-centered identity under Stalin and Mao, successors had the option of refocusing on this in the name of communism and striving to manage long-suppressed identities.

The deaths of Stalin and Mao left an identity vacuum, because both encouraged cults of their personality with claims of omniscience and attempts at omnipotence. Soviet and Chinese leaders faced not only the disruption of incorporating millions of victims back into their communities in order to revive incentives for intellectual life, but also the problem of how to deal with both the victimizers and the many who had abetted or sympathized with the horrors inflicted. This made it problematic to have any kind of identity discourse about class enemies, the impassable divide with the West, or the unacceptability of the market economy and career aspirations linked to it. Changes in covering these themes, however, did not necessarily deepen the identity vacuum because other options existed for boosting pride in the nation on many dimensions.

Communism changed irreversibly in 1956. Khrushchev's de-Stalinization speech announced the Soviet Union's intention to change course. By not consulting Mao and others, Moscow denied the shared identity of communist nations and put Beijing in the position of either succumbing or defining its identity in opposition to that of the movement's leader. De-Stalinization obliged other states in the socialist bloc to respond. In the mid-1950s, the Soviet Union was the unchallenged leader of the bloc. It had compelling reasons to refocus its identity as well as its development in a direction that involved being less resistant to elements of civil society and less hostile to the West. Yet Stalin had left a time bomb, both at home and in the communist leaderships abroad.

Khrushchev was put in a contradictory situation: To go forward with the thrust of his de-Stalinization agenda would be seen as moving against the interests of the Soviet elite and its partners in international communism; to pull back would mean taking a path leading to increasing stagnation and further isolation from capitalist states. In Hungary, it led to rebellion. In China and North Korea, it encouraged challenges to powerful leaders, which after harsh repression led to unprecedented extremism that imperiled ties with the Soviet Union and dampened interest in a new Soviet model. Failure to press forward gave an opening to Mao Zedong, Kim Il-sung, and resisters within the Soviet leadership, seizing on inconsistencies in Khrushchev's notion of communist identity. Truth about history or the international environment did not win approval from other communist leaders or from the elite left by the old order.

After Khrushchev tried to transform Soviet identity with utopian elements of communism mixed with humanistic links to a shared world community, Brezhnev's slogans were unable to make adjustments to identity required in a dynamic world. Khrushchev's thaw and peaceful coexistence had appeared at least to let Western civilization back into Soviet identity. However, in the 1960s competition with China to lead revolutionary movements and newly independent states rekindled the attacks on the West for its imperialism. A backlash protective of narrow socialist identity followed. Eventually, Brezhnev's contortions in reviving ideology exposed the outdated nature of seeking to keep this focus for identity. This proved to be a dead end for reviving the idealism of early communism, even as the socialist legacy was solidified through superpower identity and a social contract that provided security.

Soviet identity lost dynamism after Khrushchev, particularly starting in 1968, as the Prague Spring was crushed, economic reforms stalled, and ideology grew more intense. Efforts to inculcate greater loyalty, as at the time of the centennial of Lenin's birth in 1970, lacked vitality. The artificiality of identity claims grew more obvious in an environment of deepening economic stagnation and international isolation.

The contrast between Brezhnev's approach and Mao's Cultural Revolution was stark. In the face of waning support for ideology, Brezhnev advanced the theme of "developed socialism," appealing for social unity behind leaders pledging to lead the way to the forefront of global modernization. In contrast, Mao insisted on a more intense belief in ideology. Both sought to block identities supportive of society independent of the leadership, while demonizing dissenters and the outside world. Their common goal was to substitute a mythology for reality, forging identity with an idealized regime.

Brezhnev went further than Stalin in capitalizing on Russia's past, even though he also exposed Soviet identity to tension from those prepared to go much farther. Strong emphasis on the state provided for continuity. Many people with little chance to pursue careerism found certain vicarious esteem in identifying with state success. After all, space programs, sports medals, and the Soviet Union's superpower standing gave the people sources of esteem, even if they gradually grew stale as shortcomings kept spreading. In China, there was less of a basis for national esteem in the 1980s, necessitating flexibility in national identity that went well beyond Brezhnev's tolerance over two decades.

Soviet experts were at times pressured under Brezhnev to pay obeisance to ideology, but most were permitted to remain silent, and some were so valued that their limited defiance was normally overlooked. Mao feared similar developments, going to great lengths to favor "Reds" over experts. Yet Deng went much further than Brezhnev in freeing experts to focus on their own areas of specialization and careers, whether national or international. Frustrations from ideological restraints were far fewer in China under Deng, as many pursued successful paths of upward mobility.

There were parallels in the stages of socialism in the two countries, which had proceeded with a Chinese time lag of twenty-five to thirty years until the 1980s, when the gap narrowed. The demands on national identity changed in tandem. However, in the hectic decade of the 1980s, first China broke away from the pattern of lagging in its identity transformation and then Gorbachev led his country to try to leap ahead. Instead of a rather consistent time lag, the two states leapfrogged ahead, with uncertain effects.

Chinese identity in the 1980s evolved through a tug of war between what Richard Baum calls middle-aged intellectuals and technocrats on one side and the older generation of Marxist revolutionaries on the other, leading to an atmosphere of cycles, with Deng occupying the middle ground and shifting to achieve a balance. Richard Baum suggests that in the years 1992–93, as the older group were dying or becoming infirm, the "last gasp of the left" occurred, but the repudiation of their extreme ideological views did not signify that national identity would then be forged by pragmatic reformers.[1] Rather, the left put in place a process of leadership succession that marginalized the reformers in predominantly economic roles, while reproducing a conservative core of high officials who, while cautiously following Deng's advice to bide their time, had an opportunity to play the leading role in reconstructing China's national identity.

Similar to the Soviet Union, China faced a choice in the 1980s of debunking myths or spreading more lies. Leaders tolerated some exposés but decided that the myths must be protected. If campaigns in early 1984 and early 1987 failed to revive an ideologically centered national identity, they managed to forestall modernization from gaining dominance in identity in parallel to reforms freeing the economy. Rival versions of identity persisted until three shocks tilted the balance to a reconstituted ideology, which was reinterpreted to soften the image. First, the spring 1989 turmoil in China—climaxing on June 4 with the Tiananmen Square massacre—changed the balance in the leadership. Second, the collapse of the communist bloc in 1989 alarmed the leadership, bolstering the case for identity opposed to the reform worldview. Third, despite Deng reinforcing developmental identity in early 1992, the impact of the collapse of the Soviet Union favored further consolidation of a conservative identity. Deng's caution about "lying low" obscured the thrust of this shift, as academics kept alive moderate interpretations of the way national identity was evolving. Yet they were battling a mainstream force, without being able to directly challenge the growing authority of the views they opposed. The fact of leadership divisions softened the rhetoric of conservatives in the 1990s and 2000s.

The verdict of June 4, 1989, and the failed Soviet coup of August 1991 was that the vertical dimension must remain dictatorial, ready to repress dissent if collapse were to be avoided. The ideological dimension must not be confused by relaxation of the control system and propaganda. Moreover, the horizontal dimension must be seen through the lens of "bourgeois peaceful evolution," in which US subversion focuses on cultural identity, gradually undermining political national identity. When regimes under communist rule fell one after the other in 1989, blame was also put on how Gorbachev abetted (intentionally, according to many) the West in undermining all three of these dimensions of state identity. Finally, when the Soviet Union collapsed, the idea spread that "humanism and democratic socialism" weaken both cultural and vertical identity, posing a similar danger in China.[2] The lessons from these successive shocks were tempered somewhat by Deng's insistence on a low-intensity response as well as further economic reform, but they were never seriously reconsidered in China.

Denouncing Soviet history put an enormous strain on national identity, not only at the end of the Soviet era but also at the onset of the following Russian era. The Communists had "dehumanized the country's life after 1917," according to the devastating view of Gorbachev's "nihilistic" impact.[3] Critics charged that glasnost—Gorbachev's policy calling for increased openness and transparency—caused everything to be inverted. The honor of the country trumps the honor of individual victims, many believed. Stalin forged a strong country, guided the Soviet Union to victory in World War II, and brought his country into the club of superpowers. To demean these feats is tantamount to stripping Soviet citizens of their pride, which rested heavily on the collective identity of a nation steeped in success. Dwelling on human rights plays into the hands of anticommunists, whose goal is understood to be to weaken their opponents, argued some, who felt that national prestige and identity were being endangered by such human rights concerns. Others warned that "the notion of an omnipotent, omniscient and omnibenevolent state is held not only by ordinary people. . . . It penetrates our society far more deeply."[4] Exposés of bureaucratism, corruption, long-concealed crimes, and repeated lies jeopardized what was really a house of cards.

Soviet reform spoke in a loud voice but carried a small stick, whereas Chinese reform kept the promises down and the results up. Gorbachev made many promises that were not achievable compared with Deng, who said little even when he intervened to set a new course. The implications for national identity of these discrepancies are difficult to overestimate, giving China room to reaffirm its communist claims while denying Russia space to replace its long history of claims. Soviet reforms were to bring democracy through empowering local soviets, which never gained real power. They were to yield abundant consumer goods through cooperatives, but shortages spread rapidly. New relations with the West heralded large-scale foreign investment, as was promised in the 1987 program for the Russian Far East, when the conditions for investment were missing and rampant corruption greeted anyone who dared to try to invest.

In the second half of the 1980s, both China and the Soviet Union had debates that touched on every dimension of national identity. Ideology was in the forefront, and history was recognized as critical. All aspects of sectoral identity were discussed, as cultural, economic, and political identity loomed large. Vertical identity mattered, as totalitarianism was rejected and authoritarianism was debated. Foreign relations were recast in identity terms. The intensity of identity demands was lowered, even as the substance was being reexamined more energetically. In 1989, China's leaders began to increase the intensity, while when Russian leaders in 1992 failed to do so, they became increasingly vulnerable to a backlash from below demanding this revival. The contrast between how Gorbachev and Deng handled the critical period is easy to draw.

THE IDEOLOGICAL DIMENSION

Ideology dominated national identity in both countries. Its hold was so great that there was little room for reconstructing the other dimensions. Only the death of the narcissistic leader, who defined ideology while brooking no diversity, opened the door to change. This had to begin with the downgrading of ideology, as occurred in 1956 with de-Stalinization and in 1978 with the Third Plenum's decisions. The straightjacket of a single dimension narrowly deciding permissible thought was, at last, broken.

The national identities established by Stalin and Mao incorporated all aspects of identity into ideology. The immediate challenge for their successors was to dethrone a narrow interpretation of ideology, rehabilitating ideas that had been branded heresy but rejecting others that threatened to discredit the entire communist experience. For China, Mao was made off limits in 1980; therefore, much of the discussion turned to the record of Soviet ideological themes. Khrushchev allowed a rather narrow range of ideological inquiry, putting Stalin's role into a formulaic discussion of the "cult of personality." When Brezhnev drew the line tighter on Stalin but approved a wider assault on Chinese ideology, the door was open for indirect, reformist thought to explore some ideological limits as a means to revise national identity.[5] Absent this pretext, other dimensions were little more than a sideshow, with scant prospects for far-reaching Soviet transformation.

China's ideological disadvantage appeared to be the absence of a fallback to an indigenous counterpart for Lenin. To the extent that Mao was discredited, all of Chinese communism would be in jeopardy. Without such a safety valve, China went further in reconstructing other aspects of the ideological dimension, with ramifications for other dimensions. The anti-imperialist factor was far more pronounced in ideology and was refocused. The Sinocentric theme carried more weight than a dubious Russocentric effort at odds with the integrative thrust of the Soviet Union. Having experienced a shorter history of socialism and lacking superpower pretensions, China could recalibrate its socialism to an early stage, while that would have rung false in the industrialized Soviet Union.

China's ideology in the period 1979–89 never strayed far from central control. Repeatedly, leaders tightened the rope or launched campaigns, setting a clear tone in 1980 with the concept of "socialist spiritual civilization." This ideal, linked to limits on debate, soon encompassed Chinese civilization, with stress on a history of exceptionalism. Balancing the traditional identity inherited from Stalin or Mao with the newer identity forged after their deaths proved complicated in the subsequent period. China did so with vague slogans, mixing the words "socialist" and "Chinese." Soviet ideology was embedded in policies with more popular appeal, making the struggle against it more complicated and protracted.

Many see an abrupt change in Chinese national identity in the 1980s, from a radical form of communism in favor of revolutionary internationalism to a cautious, nonideological path of nation building. At the same time, they may recognize two secondary strands: a quasi-liberal approach taking peace and development as the sole objectives; and a conservative, security-oriented approach emphasizing Communist Party authority and Taiwan as the symbol of threats to China's territorial integrity.[6] Although, before June 4, 1989, outside observers were prone to weight the quasi-liberal views heavily, afterward there was more doubt that they could challenge the mainstream or even serve as a counterweight to the conservative, security-oriented school. The relationship of the mainstream to the latter group remained particularly unclear. A declining revolutionary ideology did not necessarily mean that another variant of socialist ideology was not ascendant. Indeed, the contradiction between, first, Mao's agreement to normalize relations with the United States and anti-imperialism and, second, Deng's priority for modernization and class harmony made it imperative even for conservatives to find a new anchor for national identity. The shift under way in Soviet socialism, focusing party legitimacy on state power, was repeated in China.

With the challenge of developing a modern country in the forefront, China downgraded ideology while praising science. Narrowing the ideological debate by setting limits through the "four basic principles," "socialism with Chinese characteristics," and a "socialist spiritual civilization," Deng carried forward a two-front struggle versus party leftists and those seen as rightists while trying to prevent a crisis of legitimacy by reconstructing national identity, linking Chinese patriotism with socialism. In 1986, the campaign against bourgeois liberalization tilted to the leftists before the pendulum swung toward the intellectuals, backed by Zhao Ziyang and Deng. And the intellectuals were determined not only to put an end to class struggle and the polarization of socialism and capitalism but also to link science, inclusive of the social sciences, and humanism. This paralleled developments a quarter century earlier in the Soviet Union, which also ended with a sharp turn against humanism.[7] China had a weaker base for humanism, but June 4, 1989, did not lead to the pain of Soviet-style isolation from the international community.

Glasnost was the kiss of death for Soviet communism, which rested on fabrications and secrecy. Without censorship, it could not long survive. Gorbachev tolerated the revival of suppressed identities—ethnic, religious, and Western. These were stronger in the Soviet Union than in China, except for the Tibetans and Uighurs, and they benefited from local elites who had found ways to express them in the decades since Stalin's terror was removed.

The contrast between Alexander Yakovlev, who was put in charge of the propaganda machine in 1985, and Deng Liqun, who stifled Chinese debates and kept pressing for political campaigns in the 1980s, had great bearing on national identity changes. To reform economic policies that were proving ineffective did not mean to the Chinese leadership that the core of national identity was to be reexamined, as Gorbachev had done.

Although much attention centered on breakthrough challenges to ideology in the second half of the 1980s, opposing forces mounted a fierce counterattack. In Moscow, the transfer of control from chief Communist Party ideologue Mikhail Suslov, who for two decades before his death suppressed reform thinking, to Yakovlev in only a few years gave the momentum to the reform forces. But in China, the reinforced roles of Hu Qiaomu and Deng Liqun denied the reformers similar results. However, for about two years Deng restrained the attacks that conservatives sought to launch against Gorbachev, and he later put limits on the backlash against reform thinking, preventing a full recovery of ideology as a force in identity. With "humanistic universalism," recognizing one human civilization, Gorbachev gave new substance to peaceful coexistence and principles such as democracy and freedom, crossing what had become red lines in China's ideological retrenchment.[8] As in the late 1950s, Moscow lacked insistence on the concept of East versus West demanded by Beijing.

China has taken ideology more seriously: Confucian versus tsarist differences in the "rectification of names"; Maoist versus Stalinist differences in "thought reform"; and Deng Xiaoping versus Khrushchev, Brezhnev, and Gorbachev in managing the shift away from orthodox thinking. The legacy persisted in the post–Cold War period, when the Chinese devoted more consistent attention to reconstructing identity from the top down inclusive of ideology.

THE TEMPORAL DIMENSION

Communist ideology overall and its specific application to relations between nationalities internally emphasize relative development as a marker of superiority in culture and social system. Once backwardness is acknowledged, the identity of socialism is put in jeopardy. Rather than make such an admission, strenuous efforts are made to feign superiority, lying about the conditions of capitalist societies and of one's own society. When such admissions are made, it is imperative to reconstruct national identity, as Khrushchev, Deng, and Gorbachev all discovered.

In the second half of the 1970s, Soviet claims to developed socialism smacked of ideological innovation after the stagnation that followed Khrushchev's peripatetic twists and turns. However, its thrust was more of the same: feigning democracy in the struggle between dictatorship and democracy, showcasing a more advanced stage of development while denying the themes of the communist stage raised by Khrushchev, and trumpeting ideology when it was growing stale and standing in the path of reform. China's leaders avoided this mistake, reverting to the primary stage of socialism as a signal of lesser ideological pressure and more far-reaching reform.

The temporal dimension was steeped in notions of stages of development. By situating their countries as fully socialist and on the path to communism, Stalin and Mao put the past far behind and claimed to be ahead of capitalist states as well. Yet the reality, drawing on modernization theory, was that their countries were behind, especially China at the end of the Mao era. The implications of claims of advanced development, such as Brezhnev's announcement that his country was a developed socialist state, were that nationalities were well along in converging, rural-urban differences were being erased, and public consciousness was ahead of that in other countries. Pushing one's country further ahead also widened the gap with capitalist states, reducing the need to learn from them. With a wider gap, it followed that the struggle between the two systems was intensifying. Chinese leaders drew back from such claims, culminating in Zhao Ziyang's declaration in 1987 that China was only at the primary stage of socialism. The general secretary of the Soviet Communist Party, Yuri Andropov, in late 1982 also pulled back some, by warning that his country should not get ahead of itself. It must improve developed socialism, dealing with real problems rather than dismissing them as nothing but vestiges of the past. There was little follow-up in comparison with China's reforms.

China's emphasis on stages of development allowed room for refocusing on the need to catch up and leapfrog to global levels. Instead of replacing the socialist identity, China's leaders focused on developing the foundation to resuscitate it. Room opened for a technocratic model of modernization, with little to say about authoritarianism, which, after all, had prevailed during the economic miracles of the other East Asian states. Although some argued that socialism was feudal and that the West, as seen through the lens of humanism, represented a modern outlook on values, others, favored by rising censorship in 1989, argued for a strong state to overcome backwardness and the anarchy of the Cultural Revolution, with little concern for any checks on its power.

With communist constructs of national identity in trouble in both states in the 1980s, much depended on the recovery of precommunist identities and their compatibility. The Soviets were further along in this process, given Stalin's reassessment of tsars as heroes and of Russian cultural giants as the embodiment of the nation, and Brezhnev's tolerance for proponents of Russianness even if they had doubtful views of Soviet identity. China's leaders had been harsher to the emperors and to traditional culture; yet they claimed to be introducing Chinese characteristics to socialism, particularly in spiritual civilization. It proved harder for the Russians to clarify what to accept from tsarism, as they consciously substituted it for socialism, than for the Chinese to welcome parts of Confucianism, even as socialism was shielded.

In the first half of the 1980s, Chinese reform was premised on the primacy of modernization centered on the economy. Reaffirmation of the four modernizations—industry, agriculture, defense, and science and technology—accompanied assertions that China was a developing country that must overcome backwardness through open participation in the international division of labor, regardless of its socialist system and its vast size. Amid the world's ongoing scientific and technological revolution, a failure to open China's door and reform would mean isolation and a widening gap. One author noted that backward countries cannot "avoid eating a little dirt."[9] As modernization and comprehensive national power were recognized as critical for China's future, socialist identity was reinterpreted in this new context. A similar approach was taken toward the Soviet Union, as its insularity was criticized and hints that it would open its economy were praised at the start of Gorbachev's ascent.

Under Mao, China rejected feudalism (*feng*), equated with its past; the West (*yang*), linked to imperialism; and the Soviet Union, portrayed as revisionism (*xiu*). In the 1980s, China acknowledged Confucianism (*kong*) as part of current identity, modernization (*xiandaihua*) as a positive pursuit coming from the West, and reform socialism (*gaige*), in place of any hint that there is something called revisionism. In this way, they scrambled stage theory without discarding the idea of running a race.

The second half of the 1980s brought uncertainty about national identity to a peak in both China and the Soviet Union. Politics, international relations, and, not least of all, economics were questioned for their identity implications, while culture was also part of this whirlpool of reflection. Seemingly little things could become a matter of great controversy through the newfound prism of identity. For the leadership, the challenge was to steer this search, fortifying desired elements of the identity search and starving others. China's leaders did this. The Soviet leaders feared a repeat of Khrushchev's failure, having more confidence in humanism diffused in the public, and trusting the West more. Expecting the USSR to remain a superpower, they started with a shorter timetable. Deng called for "lying low" with an extended time frame.

The Chinese leaders, however, after starting by trying to salvage the period 1949–57, decided to salvage the entire history of socialism before Deng's reforms with praise of foreign policy and censorship regarding class struggle. Gorbachev went so far as to expose Stalin's mendacious history of World War II, shaking the cult of the war on which the greatest glory was bestowed.[10] Although this was a key move toward de-Stalinization, the drumbeat of exposés as part of glasnost did not succeed in the goal of separating the people as the source of victory from Stalin, who, in extending his Great Terror, had left the country unprepared. The cult of the war could not easily be shed, as seen in the backlash that led to the recovery of wartime memories as Victory Day, not celebrations focused on communist triumphalism that kept alive the soldiers' immortal exploits.

In observing the outcomes of glasnost, the Chinese leaders saw the Soviet leaders make a fundamental error in dealing with various dimensions of national identity, especially the chronological one. Such a policy of openness greatly undermined historical claims to national identity, regarded in Chinese history and the history of the communist movement as indispensable. Criticism of the Khrushchev era guided China's management of historical memory, even before the shock of glasnost rekindled alarm that regime legitimacy depends on the past.

Both China and Russia started to rediscover their roots in the second half of the 1980s. Environmentalism was a factor, given exposés of once-concealed disasters and the shock of the Chernobyl nuclear reactor meltdown in 1986. In 1988, both states at last faced prodemocracy movements with substantial appeal, encouraged only by the Soviet leadership. Coverage of blank spots in history intensified in 1986 in the two states, to be interrupted in China just as the Soviets were accelerating it. In common, there were harsh condemnations of the 1960s and 1970s for flawed economic thinking with a negative impact on the spiritual life of society. China kept the focus on this.

The history of communism proved a stern test of national identity in the two countries. In dealing with the history of Soviet communism, they faced questions on the same topics and individual leaders. Revelations served to discredit Communist Party rule, as China's leaders strove harder to limit it. There was a possibility of rehabilitating the more reform-oriented communists, but those who pressed to do so generally saw this as a stepping-stone to revealing other secrets with more explosive potential, while leaders who resisted found scant satisfaction in a variant of socialism at odds with what they valued in national identity. There were more intellectuals in Russia engaged in this discussion, but the main interest groups separated by economic and security concerns had other objectives. Gorbachev found it possible to activate these educated big-city residents who were attentive to histori-cal questions, but talk of mobilizing interest groups in support of change in the vertical dimension proved wishful, and the only recourse was to keep going further with glasnost and joining top-down to bottom-up pressure on those preventing reform through greater democratization.

THE SECTORAL DIMENSION

Economic national identity was unsustainable in both countries. In China, the situation was so dire that there was no attempt to salvage it. The best that could be said was that China would join the universal process of modernization, which earlier had been denied, but would proceed with Chinese characteristics kept vague for a time. Allowing the responsibility system in agriculture and the breakup of *danwei* (work unit) organization in industry, China was slow to acknowledge the identity implications. For Gorbachev, economic acceleration was the priority; but there was no available labor force, and there was too much resistance from vested interests to take advantage of the end of restrictions. In the late 1980s, earlier economic claims were repudiated with no new sources of pride. This contributed to the loss of intensity in national identity.

In the Soviet Union, after a respite for nationalities in the 1920s and even early in the 1930s, the purges decimated much of their leadership and forced acceptance of a narrow Soviet identity. Despite Khrushchev's thaw, he intensified Russification, even anticipating the disappearance of "nationalism" along with religion in a rapid transition to the era of communism. With urbanization, Russian's dissemination as a second language, and intermarriage rates rising, it appeared that assimilation was accelerating and that the "identity problem" was being solved. A single Soviet people supposedly loomed just around the corner, but this proved to be a drastic miscalculation about identities and how they actually were evolving beneath the cover of censorship and coercion.

Cultural identity proved that it carries explosive potential, arousing ethnic tensions and breaking down the divide with the West. Reform leaders took the lid off this force, exposing the greater vulnerability of the Soviet Union because of its large and concentrated ethnic minorities and its ambiguity over humanism shared with the West. Once the Pandora's box of cultural identity was opened, it proved to hold intense ethnic separatism, Russian xenophobia, and narrow notions exclusive of others that also claimed to represent Russia's core. Tensions quickly deepened.

Cultural identity was confused in the 1980s. The Maoist legacy struggled to survive the fiasco of the Cultural Revolution. Traditional Chinese culture found room to begin a comeback after decades of suppression. Western culture resonated with some audiences in the "culture fever" from mid-decade. The thirst for new trends showed signs of forging a civil society, as groups gravitated from one current to the next. Hu Yaobang's initiative to "emancipate the mind" reverberated in debates over history, society, and even politics; yet the academic and cultural community never was able to keep the initiative. Political controls were never relaxed for long, even when some bold figures managed to bend the established limits. The tightening in 1989 did not eliminate all public space for cultural debates, but it did severely limit their range and their potential to influence national identity.[11] Yet at the start of the 1990s, cultural pride was quickly being reasserted, using symbols of humiliation.

At the start of glasnost, Russian cultural identity posed a challenge to Soviet identity. Focusing on monuments, ecology, and numerous other themes, giants in the world of culture pursued further openness stemming from the inroads that had been made during the previous decades. Soon the battle over culture engulfed the temporal dimension, because Russians' high regard for many whom Stalin had purged or had tried to erase from history was infectious. Warnings against the "corruption of the national spirit" by those who had imposed a "class approach" to cultural heritage paled before the more forceful response in China.[12]

Under Brezhnev, Mikhail Suslov became the ideology tsar, with a supportive attitude toward Russian identity. Although Andropov after Suslov's death proved to be more critical, the foundation was built for an upsurge, in spite of the fact that in Gorbachev's time the balance in the leadership favored Western culture, which was deemed favorable for reform, over Russian tradition, as culture became a testing ground for the direction ahead.[13] The group focusing on Russian particularism was keener on sheltering the dark side of Soviet history, including Stalin, whereas the others feared a rising amalgam of Russian and Soviet identities. This struggle intensified during the late 1980s, appearing to favor Western culture, before making an abrupt turn.

Chinese academics in 1990 groped for the proper way to treat the Confucian legacy. Following the 1980s trend, they acknowledged that it has exerted a positive role in the economic development of Japan and the four little dragons (Hong Kong, Singapore, South Korea, and Taiwan) through solidarity, ethical education, and reduced conflict. However, when approval of Confucianism seemed to threaten socialism, one symposium's findings could only go so far as to say that Marxism and traditional culture "do not appear to be absolutely contradictory."[14] At this time, ambivalence toward Western culture led to an emphasis on complementarity with Eastern cultures, with each side compensating for the other's deficiencies. The Chinese still dealt gingerly with cultural and economic national identity. By 1990, Russian confusion was even more pronounced, as attacks on old notions of identity, both Soviet and communist, raised havoc about previous sources of pride— economic, cultural, and political. Sectoral identity proved more problematic in that country.

The Brezhnev era witnessed patterns that would find some parallel in China in the 1990s and 2000s. After a wave of reform zeal, groups of intellectuals would vie to steer national identity, among which advocates of cultural identity rooted in history had the upper hand, given the policies of top leaders. Gradually allowing more open endorsement of this theme, interrupted at times by tightening, officials tolerated a revival of long-denigrated cultural themes valued as opposed to the infiltration of Western culture. They filled the void as socialist ideology was evoking yawns. This was a safety valve for intellectuals and, increasingly, for others, giving them another focus of identity, which was deemed supportive of a strong state. This posed some problems, which were not completely identical as in the Soviet Union and China. After all, the spillover to other cultural identities across the Soviet Union was more fractious and the distinction of Soviet and Russian identities resulted in tensions beyond those generated in China.

Yitzhak Brudny clearly captures the tensions of the rise of cultural identities in the Soviet Union. First, many saw their country as a Russian state and were keen to make it more so, with disruptive implications. Second, as they took up causes such as the peasantry and the Russian Orthodox Church, they confronted socialism at a time when Moscow was mired in ideological defensiveness, unlike China, which by the late 1980s had moderated its ideological identity. Yet there was a similarity in limiting criticism of the great suffering during the Stalin and Mao eras, blocking numerous revelations. Third, a backlash occurred in both countries, garnering considerable support from above, which was defensive of Stalin or Mao, vehemently hostile to the West, and prepared to turn against the leadership if it moved toward reform. In the period 1969–72, it gained ground in the Soviet Union, and in 1979–80 and again in 1983–84, Brudny points to rising resistance to Russian cultural identity.[15] Given frustration over both rising inequities and corruption, it posed a national identity threat from the left. In neither state was it easy to manage this mix of reform, precommunist, and leftist identities, while maintaining clarity about socialist ideology. Gorbachev opened the door to these forces, succeeding for a time to put reform identity ahead, while from 1989 China stifled reform identity but did so with more flexibility, allowing religion, China's historical culture, and even Western ideals to be aired, even as the left drew renewed support over causes similar to those that galvanized it after Gorbachev.

Reform cultural figures and intellectuals had a different relationship with the Communist Party leaders in Moscow than with those in Beijing. Accepting a shared cultural tradition with the West and Russian cultural identity, the Soviet leaders recognized the prestige of a second elite not fully under its control, despite its firm organizational control over the cultural community. Emerging from the Cultural Revolution, China's cultural elite was decimated and required time to regain its footing, which was complicated by the regime's determination not to allow a repeat of the Khrushchev "thaw." Cultural pluralism linked to the outside world allowed for an influx of Western culture in the Brezhnev era and then a flood under Gorbachev. Alexander Yakovlev and other new officials welcomed this, as had Khrushchev to a lesser degree three decades earlier. In accord with imperial tradition, China did not accept a cultural sphere separate from the political one. This was true of Mao, and after hesitation Deng reaffirmed it.

Cultural identity became clearer as China battled against humanism. Without economic identity reviving and with great uncertainty about political identity for a time, cultural identity filled the void. If the link seemed weak between cultural and political identities, casting a shadow on communist authority, which had been used for at least a decade to destroy much of Chinese culture, attempts to prevent such exposés may have helped to prevent things from worsening. When other types of identity were in doubt, the deep reservoir of Chinese cultural pride filled the gap.

With the rise in ethnic identity with a potential for separatism, an upsurge in Russian identity was inevitable. Russian communities in republics other than Russia felt insecure. The large security establishment was nervous. By late 1990, Gorbachev had ousted officials, including Yakovlev, who had been deemed too sympathetic to the West. However, given Boris Yeltsin's success in winning election as president of the Russian Republic, it was he who proved more adept at seizing the mantle of Russian national identity—if, for a time, it appeared that he outdid Gorbachev as a champion of the Western side.

The Chinese blamed Western culture for Gorbachev's betrayal of socialism and the collapse of the Soviet Union. Criticizing "democratic socialism" and "humanism" while tracing their impact back, at least, to Khrushchev's 1956 complete rejection of Stalin and his model, Chinese hard-liners pressed this argument in the early 1990s and returned often to this sharp contrast with China in the ensuing twenty years.[16] Yet a different message appeared in encounters with Russians, suggesting that the socialist culture had made them lazy. One article reporting on a visit to Russia made the assertion that the deepest impression was of people taking time off from work.[17]

The cultural pride of Chinese left less of a void when traditional communism fell into disrepute. When the Russians were starting to grope for the "Russian idea" as the personal aura of a glorified leader was fading, the Chinese fell back on a culture that had long been most vibrant at the family and community levels. Whereas comparison often centers on different choices by leaders, this one rests on historical patterns.

A sense of threat to cultural identity aroused a backlash, first in China before June 4, 1989, and gathering steam with official manipulation in the 1990s; and then in Russia at essentially the same time. The situation intensified as attacks on the old order mounted and Western culture flooded into the country, but the crass materialism that overshadowed it proved overwhelming. Refocusing on restoring self-esteem through cultural pride would drive the identity narrative in the 1990s.

Global culture had enormous early appeal in the 1980s, but it soon produced a backlash. Although new forces were leading to its dissemination all over the world, in the Soviet Union and especially China the disconnect from the past was particularly great. After decades of suspicion of foreign culture, acceptance did not prove easy. If the main current in the second half of the 1980s was openness, an opposing force was not far below the surface. Russia was more vulnerable, given the established belief that it is part of Western civilization and a major contributor to the great flowering of the nineteenth century. China's Cultural Revolution left it less exposed.

Political national identity was shaken in both China and the Soviet Union by many revelations about how politics had led each country into grievous abuses of human rights. Gorbachev turned to democratization to rebuild the USSR's political identity, only to find that Russian and other republic identities undercut Soviet identity. China succeeded in keeping the focus on the People's Republic of China, denying room to Tibetan and other local identities and avoiding the divide caused by Soviet versus Russian identity. Turning attention to the state's role in both reform and international relations, China conveyed optimism about top-down coordination toward a future strikingly different from the previous three decades. The Soviets' failed reforms and rapid loss of status belied such optimism.

THE VERTICAL DIMENSION

Although most attention centered on ideology as the key to break-throughs that paved the way to reforms, the vertical dimension also deserves special attention; it was the focus in class struggle and in glorification of a single leader. Even as these issues faded in impor-tance, the national identity shift failed to go nearly as far as advocates of democratization were seeking. Centralism was preserved for the most part, stratification did not change quickly, and even the idea that a technocracy was taking shape proved to be an illusion.[18] The con-trast between Deng and Gorbachev was particularly pronounced on this dimension, giving China a greater sense of its continuity through party and state authority and leaving the Soviet Union shaken.

In the Soviet Union in the late 1950s and in China in the late 1970s, coexistence had a narrow purpose, as modernization drew strong support following a leadership change. The threat to earlier national identity was serious, and the United States was expected to seize the opportunity to undermine allegiance to the regime. If, simultaneously, socialist realism was relaxed and the class struggle lost its rationale for repression, ver-tical identity would be threatened. Khrushchev's ambiguous results in sustaining it aroused a backlash. So too did Deng's mixed results, keep-ing Khrushchev's record in mind. One striking contrast was the greater centralization of Russia and relative absence of social forces prepared for decentralization. Socialism in China existed for a shorter time, and centralization had lost ground during the Cultural Revolution. In the Southeast, especially, overseas Chinese with lingering ties to local com-munities added a powerful force for bypassing the center.

Khrushchev recognized soon after Stalin's death, as Deng had done by the time of Mao's death, that the existing national identity legacy was incompatible with policy changes essential for modernization. The Soviet Union had become a superpower with a vast military-industrial complex and enormous global political reach, so it could draw on these sources of pride and competitiveness while questioning others. China could capitalize on the East Asian "economic miracles," whose eager-ness to include China in their production chains held great promise for rapid growth. The two regimes saw an opening, while striving to narrow the scope of ideology as they boosted pride in the nation. For the Soviets, this raised the question of balancing Russian and Soviet identity; but in China, there was much less of a problem, given the smaller percentage of non-Han in the population and their lesser political clout.

Building on the "big deal" of the 1930s, which diluted egalitarian ideals for incentives and identity themes that accommodated a rising middle class, Brezhnev offered a "little deal" to a broader population favoring leisure, consumerism, and even tolerance of activities on the margin of legality and political passivity.[19] Moreover, a social contract offering diverse, if limited, welfare benefits to the vast majority of citizens was reinforced through identity rhetoric.[20] This legacy limited the shift in economic identity more than was the case in China, arousing leaders to press harder on political national identity. Although claims to "developed socialism" at a time of growing stagnation were overdone, they had some comparative validity.

On the vertical dimension, ethnic minorities were kept in check, as many in the majority were receptive to notions of their backwardness and of the generosity of fraternal assistance enabling them to make up ground. As for culture, there was a parallel understanding of the benefits to them from diffusion of a more advanced culture—with education in the forefront, but with assimilation centered on control over ethnic diversity not far below the surface. When Soviet economic and cultural claims were dispelled in the Khrushchev years and similar Chinese claims were put in disrepute in the Deng era, the ramifications for minority reconsideration of past identity arguments were considerable. Given Gorbachev's decision to relax central control, China was more prepared to suppress ethnic aspirations, using coercion.

One factor driving a focus on Russian identity was resentment of the other nationalities of the Soviet Union, which were seen as benefiting from unfair budget allocations. The leveling effect appeared more pernicious in an atmosphere of stagnation. As a sense of dissatisfaction was spreading, such targets undercut the notion of Soviet identity. As titular nationalities pressed their own identity claims, Russians were mobilizing around resentments, encouraged by democratization.

Although suppressed by communism and in 1991 seen as having defeated its rival identity, Russian identity tied to the Orthodox Church and a rejection of shared identity with other non-Slavic ethnic groups had a complex relationship with Soviet identity. In the Brezhnev era, this identity gained ground through tolerance of its critique of declining moral values; disintegrating family life; a devastating treatment of the environment, as symbolized by several mammoth, controversial projects; and failure to maintain the architectural treasures from Russia's past.[21] Affirmation of this Russianness helped to salvage Soviet identity along many dimensions, as even the Orthodox Church proved to be wedded to a strong state and anti-Western exclusivity.

Provincial and local identities have a richer tradition in China than in Russia. With China's greater success in decentralized economic growth, calling attention to sharp contrasts across provinces, the potential rose for a revival of localism. During the peak period of political decentralization in Russia in the 1990s, this tendency was even more visible. But recentralization under Putin quickly exposed the weak foundation for localism in economic dynamism, cultural discourse, and political tradition. In contrast, provincial identity revived China's native-place traditions, reinvented the earlier entrepreneurial culture as a source of prestige, and claimed an edge in economic development based on specific local conditions. However, by invoking Chineseness and avoiding challenges to the approved national identity discourse, they had little prospect of solidifying a collective identity to balance the center.[22]

The identity difference that may have exerted the greatest impact on reform was the incomparably stronger legacy of localism in China, which gained new life under Mao and proved amenable to market competition under Deng. Leaders gave encouragement to it, authorizing special economic zones, judging local officials on how well their areas performed economically compared with others, and urging poor areas to find a way to compete in a market economy.[23] Yet leaders reined in efforts to ground localism in identity terms, fiercely resisting ethnic identities and eagerly supporting developmental experiments as long as they avoided political pretenses.

China, in contrast to Russia, visualized subregional identities centered on economic development. Southeast China found a hospitable environment in Hong Kong, Taiwan, and the overseas Chinese communities of Southeast Asia. Northeast China had its sights on Japan, South Korea, and the Russian Far East—even if the last of these areas proved difficult to open. The overlay of subregional and national identities contrasted with Russia's competition for sovereignty and the dearth of local initiative in economic reform and external relations. Decentralization in China was denied political identity, which was present in Russia in ethnic republics above all, while far outdistancing Russia in economic identities, which were associated with divergent local models.

Reducing the grip of a single, simplistic identity, Russia opened itself to more identity challenges than China did. It was more vulnerable to the gap between Soviet and Russian national identity, for which there was no Chinese parallel; to the spread of Western identity, deeply rooted before 1917 and revived after Khrushchev's era; and to the volatility of ethnic identities focused on sovereignty, which incubated in the Brezhnev era through greater accommodations with titular nationalities. China was keenly attuned to these potential challenges, intensifying its defenses after June 1989 and in response to the lessons learned from observing the Soviet experience.

An identity hiatus opened in the 1980s in both countries. China had the edge, because it could reawaken local and provincial identities, which were more intense due to both the premodern legacy and Maoist attacks on centralization. When interests tied to regionalism were aroused in 1987 in the Soviet Union, there was nary a response, apart from seeking more revenues from Moscow, in contrast to what had happened in China. The command economy and relentless political controls had snuffed out official initiative. Environmental causes had some impact in awakening society, but even with encouragement from above, they did not overcome bureaucratic inertia.[24]

The discrediting of the national identity needed for Soviet reform undermined the foundation for rebuilding. China had the option of the responsibility system to transform rural production and special economic zones to induce foreign direct investment. The foundation of the old order could be bypassed while economic growth increased. There was no way to transform the more bureaucratized and industrialized Soviet system without tackling the heart of the old order. This led to a decade-long confusion over the nature of vertical identity, exceeding China's doubts.

The Soviet leadership shook things up, exposing social injustice—such as elite privileges, special schools, and stores catering to a favored minority—and corruption. China's leaders refused to do the same, after brief exceptions showed where this could lead. The Soviet leaders expected to maintain essential order through the replacement of the discredited elite, but they failed to replace many. China's leaders decided that only protection of the elite with an orderly transition would prevent instability anew.

Popular culture had made considerable inroads in the Soviet Union, undermining interest in the official culture and serving to incubate an alternate cultural identity, which narrowed the gap with the West. Even with respect to high culture, memories of icons who were killed in Stalin's purges left strong resentments. In the 1980s, for China, pop culture remained stifled and the rehabilitation of cultural victims was unable to emerge as a central concern linked to shared Western culture. The cultural factor proved more disorienting in the Soviet Union, despite China's Cultural Revolution.

China and the Soviet Union forged a privileged elite, which saw the construction of national identity as its province, even if Stalin and Mao totally usurped it. By the early 1980s, the established national identity had few challengers, apart from a few pesky reform advocates on the fringes of the Communist Party or the academic establishment, who were no match for the party elite, the military and security apparatus, the leaders of the military-industrial complex, and the propaganda establishment. When, for a time, more voices were heard in debates about national identity, a backlash was soon building steam. Rival notions of the 1980s and 1990s had little prospect, because the residual elements of national identity had powerful defenders who could take advantage of either new confidence or new symbols of vulnerability. The greatest confusion over the role of the state left these defenders in the shadows for a time, but this proved deceptive.

China's leaders saw dropping a country's ideological guard as leading to the rapid penetration of external values and then undermining the vertical order of society. Soviet vulnerability to Western values was a theme of the Sino-Soviet split, and it resurfaced as a theme of the Gorbachev and Yeltsin eras. Noting the fate of the Soviet Union, China tightened control through the Communist Party's propaganda and organization departments, while keeping close watch over how potential cosmopolitans addressed identity issues.

THE HORIZONTAL DIMENSION

Soviet identity shifted decisively from revolution to statism in the mid-1950s, while China's sank deeper into revolution. This led to a sharp split between their policies toward the United States, India, and other countries. However, Moscow proved unwilling to press a statist perspective, as seen in the failure of détente. Only a crisis atmosphere in Moscow, after Beijing had proven that international cooperation beckoned, could turn things around, beginning with a decision to end the Cold War. China made a similar decision in the 1970s, which shows that the horizontal dimension played a critical role in the transformation of national identity that brought internal reforms.

Soviet views of national interest became overtly ideological when, in 1969, the Brezhnev Doctrine was defined through repression of the Prague Spring. This represented a setback for US relations, a source of alarm in China, and a declaration that socialist identity justified disregard for sovereignty.[25] Socialist internationalism proved to be an element of identity interfering with reconciliation both in Europe and Asia. When, in 1974–75, it was bolstered by accusations of imperialism regrouping its forces, the cause of détente faded.[26] Instead of capitalizing on "peaceful coexistence" with an intense effort at economic integration with the West, the Soviet leaders rekindled anger toward the West and animosity toward Japan grounded in superpower arrogance.

Deng's shift to the open door came well after Mao's approval for a strategic partnership with the United States. It was accompanied by further distancing from the United States, as in the 1982 foreign policy move to equidistance and the 1984 anti–spiritual pollution campaign. The jolt was greater from Gorbachev's about-face toward the United States, which abruptly ended this obsessive superpower rivalry. Given the growing weight of opposition to the United States in Soviet national identity in the Brezhnev era, Gorbachev's "new thinking" caused considerable confusion. This change occurred at a time when divisive national identities also challenged Soviet identity.

National identity changes under Khrushchev, Gorbachev, and Deng failed to win approval from the armed forces and others that prioritized security. In the two countries, these might be quieted for a time, but they had a formidable presence. If support for economic integration with the capitalist states was growing, wariness about letting down the security guard remained strong. Similarly, the political elite was reluctant to abandon its posts and the identity that justified them. For many in the populace, anti-elitism and the exposure of hidden privileges and other injustices did resonate well, and Gorbachev relied on this to build support while Deng drew the line as he sustained a coalition with more conservative leaders. Security identity was so central in the Soviet Union, given the militarization of society and the rhetoric prioritizing this theme, that it had to be addressed early, with uncertain effects. The rise and fall of cooperation with the United States was rooted in the fragility of new security thinking against the backdrop of intense views of its impact on identity.

Soviet leaders stayed obsessed with their competition with the United States. Shifting to cooperation and acknowledging defeat would not be easy. But the Chinese pursuit of competition came only after 2000, freeing Deng and Jiang to be more flexible. Mao had cleared the way to look outside, not necessarily only to the Soviet Union, as he endorsed US ties. Thus, China maintained a bifurcated attitude about cooperation with the United States, continuing to warn against hegemonism while welcoming the breakdown of a great many barriers. Even when Gorbachev opened the door to closer ties, as long as the focus was on arms control, a kind of Group of Two seemed to be in operation, but when Soviet weakness showed that this was not the case, there was a great letdown. The blow to national identity was much greater than the impact of US ties in China, especially starting in June 1989, when China's leaders railed against "bourgeois peaceful evolution."

In 1987, the Soviet Union stopped demonizing the United States. Telebridges (i.e., joint television shows with audience participation), were one means to achieve mutual understanding, discussing real problems while reducing the cultural divide, especially as the Soviet participants acknowledged shared values as part of the Western tradition. China's leaders kept a tighter rein, denying those eager to expose the excesses of the past and to give voice to shared values similar exposure, with rare exceptions. Whereas a loss of state or party dignity left China's establishment fearful of anarchy and of a groundswell against the cruel realities of their time in power, Russia's large intellectual community and many of its technocratic officials, long removed from Stalin's purges, trusted in shared values with the West to enable a transition without anarchy or total loss of state dignity. If the Soviets also bemoaned the state-society gap and sought policies to narrow it, such as strengthening local soviets and involving workers in management, China's bosses were so distrustful of the masses, particularly after Mao's cynical manipulation of them under the slogan the "mass line," that only economic openings were welcome. Soviet sociologists discussed the problem of excess dependency on the state and the fear many had of losing their crutch, while Chinese leaders faced that problem only in manufacturing and public services, while finding it easier to energize others.

Russia had long been a peripheral country aspiring to move to the center, reflected in the nineteenth-century aspirations of many Russian intellectuals and political figures and in the twentieth-century claims of Soviet leaders. Territorial advances were seen as unification, while hierarchical relations with other states seemed to be natural extensions of Russia's quest for stable boundaries and a lasting balance of power.[27] In contrast, China was for many years a state accustomed to its centrality that had been abruptly relegated to the periphery, but, as in the case of Russia in the 1990s and 2000s, it was determined to regain its centrality. Reunification with Taiwan became an obsession, but many also sought the reestablishment of a Sinocentric order in East Asia. Russia repeatedly faced the challenge of multi-nationalism, readjusting its national identity without seriously risking accommodation, while China denied any such challenge, confidently reasserting its identity. Whether in premodern times or in the shift away from its radical communist identity, Russia encountered more ambivalence than China due to its pretensions to be part of Europe and the West. Whereas Russia faced a legacy of insecurity, fragmented national identity without coherence, and the dilemma of a nationalizing empire, as Ronald Suny argues,[28] China's identity was the picture of security and coherence with little impact from its imperial gains.

The *mezhdunarodniki* (internationalists through experience or expertise) had no counterpart in China. They knew the West from personal experience, were well placed to advocate reform, and saw themselves as a bridge, both politically and culturally. Many had survived from the earlier opening of the 1950s, had found ways to broaden their knowledge and continue at least kitchen-table discussions of bold ideas in the Brezhnev years, and had waited for another chance to expose Stalin's heinous crimes and refocus their country. The confidence of a superpower had caused leaders to accept this situation, while similar types among China's elites had been cleaning pig manure and had no such input. In refocusing international relations, the Soviet elites' sympathy for the West proved to be stronger.

The Soviet Union's pride rested heavily on its military might and global military and political reach, but these were hard to maintain with energetic reforms and a narrowing gap with the West. China's international pride had been so badly wounded that there were few barriers to taking a fresh look at the international community. The Chinese had more flexibility in foreign policy without undermining other dimensions of their identity. Soviet claims to setting US relations on a new course had to be buttressed by results befitting past Soviet pretenses.

The Soviets saw their region through the lens of satellite states, while the Chinese awoke to states with similar Confucian traditions prospering through capitalism. This resulted in contrasting regional identities with reassuring implications for China's economic globalization. If the Russians looked beyond socialism to Slavic brotherhood, this was from memory of struggles against Western influence expanding, not for building bridges to the thriving West.

THE INTENSITY DIMENSION

The Khrushchev years and the early Deng years had similarities, seen from an identity perspective. How should the extremism of a recently dead dictator be handled? How should ties to the outside world be improved? What means should be chosen to incentivize a population downtrodden from coercion? And what narrative could replace the wild lies told over decades without destroying the regime's legitimacy? There were a number of critical differences in their identity responses. Deng went much further in breaking down barriers to the outside world and offering incentives to the Chinese people, but he was more circumspect in handling temporal identity and in accepting the premises of Western civilization, while lowering the intensity of national identity to make room for pragmatism and long-term cautious advances.

Robert English describes the Soviet populations as "repeatedly terrorized, ceaselessly propagandized, and effectively isolated" for decades, leading to a generation left with dogma, which only slowly and partially was replaced as a new generation was beguiled by ideas emerging in numerous fields over the three decades after 1956.[29] Without a reconstructed economic national identity until the mid-1980s, leaders were timid about shifting the focus from the tense superpower competition. The impact of the West grew through fascination at a distance, which was suppressed, unlike what happened in China starting in the 1980s, as access to travel and ideas grew ever easier. In Gorbachev, Moscow had a leader who was attentive to truth and ready to discount the inflated threats officials had used to sustain an identity hostile to the outside world, discarding the "psychology of a besieged fortress."[30] Unlike Beijing, Moscow rejected the idea of American imperialism, opening a window for some years for identity discussions that far transcended what was tolerated in China, even as a parallel backlash arose.

The Soviet Union and China moved from insisting on total identity control to accepting some collective identities and apathy toward certain identity themes. For the two countries, a shared concern was how to turn belief in the preceding communist identity into trust in a new identity. One adjustment was tolerance for religious identity, if it did not lead to ethnic identity at odds with Russian or Han loyalty. Another one was acceptance of unmitigated pride in prerevolutionary cultural identity. Lowered intensity allowed for accommodations to multiple types of identities and a narrow pursuit of money or careers with little regard to identity concerns. China succeeded in opening the way for many safety valves, while growing discontent in the Soviet Union prevented this.

CONCLUSION

For China's more impoverished, less educated populace, meeting economic goals postponed demands for humanist ones. In the Soviet Union, by contrast, many educated Soviets recalled the thaw and were focused on seeking truth, recognizing dissidents and prior cultural martyrs as moral guides. A combination of Russian cultural identity and shared humanism with the West was well engrained in a group that took pride in being known as the intelligentsia. The fact that such an elite had been given space to develop over decades contrasts with China's record. Although Deng and others at the top had been victims of Mao, they were complicit in the antirightist campaign of 1957 that decimated the very type of member of the intelligentsia who had come to the fore under Khrushchev. The humanist elite was more fully blocked in China, despite signs of its emergence in the 1980s and rumblings of discontent thereafter, which were stifled. The coalition of officials and cultural elite members who grew vocal under Gorbachev never coalesced in China, denying an alternate national identity a chance to gain traction.

Chinese problems were so serious after Mao that a consensus was reached on a succession of reforms, while conservatives in the ruling group were able to limit the impact of reforms on national identity. Soviet problems were less severe, preventing a consensus and leading to conservatives having less say, as Gorbachev considered their opposition insurmountable without a strong assault. When a cover-up of the Chernobyl nuclear reactor disaster coincided with the blockage of economic reform, a decision was reached to sharpen the divide and to make much deeper changes in ideology.

If narrow economic ideology was an obvious target in dismantling the Soviet Union's legacy of communism, obsessive security against exaggerated threats proved to be a much greater challenge. Khrushchev gingerly tackled it with talk of peaceful coexistence. Gorbachev was bolder, suggesting that conservatives at home were a more serious enemy than the United States. In China, Deng had the luxury of not having a massive military budget and establishment; so he could put security goals on the back burner for a decade, while also avoiding Gorbachev's optimism in dealing with the legacy of the Cold War— whether Taiwan, North Korea, or the dangers of Western hegemonism.

Khrushchev most deliberately tried to replace the ideological straitjacket of the past decades with utopian ideological assertions. Deng took pains to avoid doing the same in the aftermath of Mao. Brezhnev avoided utopianism, but reemphasized the rigidity of ideology. Deng also avoided that, insisting on its flexibility, notably with regard to the market economy. The association of decentralization and markets in China was far greater, given Chinese history. Glorification of the state was less pronounced than Russian *gosudarstvennost'*, which Gorbachev dared to challenge. In seeking a civil society to limit authoritarianism, Gorbachev overestimated how far Soviet modernization had proceeded and how easy it would be in a society heavily dependent on the state to forge a counterweight. Instead of forging a civil society, Deng turned to those less dependent on the state with benefits to win their support.

Gorbachev dismantled authoritarianism without succeeding in establishing a system of control to replace it or fill the vacuum in Soviet national identity. He loosened controls over the nation's regions, allowing room for ethnic identities hostile to the Soviet state. He downplayed great power competition, contradicting the long-standing message of irreconcilable rivalry and Soviet identity through it. He contradicted insistent claims that Soviet citizens enjoyed unrivaled security, threatening to break the social contract to which vast numbers were wedded. This disconnect sharply differs from Deng's preoccupation with finding strands of continuity amid change.

China's decision to tighten control over theory and remove those most set on questioning it contrasted with the Soviet decision in the same year, 1987, to open wide the door for rethinking theory. This was the decisive point when, after a decade of great uncertainty about the future of Chinese national identity, the doubts about Soviet national identity became more serious. Glasnost intensified, arousing intense blame for the Soviet communist system and state, the lynchpins of identity. Avoiding introspection, China let markets develop while guiding an identity transformation.

The Gorbachev period starting in 1987 contrasts with China's developments starting in 1989 on national identity matters. Exposés were deemed essential to transform identity, whereas the Chinese approach was to prevent them, taking the fate of the Soviet Union as proof of what must be avoided. The sharpest contrast was in the vertical dimension, with one case witnessing the empowerment of society but the other its narrow manipulation from above. Many have contrasted the political and economic policies of Gorbachev and Deng, and their divergence in managing national identity adds to this picture.

Glasnost opened the way for turning one element of identity against another—Lenin versus Stalin, Russian versus Soviet, society versus state, nature versus ideology, and even the masses versus a privileged elite. These opposing elements could work for a time, but they left a vacuum that could only be filled by universal values identified with the West or ethnic identities. Tsarist Russia had proven incapable of reconciling the contradictions involving many of these identities, and the consequences of seven decades of communist rule reduced this possibility further, so Russia's identity flux proved more serious than China's.

Identity extremes also come easier to Russian intellectuals, who are known for sitting around the kitchen table pontificating on grand philosophical themes, as opposed to the Chinese, whose Confucian traditions avoid transcendental issues in favor of fine-tuning state-society relations. Gorbachev's quest for far-reaching ideals stands in contrast to

Deng's heralded pragmatism, groping from stone to stone to find a way across the river. Released from Mao's ill-fitting ideological cause, the Chinese reverted to humble thoughts, despite anxious leaders serving with Deng and in his wake fervently striving to reconstruct identity to restore party legitimacy.

China's leaders, many of whom had been marginalized for a decade or longer, assumed that their system had failed; yet they were determined to sustain it in critical respects. The Soviet leaders believed that their system had realized enormous success, but they were driven to seek its replacement in important respects. On the whole, they recognized the positive prospects of convergence, accepting the West as a standard. In contrast, China's leaders had less trust in the West and in their neighbors, but they had to hold onto the system because the alternatives were beyond the pale. Gorbachev and those closest to him expected to remake their system, more closely connected to the West, and to survive personally with a country better prepared in the future. The Soviet Union was more impatient. In an echo of the Meiji Restoration or Japan's postwar reforms, China's leaders gave the nod to openness and reform, while protecting the core of their national identity. They did so through their communist legacy, which shaped the course of transformation.

CHAPTER 3

RUSSIAN NATIONAL IDENTITY FROM THE 1990s TO THE 2010s

When Vladimir Putin made clarification of national identity a major priority as he began what seems likely to be a run lasting through the first quarter of the twenty-first century as Russia's president or prime minister, he was following in the footsteps of Tsar Nicholas I during the second quarter of the nineteenth century and Communist Party boss Josef Stalin in the second quarter of the twentieth century. Although Stalin came to power amid a torrent of denunciation of the tsarist era that Nicholas represented, and Putin took power after a wave of repudiation of the period of communism symbolized by Stalin, there is unquestionable continuity in what these three giants of Russian history propounded as the crux of national identity. Each glorified the state and its leadership, renouncing both democratic values and any sort of civil society capable of checks and balances. Each leader demonized the West, warning against the threat it posed to the civilization he protectively guarded. And all three shared an obsession with constructing a shield for their country of such intensity that the dangerous currents of Western thought would no longer be able to penetrate it. Alexander I, Nicholas II, and Mikhail Gorbachev, followed by Boris Yeltsin, had been vilified for dropping their country's guard. Their successors fixated on reinforcing it for the indefinite future.

The ideological challenge after the Cold War resembles others repeatedly faced since at least the time of Peter I. The West represents modernization, which remains very closely associated with a different sense of political, economic, and cultural identity. Given the temptation of modernization and the appeal of Western culture as shared with Russian culture, Russians have been hard-pressed to differentiate their state's identity in an appealing manner, except when communism drew an absolute line.

Catherine II, following Peter I, and Yeltsin, after Gorbachev, appeared to tear down barriers to European identity, but the "idea of Europe" proved to be too dangerous to embrace.[1] It threatened Russia's political identity, centered on state power, close ties to autocratic regimes, and rivalry with the West. It also cast doubt on Russia's cultural national identity, which remains fragile since the collapse of communism.

As had happened at various times in history, the emphasis under Yeltsin shifted to shedding outmoded thinking in order to catch up with the West, borrowing intensively, with ideas in the forefront. An atmosphere was created in support of disassembling a structure that was passé, accompanied by discrediting a well-established worldview, and replacing it with a model taken from the West and understood to be more successful. Yet well before Putin replaced Yeltsin, the popular mood had shifted toward filling the vacuum that had been created by the tearing down of the old order. A backlash was gaining momentum to substitute an authentic Russian national identity for the imported ideals that appeared to take precedence in the early 1990s. The problem was that there was no clarity on what constitutes Russian identity, resulting in a situation where people awaited a strong leader to instruct them. Putin filled this vacuum.

Could a reformer have played a similar leadership role? There were alternate examples in Russian history that had led to alliances with democratic states, short-term democratic institution building, and cultural identification with the West. Yet they mostly symbolized pragmatic reforms, not an enduring case for Russia's distinctive identity. National identity is not destiny, and at times pragmatism and even idealism drawing on some broader identity will trump it. The argument that Russia has no identity capable in the foreseeable future of dislodging the essence of what is now present is not an argument that Putin will not lose credibility and a reform coalition gain ground, but its durability will depend on another identity transition.

Dismantling communism gave way to reconstructing identity. Putin's return to the post of president in 2012 clarified his impact, which had been building during his two prior terms as president and was never seriously eclipsed in the term he served as prime minister.

In contrast to the narrative of the early Yeltsin years, discourse increasingly reaffirmed the tone of Soviet communism. Although socialism did not reemerge as an ideological theme, a combination of anti-imperialism and Russocentrism gained what should be called quasi-ideological status. Looking back, the Soviet era acquired increasingly positive value and the post–Cold War period, including the Gorbachev era, became a temporary aberration that had to give way to an entirely new era for Russia and the world order. As opposed to the loss of confidence in the 1990s in economic, cultural, and political identity, Putin gave Russia assertive answers to identity questions. On the vertical dimension, newfound pride in the state as the focus of identity dismissed universal values drawn from the outside and downplayed ethnic identity apart from Russian identity. Continuity with Soviet times was particularly pronounced in raging anti-Americanism, accompanying calls for regionalism under Moscow's aegis and great power balancing opposed to an international community centered on the West. The intensity of national identity, trumping pragmatic diplomacy, even revived some elements of the tone found in the Soviet period, Putin showing the way.

THE DECADE OF THE 1990s

Gorbachev set in motion a struggle lasting roughly a decade between rival notions of national identity. Within the top leadership, Gorbachev was opposed by Yegor Ligachev, who sought to keep the existing identity mix, but Gorbachev was successful in downgrading ideology and challenging the highly vertical concept of identity focused on obedience to the Communist Party and the antiforeign concept of "internationalist" identity in fierce opposition to a "globalizing" outside world. The result was a vacuum that Yeltsin was no more successful than Gorbachev in filling with a sustainable identity narrative. Calling for "socialist democracy" or "democracy," leaders could find small groups of vocal support but no basis for strong interest group backing.

Gorbachev allowed local communities to rekindle ethnic pride, purging many of the leaders who had suppressed it. He approved shocking revelations of past injustice, which exposed much of Soviet national identity as based on lies. Opening the floodgates to harsh accusations against the wanton abuse of power, he implied that nothing was sacrosanct any more. All dimensions of national identity felt the consequences of these great changes throughout the chaotic 1990s.

In the years 1990–91, the national identity debate reached high intensity. On one side were revelations of the falsity of Soviet identity, such as a newspaper article exposing the truth about the Korean War: Stalin gave the order to attack, a Soviet aviation division relocated to North Korea from China and participated, and not only did more than 10 million people die from the war but the Cold War was greatly intensified, with lasting consequences.[2] On the other side were charges that ideological opponents inside Russia wanted to destroy the state to its very foundation, beginning with the armed forces.[3] The outcome remained unclear, even as Yeltsin's victory gave a boost to democracy and openness, notably relations with the West.

At the start of the Yeltsin era, Russia faced a national identity void. It seemed as if the identity of the communist era was lost, but there was no identity to replace it. Some argued that the identity of a democratic state with a free market entering the international community would be appealing. Not only were Russians suspicious of these ideals; they also doubted that Russia would follow them. Democracy was soon associated with disorder, a free market with kleptocracy, and globalization with irrelevance and dependency. Calls for patience through a necessary transition fell on deaf ears; conditions did not improve. The Soviet legacy provided different ideals, revived for reconstructing national identity. It reinforced a deep sense of the messianism of the tsarist era, which entailed a reliance on strong leadership claiming to have all the answers, and the presence of the "new Soviet man," who believed in the old order despite misgivings and recent arousal against certain blatant shortcomings.[4]

James Billington writes about the struggle around the collapse of the Soviet Union that "the inner force of Russian culture was breaking through the outer shell of Soviet power," which led to "one of the most wide-ranging discussions of a nation's identity in modern history."[5] He lists such themes as "a single leader who would restore moral order through a reestablished Russian Orthodox Church"; the appeal of Eurasianism, which was associated with the rejection of the insidious force of globalization; and the "perceived 'Russophobia' of the new Westward-looking liberal elites," which could be countered not through "blending the culture[s] of two continents as isolating themselves from either . . . in Russia's islandness." Accompanied by writings describing Russia as a "special type of civilization," not just an ordinary nation-state, the converging views of the right and left revered power, winning support among officials and beneficiaries of the reallocation of state resources, but also among many who had lost all hope during the 1990s and were ready to embrace simplistic answers.[6]

Yeltsin exercised power with an unstable coalition; some opposed Gorbachev as a failure in sustaining the Soviet system and envisioned a Russian state with many features of the Soviet era; and others were persuaded by anticommunism and were eager for a speedy transition. In short order, hopes for the transition were dashed, and Yeltsin had to yield to an identity surge in support of a strong state, in which he was backed by many who had joined his coalition and most who had joined the opposition, whether under the communists or grouped as ultranationalists. Divisions persisted, as the spoils of the economic transition placated one group but not others. Yeltsin's moderate tendencies meant that the extremists were kept at a distance in policy decisions, but they were given almost free rein in arousing support.

Russian national identity in the 1990s passed through two primary phases. During Yeltsin's first presidential term, for the most part, there was balance between commitment to join the United States–led international community and renewal of Russian identity combined in unclear ways with Soviet identity. This was depicted as a struggle between "Atlanticism" and the "Russian idea." In 1996, with Evgenyi Primakov's appointment as foreign minister and then the start of Yeltsin's second term, national identity tilted sharply away from the West, with more urgency for clarifying the "Russian idea" and greater priority for Asia. The term "Eurasianism" was added to the mix, along with "anti-Americanism," which accompanied it.

Russia, arguably, faced more uncertainty about its identity than at any point in its history, apart from the first years of Bolshevik rule. Still fresh in people's memories was Soviet identity. Already suspect was European identity or Atlanticism in foreign policy. Gaining ground but still poorly defined was Russian identity, looking back to the era before 1917.

European identity meant joining the West and abandoning the authoritarian claims associated with the vertical dimension. It had far-reaching implications for the hierarchical structure of power and for the foreign policy choices facing Russia. Despite giving lip service to this ideal, few in the elite could stomach the consequences of such a momentous shift. After all, it would signify acceptance of all that the Soviet Union had demonized over three-quarters of a century. In contrast, Soviet identity could be partially salvaged by repackaging it as Russian identity and Eurasianism. This troika stood in the path of European identity. Apart from the Baltic states, the leaders of the states that had been carved from the former Soviet republics were suspicious of European identity. The security establishment had rejected it. Only the newly vocal liberal elite embraced it, and they soon found that they exercised little power and would have to temper their message even to be heard in the midst of a virulent blowback.

Whereas there were relatively clear markers for understanding Soviet and Western identity, Russian identity and Eurasianism were hard to pin down. Democrats, embracing a Western model, and communists, harking back to the Soviet model, found wide-ranging resistance to their ideas of national identity. Self-proclaimed patriots, who sought answers in Russian history, soon found the public distrustful of the European idea and gravitating to the Soviet model. They rejected Western ideas as denying the existence of Russian identity. Claiming that only a Russian identity would overcome immorality, they concentrated on blaming supposed villains. And for them, the task of explaining Russian identity became an obsession, generally leading back to overlapping themes with Soviet identity. In mid-1996, Yeltsin challenged Russians to uncover the "Russian idea" within a year, but this goal proved more elusive than the gathering storm against the Western model as the source of this vacuum.

In the mid-1990s, the mainstream message from Russia was of failed reform and a tragic loss of continuity. The idea that Soviet identity could be replaced by the kind of national identity advocated by Western theories was blamed. It was increasingly assumed that socialism was not some vile growth that could be cut away for a healthy organism to reemerge, but the essential basis for a transition. To recover, Russia had to strengthen its state, forge an orderly society, regain respect in the world, and end its dependence on the West. Given this outlook, China served as a model as well as the critical partner for devising a new foreign policy. Although Western advisers insisted that Russia was on track to be a "normal country," if only it would deepen its ties to the West and weaken the state in order to boost the market and fight corruption, most thought differently about a "normal Russia."[7]

Identity themes raised over a decade proved fragile and were easily overwhelmed. Given the importance of the state as the traditional basis for national identity, its recovery proved to be a compelling theme. Individual space was welcomed, but individual rights versus the state did not elicit similar concern. Under the impression that the United States and its type of globalization are inimical to state identity, Russia turned to China for full support.

Restoring national status that had been unfairly or temporarily lost became a rallying cry in the upsurge of national identity debates in Russia, as in China, in the 1990s. This theme served to consolidate opposition to Yeltsin and was preempted by his followers. In China, it was tempered by an awareness that China had squandered its opportunities in the 1960s and 1970s and needed time to press claims for status. Russians were more prone to place the blame on a small leadership group under Gorbachev and on the West, specifically the United States. In the mid-1990s, the *derzhavniki* (great power nationalists) were gaining momentum, calling for early restoration of greatness, rekindling anti-Western emotions, and also affirming a positive outlook on Soviet history. Instead of the Communist Party serving as the object of identity claims, the state was glorified in opposition to globalization. State policies deemed to be weakening Russia were blamed on pressure from foreign countries. Alert to these fears, the Yeltsin leadership group catered to the popular mood and drove it further to the extreme, sending troops to Chechnya in late 1994 and changing its tune on ethnic policies and on international relations. The identity narrative had shifted decisively even before Putin.

In response to the troubles faced over these years, many focused on *derzhavnost'*, a call for a powerful state asserting itself as a great power. If the communists coupled this with nostalgia for an omnipotent state and the nationalists who rallied behind Vladimir Zhirinovskii added an expansionist tone, the prevailing message was to bolster the center without denying market or regional forces and to exert influence without alienating states wary of Soviet-style pressure. This ideal joined the vertical and horizontal dimensions, while prioritizing the sectoral dimension of cultural pride, economic self-reliance, and political identity opposed to the outside as the secret to Russia's regaining its self-respect.[8]

With the explosion of anti-Americanism came an effort to glorify Russia's history as distinct from the West. Thus victories in war, heroism that had allegedly saved humankind, and a focus on voices that spoke in defense of Russian uniqueness gained new prominence.[9]

Looking back on the first half of the 1990s, many described those years as a fiasco, using the logic that Soviet and Russian identity are roughly the same and that both were decimated under the onslaught of a "European orientation."[10] Rather than democracy, ethnic and religious identities gained the lion's share of attention in the vacuum left by "new thinking." These worked against international identity. Fearful of the spread of other religions, the Eastern Orthodox Church firmly supported a revived state-centered identity and the obsession with the existence of a separate Russian civilization, which needed strengthening.

Even before fixating on China's model, Russians found some solace in the image of East Asian capitalism—with its state-led development, trade protectionism, and heightened cultural claims to a distinctive type of management—as an alternative to the West. Yet interest was late to arise.[11] In the second half of the 1990s, China's dual success in achieving an "economic miracle" and resisting the Western world order won praise. China showed Russia the path to defiance, tapping many of the very same themes of traditional communist identity that had resonated well with both Russia's elite and its impoverished masses.

Russian misgivings about the threat of US power and values are not transient, capable of being allayed by a "reset" in relations, an upbeat summit, or an act of Islamic fundamentalist terrorism. They are embedded in national identities inherited from the past and have intensified in recent years. Because many had different expectations for Russia in the 1990s, and even as recently as right after the September 11, 2001, terrorist attacks on the United States, this conclusion may be doubted. Yet the leaders who have decided Russia's fate in the past three hundred or more years, perhaps after a period of uncertain reform, have proven this point. Although he started slowly in demonizing the United States and the West, Putin was quick to focus on the vertical dimension and cultural national identity, as he set a new direction for Russia. His own rule and exaggerated thinking may be repudiated, which would reopen identity debates, but this is not the equivalent of abandoning the thrust of recent identity arguments.

THE PERIOD 2000–2007

On December 29, 1999, a government Web site posted Putin's article "Russia at the Turn of the Millennium." Two days later when Yeltsin resigned, transferring power to Putin, attention was drawn to what became known as the Millennium Manifesto. A pervasive theme is that Russia's standing depends on the unity of its people, not the vibrancy of its democracy; and on the distinctiveness of its values, rather than on its acceptance of universal values. Putin thus provided an answer to the question Yeltsin had posed, befuddling the nation. For him, the "Russian idea" combines *gosudarstvennost'* (identification with the state), patriotism, collectivism, and solidarity. It sets Russia apart. Instead of rejecting a strong state as an abnormality regrettably imposed as part of communism, he embraced it as quintessentially Russian, which was critical to order and the sort of change desired by society. He reinforced the view that the state takes precedence over the individual and that the prime task ahead was to strengthen the state and glorify it as the collective expression of the nation. Drawing on Russian history and on concepts popular in the tsarist era such as *narodnost'* (belonging to the collective of the Russian people), which could easily be interpreted as consistent with Soviet notions of collectivity, Putin synthesized the national identity.[12] This was the culmination of trends that had been emerging since the 1990s, but it may carry them to an extreme that will result in a backlash, as a subsequent transition in national identity is taking shape.

Two primary phases were associated with the first terms of Putin's presidency. In the first phase, there was a mix of identities. Russia was drifting toward a vertical identity centered on a strong state, but it kept alive elements of decentralization and democracy. By the time of Putin's reelection, "sovereign democracy" was beginning to take hold as an updated version of "democratic centralism," in that the democracy part was mostly window-dressing. Similarly, there was a shift from cooperation with the West to vilification of it. In the period 2004–8, the tone grew increasingly strident in defense of these approaches to identity.

The reconstructing of national identity in the 2000s occurred relatively smoothly. The vertical dimension faced little resistance, as local leaders had failed to forge localism of any consequence, given economic as well as political realities. The longing for greater cohesion facilitated Putin's unhindered march to recentralization. A vacuum was filled with renewed pride in the landmarks of Soviet history, ranging from World War II to the struggles of the Cold War. The aura around Putin helped to reinvigorate political national identity, as did the new attention being given to Russia's nuclear weapons power. The nation's claims to be an energy superpower fueled pride in its economic national identity. And its cultural national identity, which had suffered in the 1990s, also made a partial comeback, linked to xenophobia toward its neighbors and disparagement of the West. The horizontal dimension changed abruptly from the 1990s, owing in no small part to China's value as a balance to the United States. Even elements of a new ideology mattered, however tenuous were the linkages between the usually unacknowledged legacy of socialism, the "Russian idea," and anti-imperialism.

Russia's transition in the years 2003–4 marked the culmination of a decade of revival of national identity, drawing on the Soviet legacy. The arrest of oil oligarch Mikhail Khodorkovsky on charges of fraud and the administrative centralization following the terrorist attack on a school in Beslan showed the priority on the vertical dimension. Responses to the "color revolutions" in states of the former Soviet Union and a more hostile tone toward the United States reflected the importance of the horizontal dimension. Prioritizing external threats to security— first, as US policies and NATO expansion; second, as Central Asian instability and the spread of terrorism from Afghanistan; and only third, as China's rise and its ambitions for expanded influence—meant that identity linking those seen as external and internal enemies recalled Soviet thinking about the West and its sympathizers. Legitimation of authoritarian power linked to Mafia groups took priority. Russia's great power identity was as a nuclear superpower, a permanent member of the UN Security Council, and a decisive force reshaping the world order. In 2000, Putin used the term "common Asian house," putting the East on a par with the West.

In early 2004, China was nervous about Russia's disinterest and flirtation with Japan on an oil pipeline earlier promised to China, North Korea was angry that Russia blamed North Korea alone in the Six-Party Talks on North Korea's nuclear program, and the United States and Japan offered far less support than anticipated with tough conditions. Putin's new direction prioritized China, calmed North Korea, and made the United States and its allies take notice that they could no longer count on a partner. By the end of his second term, the idea of Russia as a civilizational bridge was spreading; it was equal to China in the Shanghai Cooperation Organization, a player in the Six-Party Talks, and a link between East and West.

THE PERIOD 2008–13

If the chronology is extended to the period 2008–13, two more phases enter the picture. First was the renewal under Dmitry Medvedev's presidency of more balanced rhetoric toward the vertical, horizontal, and sectoral identities, and then a more extreme version of the narrative than was present in Putin's second term after he switched from serving as prime minister to being elected to a third presidential term. Although the four years when Medvedev was on top interrupted the post–Cold War trend, the overall pattern was of greater intensity, capped by Putin's pitch in 2012–13. In the period 2009–11, China had become the more assertive partner in pressing for coordination against the United States, reversing earlier roles, but in 2012–13 the two states appeared to be similarly adamant. Medvedev's tone was decisively replaced by Putin's.

Medvedev's appeal, especially in 2009–10, to different national identity themes shows that Russia continues to face uncertainty in its relations with the West and reform prospects. Even if democracy is discredited as an ideological crusade that undermined the Russian state, the West continues to be associated with modernization, which is desired to overcome what many fear is a dead-end strategy of reliance on high commodity prices. Tolerance for dissent was also growing in these years when Putin kept a somewhat lower profile. Yet Medvedev's record was marred by several things. First, he appeared helpless in pronouncing goals with no semblance of policy follow-up or narrative that could link them together into a vision of where Russia was heading. Second, he managed international relations pragmatically for the most part, without articulating what particular steps, such as the "reset" with the United States or the expected 2012 regional blueprint for the Asia-Pacific region, might signify, especially in light of Putin's legacy of anti-Americanism and China-centered Asian diplomacy. Third, the way he announced the decision that he would not run for reelection and that Putin would be the candidate for president, explaining that the decision had been made long ago, left the public feeling duped, and humiliated him as little more than a puppet. Though he was then still president for the following half year, he was marginal to the national spotlight. As Putin brought national identity themes to the forefront, it was clear that he found Medvedev incapable of being the leader Putin believed was needed. Medvedev offered some pragmatism but had little impact on national identity rhetoric.

The tone changed abruptly as Putin was running for office to replace Medvedev, and it grew more extreme after he resumed the presidency, cracking down on NGOs, which were now obliged to register as "foreign agents" if they accepted external funds, and putting new barriers in the path of demonstrations. Medvedev's theme of modernization, which had been reassuring to the international community, was gone. Facing a more active opposition at home, Putin twisted identity against it.

Gorbachev, Yeltsin, and Medvedev all articulated strands of national identity that encouraged reformers critical of anti-Western ethnocentrism, or pride in the legacy of Stalin and those close to him. However, in his return to the top position, Putin clarified an identity beholden to the very forces the others had criticized. Given the six-year term before him and the possibility of reelection, Putin has a chance to set the long-term direction for Russian identity. Yet in carrying things to an extreme, he may be sowing the seeds for a further transition away from the synthesis he had constructed.

THE IDEOLOGICAL DIMENSION

After three-quarters of a century of ideology in the forefront, Moscow faced a vacuum in the 1990s. In contrast to Deng Xiaoping's early clarification in 1979 that ideology still matters, which was reaffirmed in 1989 and on other occasions, Yeltsin denied it any role. If for a time it appeared that he wholeheartedly embraced democracy in a battle against the Communist Party of the Soviet Union and then the Russian Communist Party, his main opposition, and the free market through "shock therapy" in order to replace the command economy, he did not raise these to the level of lasting ideological concerns. As for the Russian public, they had to prove their value through results, and they failed to do so amid disorder and economic collapse. A void made room for other dimensions of identity to rise to the forefront, but ideology was not dead.

Of ideological significance under Gorbachev, de-Stalinization reached its ultimate conclusion of exposing one of the world's most heinous tyrants. Efforts to spare Lenin or salvage part of a Marxist-Leninist worldview also did not fare well after glasnost moved beyond its opening rounds. To the extent that Lenin's demonization of imperialism was also a pillar of the ideology used to justify the existence of two opposing blocs, Gorbachev's rejection of this dichotomy, coupled with more nuanced treatment of developing countries, undercut the ideology. Growing interest in Russian national identity did not bolster the ideology because it served as a contrast with Soviet identity, rejecting the amalgam that some had advanced since Stalin's reconsideration of Russian history and literature in the 1930s. Falsehoods came under attack, with no substitute offered except a vague European or global identity. Intense belief in ideology was left to the elderly and uneducated, who had placed so much of their identity aspirations in it that they could rationalize criticism.

In the absence of socialism, anti-imperialism kept alive the ideological mantle during the 1990s. The notion that Russia was the victim of betrayal covered many US failures—to abide by promises that NATO would not expand; to assist Russia's transition as expected, allegedly due to a plot to weaken it; to respect Russia's national interests by not striving to turn former republics and earlier dependent states away from it; and so on. Primakov voiced this worldview, winning popularity as Yeltsin was disappearing for long periods owing to his deteriorating health. Although many called this realism, reviving balance-of-power thinking, it became a matter of faith, echoing critiques of capitalist imperialism.

The foundation of identity claims in traditional communism is revolution, and in recent times it has been sovereignty. Revolution proclaimed harmony on the basis of policies to overcome class conflict, whereas sovereignty viewed harmony arising from shared support for defending and boosting state control over territory. In both cases, the state is the driving force, preempting lines of cleavage. Vladislav Surkov—who in 2005 helped to found the youth organization Nashi, which harks back to Soviet organizations and takes as its most important symbol the victory in the Great Patriotic War—emerged as a kind of ideologist, known for the phrase "sovereign democracy," who opposed the democratization associated with the West. He championed the return of the state as an ideological focus, boosting sovereignty through top-down cohesion and the demonization of various outside threats.

Putin put matters of identity in the forefront, increasingly singling out some as the basis for what should be considered an ideology. Anti-hegemonism was the centerpiece of his worldview. Without reviving communism, he glorified the state. As he entered his third term in 2012, he broached the idea of a Russocentric cultural sphere, using the term "Eurasian Union" while presenting it first in economic terms. But the shadow of communist ideology hovered over his efforts. On one side, he faced opposition from the Communist Party, whose ideology might undermine the kleptocracy he represents. On the other side, reformers remained attached to democratic ideology, which serves a legitimating purpose, given the continuation of national elections. Putin has propounded ideology rather cautiously, leaving it as still the weakest dimension of Russian national identity,

Putin's election campaign highlighted cultural and political identity, morphing into a strategy for a unique civilization. It called for a strong nation, saved from the threat of "color revolutions" by a state that commands allegiance at home and respect abroad due to public accord and its ability to extend its reach, such as through a Eurasian Union. Apart from Russia's own attributes, it is seen as benefiting from a global environment split between East and West and between North and South, not just through a balance of power but also through cultural conflict, allowing Russia to become a center of gravity for cultural change. Joining anti-imperialism to Russocentrism, this appeal outweighs the appeal of what has been branded Western ideology in charges that an ideological struggle has been forced on Russia by the intense ideological nature of US identity, as in the Cold War. If the result is confrontation, however, Putin's lack of restraint may lead to a backlash.

THE TEMPORAL DIMENSION

Communism puts history at the center of identity. Dismantling its legacy keeps the spotlight on history. If Gorbachev and Deng had a big impact on how Stalin and Mao respectively would be viewed over the following decades, assessments of them remained the litmus test for how history as a whole would be interpreted. The critical years of 1917 and 1949 served as touchstones for looking backward and forward. After class struggle was discarded as a standard for judging the present, it played a much-diminished role in evaluating the past. Far more important was the way that state building loomed as the most positive aspect of historical change. Russians as well as Chinese leaders glorified their predecessors who had expanded national territory, strengthened the state, or dealt firmly with other states. If Stalin had singled out Ivan the Terrible and Mao had made Emperor Qing Shi Hwang his model—the two most notorious autocrats in the histories of their states who acted with unparalleled terrorism toward their people—the emphasis now shifted more to autocrats with a more stable legacy, such as Peter the Great and the long-serving emperors of late imperial China.

For a time in the 1990s, the Russians appeared to accept a worldview that demonized their history while glorifying that of the United States. But this did not last long, even after efforts to reconnect prerevolutionary and post-Soviet Russia offered something positive. By 2007, a positive image combining Russian and Soviet glory was well entrenched. New historical education stressing patriotism was ascendant. Putin had met with educators over the summer in preparation for the new school year and the implementation of a new program, slighting the evils of the Stalin system and his purges, praising "sovereign democracy" as an alternative political path, and ending deference to the United States.[13]

Russia's reconstruction of national identity drew widely from the past. The irony in Russia, as in China, was that the once-vilified "feudal" past was assigned a critical role in saving the "communist" past from rejection. The Orthodox Church gained an even stronger following than Confucianism, given the ambivalence of communist leaders in China. As two in a string of leaders building a strong Russian state, Lenin and Stalin, like Mao, were to some degree salvaged among a pantheon of heroes. Yet, though Chinese leaders censored criticism of Mao, a debate over Stalin and Lenin—should the latter's preserved remains be removed from the mausoleum in Red Square?—continued among Russians.

Rehabilitating Stalin posed a problem because of opposition from the Orthodox Church and others who consider Soviet identity to be opposed to Russian identity, but also because it would needlessly revive an identity standing in the way of modernization and international cooperation. Other steps, such as reviving the national anthem, serve the purposes of nostalgia without crossing a red line. Cutting back on criticism of Stalin and justifying his excesses, even arguing that terror was essential due to the Japanese and German threats, which states in the West refused to confront, shifts the identity narrative sufficiently.[14] Along with this approach was deep resentment shown toward those, such as Eastern Europeans, who equated Stalinism and Nazism. Thus, de-Stalinization has been left incomplete. After all, if the main identity themes are strengthening the state and resisting the Western identity threat, then targeting Stalin, who pursued these aims, is not productive. Medvedev's more critical words have been overshadowed by Putin's themes.

In response to criticisms of Soviet history for past imperialist treatment of ethnic minorities and repression of satellite states, Russians respond with rationalizations. They renew Soviet claims to have played a positive role overcoming backwardness inside the Soviet Union and being obliged by Cold War realities to carve out a sphere of influence elsewhere. The problems of the Soviet era are not so much refuted as put in the context of challenges that had to be met, many of them blamed on the need to prepare for war caused by not only Germany but also the imperialist states. This perspective salvages communist leadership, as does the industrialization and military strength left as a superpower legacy to today's Russia.

Identity issues have loomed large in Russia's relations with Ukraine, Georgia, the Baltic states, and other former Soviet republics. Their views of history often clash with those of the Putin administration, leading to actions such as removing World War II monuments. Pride in this victory is much more easily justified in Russia than pride in Stalin's policies. The glorious victory in World War II remains a symbol of great success, alleged to be due to Stalin's personal leadership and state building and paving the way to postwar triumphs.

Given their preoccupation with building a strong state, Russia's leaders shifted away from Gorbachev's perception of Brezhnev-era stagnation to overall praise of the powerful military-industrial establishment over which he had presided. Brezhnev has made a comeback. He presided over the high point in Soviet power, providing a sense of security that was missing later. He gave people reasons to feel proud, something sought in the chaotic post-Soviet era. As criticism turned to Gorbachev's weakening of Soviet power, the contrast favored his predecessor. Gorbachev became the villain, but there is also ambivalence about Yeltsin. It follows that 1989 and 1991 are remembered as times of weakness that needed to be overcome, leading to the conclusion that a transitional rebuilding period will give rise to a new era of strength, unlike the 1990s and 2000s, when Russia remained marginal.

Putin sees himself as a transformative figure in the tradition of Peter I and Peter Stolypin, had the last been given more time and authority. Consonant with a heroic vision of Russian history, Putin considers Russian destiny to be in his personal hands. In reclaiming the presidency in 2012, he was committed to strengthening the historical narrative aimed at contrasting strong state builders resistant to the threat from the West to weak reformers who naively capitulated to its blandishments. The post–Cold War era serves as his arena for continuing this struggle, when economics requires some openness, as in 2012, when Russia joined the World Trade Organization, but geopolitical and civilizational competition is only intensifying.

THE SECTORAL DIMENSION

Russia lost all its bearings in economic, cultural, and political identity from 1987 to 1992. Assertions confidently repeated for decades suddenly lost any validity. Without the Communist Party in charge or the

Soviet Union in existence, the Russian political identity lacked clarity. Embracing Western assistance and the long-disparaged theory of modernization, Russia turned its back on seven decades of insistence on irreconcilable differences between its command economy and its rivals' market economies. Yet it failed to prevent an economic downward spiral, continuing for a decade, or to demonstrate that a model of oligarch and Mafia corruption served the needs of more than a small minority. At the end of the Yeltsin period, economic confidence was at its nadir. Cultural and political identity struggled to recover with little consensus.

In the 1990s, many Russians were exhilarated about entering the once-off-limits economic and cultural world of the West. They embraced the idea that, rather than two blocs divided into socialism and capitalism, a single civilized world exists sharing a transnational market economy and humanist ideals. Yet most doubted the existence of a common political identity, distrusting the notion of democratic values. At the same time, there was widespread suspicion about relaxing economic boundaries, given the long association between the state and economic identity, and there was an upsurge in Russian cultural identity in uncertain times. The brief heyday of shared sectoral identity was fading fast.

Russian efforts in the early 1990s to build a democratic political identity had little backing from economic and cultural identity. A world where democracy was spreading and human rights was prioritized was anathema in the Soviet era and did not appear positive for rebuilding state identity or reviving Russia's influence as a great power, the preoccupations of the elite. Above all, Russians awakened to the threat to their shaky notions of their nation's culture from the onslaught of Westernization in the first half of the 1990s. The prospect of a single civilization prevailing around the world meant the marginalization of critical aspects of the identity they had inherited from the Soviet Union and attributed to imperial Russia as well. If vocal liberal reformers welcomed this outcome for a time, they were quickly marginalized by an outpouring of defensive arguments based on national identity. In the case of social democrats who appealed to an international community separate from the West that would allow Russia to cultivate its own identity, there was no community to which to turn that was not dominated by the West. Already in the late

1990s, statists had won the debate on the "Russian idea," even if they agreed on few specifics apart from sovereignty first, great power assertiveness in seeking a multipolar world, and a defense of civilization against values imported from the West. Their view overlapped with the communist one, offering more flexibility in shifting from the Soviet legacy and in countering the West.[15] The line between the two was not fixed as elements of communist thinking were revived.

Culture proved to be at the center of Russian concern about a narrowing national identity gap. Accepting universal values as meaning more than Western values threatened efforts to forge a distinctive identity and the legacy of past identity. Such values stand in the way of the vertical identity that Putin was determined to rebuild. Looking back to the tsarist era, they also stand in opposition to the troika of orthodoxy, autocracy, and nationality. The Russian Orthodox Church feared that these values would lead both to the onrush of foreign religions, whose missionaries had arrived in the 1990s, and to secularism. The clergy required a narrower orientation in order to rebuild their flocks after the Soviet anticlerical period. Instead of individualism, the state looms as the defender of values, with support from the Orthodox Church, which filled a gap in public rituals, reestablished the church-state partnership, and linked orthodoxy to nationality.[16] Boosters of a strong state likewise feared that Western ideals—especially those about political checks and balances, and democracy—were being directed against Russian unity and power. The necessity of opposing the West and its impact on the social order served as their rationale. Finally, at a time when Russians were struggling to define the meaning of their nationality, attacking others served to heighten cohesion. Thus, insisting that no shared concept of human rights exists replaced Gorbachev's arguments to the contrary. Many who take up the civilizational cudgel praise Stalin as its defender, but not Khrushchev and Gorbachev, who supposedly threatened it.[17] With national elections for the presidency and State Duma continuing, a veneer of democratic identity obscured its deteriorating substance and the shifting focus that strongly contradicted it.

Russia faced a perfect storm: a sudden loss of past identity, inundation of global culture in sharp defiance of past limits, alarm over numerous ethnic fellows abruptly left behind foreign borders under pressure to yield to rival national identities, and anger that the Russian state did not protect what most deemed essential for cultural identity. Under pressure, Yeltsin responded, seeing the Orthodox Church as an indispensable partner. It was Putin, however, who brought culture to the forefront in reconstructing identity. In one of his first moves as acting president, in early 2000 he declared that the security of Russia depends on blocking cultural and religious expansion and building vertical power in defense of Russia's exceptionalism. Given the weak sense of civic identity, associated with low levels of trust and elite resistance to civic organizations, ethnic identities filled the void. Russians grew supportive of the slogan "Russia for ethnic Russians" and the goal of restricting immigration. Migrants were blamed for all sorts of problems, serving as a convenient scapegoat. Increasingly, Islamic identity was the focus of differences, as the shared legacy of Soviet culture, even knowledge of Russian, was fading.[18]

Alexander Dugin, who had long advocated Eurasianism, argued that despite Putin's initial emphasis on economic ties, the civilizational factor should be in the forefront of the integration ahead. People in the nearby states should join Russians in recognizing that they belong to "a single civilization, a single pole, a single society, a society united by its historical fate."[19] Once seen as extreme, these views now gained support.

Whether called Slavophilism, communism, or the "Russian idea," thinking hostile to Western civilization had mixed cultural exceptionalism insistent on the uniqueness of Russian civilization (*samobytnost'*), claims to Russia's special role in international affairs, and dismissal of freedom at odds with Russian ideals of community (*sobornost'*). Although Gorbachev appealed to other periods in history when reform thinking was robust, Putin gravitated to the precedents of these conservative periods in advocating identity themes.

Economic identity raises the question of modernization theory and how far Russia is willing to embrace it. In the first half of the 1960s, hopes rose that the modernization of science and technology as well as economic reform were not only compatible with socialism but easier for it to achieve due to state control. Yet control trumped both borrowing and integration into the global order. The same thing happened again in the Gorbachev and Yeltsin eras as well as during the Medvedev era, when the concepts of modernization and Silicon Valley high technology were invoked without the substance of real innovation independent of a criminalized state system. That left a narrow notion of economic autonomy, which was challenged in 2012 when Russia joined the World Trade Organization, even as it was sustained by natural resource exports that had been in high demand for a decade, allowing the pretense of autonomy to persist.

Putin returned as president in 2012 with a message that the recovery period had now ended. In both Russian and global history, this time of harsh foreign policy and foreign economic conditions was over, offering Russia a great opportunity, and it is prepared because it has national unity and has established sovereignty. Unable to point to a society poised for modernization, as Medvedev had sought, Putin stressed state power in contrast to anarchy in the 1990s. He argued that "Russia can and must play a role predicated upon its civilization model, its great history, geography and its cultural 'genome' that organically combines the fundamental principles of European civilization and many centuries of cooperation with the East, where new centers of economic and political influence are rapidly emerging."[20] Above all, Putin seemed to be suggesting that Russia would ride the coattails of China's challenge to the United States and the West. Appealing to the legacy of Alexander Nevskii in the thirteenth century, Putin links defense of Russia's distinctive civilization, including religion, with today's struggle against multiple threats from the West, whether ideals of freedom or programs to develop missile defense. Cultural and political identity are joined to resist what is portrayed as an existential threat to Russia.

THE VERTICAL DIMENSION

In the first half of the 1990s, the Soviet model was judged a failure for its central planning at the expense of the market and militarization without developing much of a consumer economy. This bureaucratized leviathan stood in the way of "normality," liberating the forces of civil society. Yet, however justified this negative image was, it did not serve to reconstruct national identity. Insisting on the need to abandon the past, it failed to guide Russians toward a future linked to their past. Thinking on many dimensions of national identity would not change abruptly, reforms would inevitably be distorted by officials steeped in old approaches, and civil society had no prospect of eclipsing state power.

The reform intellectuals who had been vocal in China and Russia quieted down. In the case of China, it was the impact of June 4, 1989, with its terrifying message. For Russia, there was no single turning point, but the electoral surprise in December 1993 of the ultranationalist Vladimir Zhirinovskii left in doubt the public's support for their agenda. Preoccupation with material needs was another factor. They had outlets for their views, unlike China's government critics, and they had spokesmen in the administration, but they had come to realize that the issue was no longer communism versus humanism and needed to address other identity themes.[21] The debate shifted abruptly by the mid-1990s.

Collective identities remained weak after the collapse of the Soviet Union, which strove to transfer any sense of identity to the party-state. Attacks on individualism or any abstract principles with universal applicability served this transposition. Loss of pride in the state caused a vacuum, which was not filled, leading to receptivity for renewed state-centered identity. To the extent that individuals lacked self-esteem, this quest for state pride grew. If collective identities such as feminism that were popular in the West drew attention as notions of social class identity lost appeal, Russians were ill prepared to trumpet diversity and welcome civil society.[22] NGOs with these goals did not transform identity.

Loss of confidence is associated with a decline in the social order, which became a major focus in national identity narratives. Pride in the military, criticism of social groups alleged to endanger order, and appeals for a strong state abound in these narratives. Although in China this talk seemed contrived, given minimal problems with disorder beyond village demonstrations for justice, in Russia a loss of order proved to be a critical justification for a shift not only in policies but also in identity. More than crime was of concern. Indeed, the state manipulated the discontent without any serious interest in reducing corruption or arbitrary exercise of authority on behalf of the political elite. Popular sentiments veered from fear of an Islamic threat to anti-Semitism to talk of a "yellow peril" to worry about Russian civilization under threat from the West or globalization. Putin captured the mood with appeals to ideals, co-opting the themes of communists and the Zhirinovskii faction and finding symbols to refocus public sentiment on state power and often on himself.

Historically, China had strong regional identities. In Russia, the regional identity most emphasized, other than those based on ethnicity, is Siberian. In the early 1990s, there was talk of resurgent Siberian identity, or Russian Far East identity, drawing on currents of a century earlier. One argument was that the exploitation of resources was of a colonialist nature, while the construction of infrastructure lagged far behind that in European Russia. Relying on Yeltsin's support for regionalism, calls for autonomy were heard. Environmentalism served as one of the rallying themes. Exposés of repression against symbols of localism were widely publicized. Loss of economic benefits fueled efforts to put political pressure on Moscow, including demands for new types of autonomy. Yet the foundation stayed weak for regional identity; separate governments struck their own deals with the center.[23] As Putin consolidated power, localism was brushed aside with scant resistance.

Complicating clarity about Russian national identity in the first half of the 1990s were the cynical claims to sovereignty and priority identity made by many regions around the country, usually as a means for local elites to seize control of resources. Eventually, the hollowness of these claims was exposed, making it easier to refocus on identity at the national level, whose ample levers to reassert control prevailed. Regional associations, such as those for the Russian Far East, talked in 1992–93 of ambitious plans buttressed by identity claims, but these abruptly faded. Most ethnic republics found it difficult to keep strong identity claims as they were stripped of power, but Moslem identities were rising.

In the Soviet era, the institutions of civil society had atrophied. Local Communist Party bosses and their cronies could wield power with little regard to the law or checks from below. In the 1990s, these local authorities built a Mafia state, in which there were again few limits on lawlessness. Instead of persevering in building institutions from the ground up to limit this, Russians pleaded for the state to reassert its central authority. This was the response expected from past identity. They were accustomed to a state that was responsible for everything, from job allocations to social welfare. With recentralization came the repression of civil society and the hollowing out of what had been seen as democratic institutions.

Russia's quest for normalcy is skewed by the Soviet legacy. Reindustrializing is an elusive goal when modernized states are mainly deindustrializing as part of the new global division of labor and when international chains of production leave little room for the autarchic ideal of the Soviet era. Remilitarizing in an age of advanced technology in the forefront obliges Russia to revert to its nuclear arsenal, however unlikely that is to be usable in the conflicts of the next decades. Putin's credentials as a champion of the social order, social conservatism, and patriotism that brooks no interference in Russia's internal affairs struck a positive chord at a time when disconcerted people clung to symbols of continuity, and Putin took advantage of the surge in prices for energy and other natural resources to provide relief for the lower classes and the sizable population of retired people. Even Medvedev's tenure was facilitated by the sense that Russia's economy had again fallen into jeopardy and that recovery in 2009–11 must be prioritized. In addition, Medvedev soothed middle-class anxiety with rhetoric in support of a less confrontational and more reform-oriented national identity. Reviving the notion of a besieged Russia, Putin risked alienating this vital group, perceiving a subterfuge for repressing popular unrest. Putin took a more extreme posture, putting even more emphasis on a strong Russian identity.

Soviet claims of convergence of identities among ethnic groups proved to be an illusion. The notion of the "new Soviet man," who cared little for ethnicity and religion, and lived harmoniously accepting the Russian language as primary, was as misleading as China's claims of a "harmonious society" based on similar ideals. Yet, gravitating again to a singular ideal for ethnicity, Russians put diffusion to other groups aside.

Fearing that the Russian Federation would split apart, they grasped for unity on the basis of culture and then through centralization that rejected formal legal differences between republics or tolerance for local leaders who could claim a mandate through democratic elections. With the Communist Party removed from power and the central state in disarray, Russia had fertile soil for new identities or identities long suppressed to rise to the fore. Political and economic arguments took a backseat to cultural ones in these fluid times, as in other times of upheaval. It is testimony to the falsity of Soviet pretensions to have relegated ethnic nationalism to marginal importance and to have established a deeply rooted Soviet identity distinct from it. Increasingly, Soviet identity had morphed into Russian national identity, and titular nationalities had managed to establish their own embryonic national identity. Lenin had left a legacy of ethnofederalism for titular ethnic groups; and as coercion was reduced, it was more easily manifested. Multiple grievances were unresolved in the overly centralized Soviet system, giving rise to resentments directed against the center and a backlash from Russians at the center. When in the late 1980s and early 1990s stagnation turned into decline, frustrations over limited social mobility led to charges against other ethnic groups.[24] This was a blow to vertical identity.

Throughout the 1990s, Russians were struggling to define who was Russian. If many in the other former republics of the Soviet Union disavowed a Russian identity as they consolidated around one national identity each, the nationalities left inside the Russian Federation were bifurcated into Russians and non-Russians with tensions on how to apply Russian identity to others. Sorting out civic and ethnic identity in the chaotic environment of the 1990s proved complicated. The answers were more clear-cut in Putin's Russia. The two were essentially equated. Russian ethnic identity faced few bounds. Although the rise of xenophobia was not directly promoted by the top leadership, there was little in its path.

Incidents of terrorism by Muslims from the Caucasus played a role, but the complaints against immigrants center mostly on their occupying the places of Russian workers, squeezing locals from the job market, or exploiting people in the market and operating illegally with bribes. The real source of concern seems to be the failure of these groups to assimilate—their tendency to stick together. In the Soviet era, there was no recognition of subcultures or means for their expression. This legacy leads to demands for integration on terms set by the majority. Migration is perceived in the context of cultural identity. Even if the vast majority of migrants are from states from the Soviet Union and are driven by economic motives alone, filling labor shortages, Russians are disposed to demonize them.

Russia also rebuilt its cultural identity through alarm about the fate of Russians left behind in the newly independent states of the former Soviet Union, and especially about the threat from the West to Russian culture. Fear of helplessness over culture remained a preoccupation, compounding the sense of loss over shock therapy.[25] An alternative was available: Embrace multiculturalism in support of a broad Russian (*Rossiiskaia*) federation based on shared political identity. Russian (*Russkaia*) ethnic identity trumped common citizenship, as Putin set about reconstructing identity. If Putin did not embrace xenophobes with an exclusive notion of Russiannness at the expense of ethnic minorities, he also left multiculturalism aside and did not articulate an identity welcoming to the 20 percent who are non-Russians or use Yeltsin's term *Rossisskii* for a civic identity, instead stressing a civilizational identity based on Russian culture, echoing the Soviet ideal of a single civilization rooted in Russia's more advanced level of cultural development. Culture was central for Putin.

As ethnic homogeneity rose through the replacement of the Soviet Union by the Russian Federation, national identity refocused on the Russian population in place of the "new Soviet man." This revision of national identity occurred despite the fact that 20 percent of the population was non-Russian and that large numbers of non-Russians arrived as migrant workers. Many of these people felt entitled to be in Russia because of the Soviet legacy, but Russian ethnic identity aroused xenophobia without balance from weak civic identity. The Russification of consciousness, accompanied by concern about the demographic dilution of the country, exerted a powerful force in the emerging identity. Areas known as the "near abroad" lost their appeal as part of a shared nation, as territorial boundaries acquired great significance. Deeply embedded in Russian tradition was the notion that a vast, ever-expanding territory is essential to Russian power, however, which kept alive claims to exercise control over nearby states even if their citizens, apart from Russians, were treated with hostility in Russia's cities.[26]

The failure of multiculturalism and of efforts to establish the Rossiiskaia nationality as a melting pot based on civic identity left many clinging to strong ethnic identifiers and responding with slurs (e.g., "Russia for the Russians") and sometimes violence to labor migrants, army recruits, fellow prisoners, and just "dark" people on the street. Boosting hostility to the West and civilizational arguments by 2006, Putin was legitimizing xenophobes, even if he officially supports interethnic harmony. Although anti-Chinese sentiments often are held by skinheads and other bigots, these are overshadowed by the primary targets.

As long as social injustice rose to the forefront, old assumptions of identity were questioned. The state appeared to fail in meeting recognized goals. But if state weakness became the focus, then old identity loomed high. Suddenly, Brezhnev-era stability looked appealing. Gorbachev's reforms, offering more freedom to educated persons and young people, gave way to calls for more control.[27] This shift came quickly in the chaotic 1990s.

The shock to vertical national identity was decisive. Turning from the state to the individual or the global community failed to meet expectations. Only a strong state at the center of Russian identity would have been able to steer expectations toward trust in the United States and the international community it leads. Focusing on democratization as the key to identity change turned out to be deceptive. Instead, making this the centerpiece may have unwittingly been a stimulus to an identity backlash led by those who insisted that only a strong state undiminished by democracy could restore the essential identity.

The prolonged debate over what is Russia is premised on uncertainty, in contrast to the certitude of China's elite. This extends from doubts about where to locate Russian civilization in the dichotomy of East versus West all the way to concerns about what should remain of the legacy of socialism. Critical to these uncertainties is how to reconcile claims of democracy with a growing awareness that most of the attributes of this system are missing. China is more consistent in its identity claims versus the West and supportive of a communist autocracy.

THE HORIZONTAL DIMENSION

In 1999, Yeltsin criticized the United States and the European Union for their "double standards" related to Kosovo. In 2003, Putin's initially cooperative attitude toward the West was changing. In 2007 in Munich, he spoke so critically of the United States that some saw a revival of the Cold War. In 2012, his tone was even harsher, demonizing it on all dimensions of identity. Evaluating the breakup of the Soviet Union as a "major geopolitical catastrophe," Putin linked the horizontal to the vertical dimension, objecting to interference in internal affairs that could impede his concentration of power. Because Soviet identity had come to center on international competitiveness, it should be no surprise that the same alleged threats reemerged as the focus of Russian identity. Only a strong state, whose identity overrides all other domestic identities, forestalls dangerous external threats, even from soft power.

Putin vehemently attacked the existing international system, blaming states in the West for destructive forces threatening global security, both for the way they "export democracy" and for risky economic behavior that adds to tensions. Noting a "systemic crisis, a tectonic process of global transformation," he welcomed a new era in cultural, economic, technological, and geopolitical respects. Critical of the two decades that had brought the collapse of the Soviet Union and the rise of unilateralism, he called for overcoming "ideological prejudices" through greater reliance on the UN Security Council and the Group of Twenty as well as the Group of Eight, all of which limit US power. In his January 2012 *Izvestiia* article, Putin qualified the scope of freedom, insisting that Russia has a "long-standing tradition to respect the state, public interest and the nation's needs. An absolute majority of Russians wants to see their country strong and powerful. . . . Freedom which is not based on morality turns into anarchy." This call for cohesion in society, trust in the state, and self-confidence based on state power joins the vertical and horizontal dimensions while pretending that ideology is an evil coming only from the other side.[28]

A refusal to accept Russia's strategic parity was equated with the United States' dismissal of Russia's national identity. In turn, Russian cooperation with so-called rogue states was justified as defensive in the face of US hegemonism and unilateralism. Citing the threat of US world domination, Russia justified its foreign policy and national identity. Great power status depends on blocking US power and on regional integration on the basis of separate poles, which stay in a kind of balance of power and limit globalization. Neoimperialism in the former Soviet space is not just tied to preserving Russia's current political system; it is a precondition of the survival of the state. The 2008 war against Georgia proved cathartic in a way, along with the sobering effect of the world financial crisis. A message was directed more at the United States than at Georgia, drawing a red line against further NATO expansion. A confidence booster, it dispelled two decades of retreat. Although in 2009–11 the Obama-Medvedev "reset" obscured the national identity message for a time, Putin's return to the top post gave it new reinforcement.

Putin inherited the term "multipolarity" from the Yeltsin era and gave additional substance to it. In his second term as president, he emphasized anti-hegemonism. Campaigning in 2011, Putin called for an "active foreign policy, . . . creating a more just political and economic order." He insisted on a dialogue of equals, warning against imposing anything on Russia from the outside, such as by trying to influence the election campaign through traitors in Russia. At the start of his return to the office in 2012, he proposed establishing a Eurasian Union as an integration project to create a new center of geopolitical influence, building on increased unity among former Soviet states. Major financial outlays are required for the armed forces, he added, to defend Russian sovereignty and independence.[29] At the same time, Medvedev boasted of the impact of the Eurasian Union in boosting Russian feelings of "geopolitical greatness" and its international standing in the world arena by broadening not only its economic but also its cultural expanse that shrank with the demise of the Soviet Union.[30]

Given China's rise and the perceived weakening of the United States along with the chaotic state of the EU, this was virtually a claim to tripolar geopolitics. It promised a bridge between Europe and the Asia-Pacific region, harking back to the glory of the Soviet Union as a supra-national structure. With Belarus and Kazakhstan in tow, Russia pressured other states to join. In highlighting the economic identity of the group, Putin skirted other dimensions, despite brief claims of being "united by commonly shared values of freedom, democracy, and free market."[31] The continued existence of the Collective Security Treaty Organization adds another element to the notion of a union. But requirements for unanimity and the absence of actual military cooperation left the significance of this element in doubt. In addition, the backward-looking economic orientation of Belarus and uncertainty over Russia's model left identity confused. It was assumed that Putin sought to reestablish a variant of the Soviet Union with Russia in the driver's seat, which would be unacceptable to others. For them, economic benefits from Russia were a lure, as long as few strings were attached.

What does the concept "Eurasia" mean? In early 2013, Dmitry Trenin reconceptualized this idea for an era of bipolar Sino-American competition and growing Chinese ambitions that are putting it in conflict with many neighbors, arguing for an inclusive interpretation. He mentioned Japan, South Korea, the Association of Southeast Asian Nations, India, and Turkey as key components of the "new Eurasia."[32] Many others, however, preferred to think of this as well as the Eurasian Union as an exclusive sphere under Russian tutelage, approximating as closely as possible the former Soviet Union. The future of Eurasianism is closely bound to the choices that Russia is making in dealing with China. Despite Trenin's idea, Eurasianism essentially means an anti-West coalition. It provides reassurance that Russia stands at the center, whether that means a revived imperial destiny or a polarized globe ripe for the ascent of a third civilizational center.[33]

The "Eurasian Union" combines the identity theme of Eurasianism and the idea of a union, reminiscent of the Soviet Union. It is a response to the West, rejecting the notion that Russia is part of it without dis-associating completely. At the same time, it stakes out a bridging role between the West, centered in the United States, and Asia, centered in China. If Russia is alone as the leader of its region, it sees the EU and India as divisive forces in the other regions. Yet, whereas the other regions have long-standing pedigrees and great heft, Russia's vision tenuously refers to the discredited Soviet model and has a flimsy basis in economic integration that is slipping away. The theme caters to the nostalgia of the Russian public, keeping alive an element of nation-al identity that can buttress others. It counters the impression that Central Asia is being pulled into China's orbit or that other areas of the former Soviet Union will be further drawn into the EU's orbit. In this way, despite its elusive nature, it serves self-confident national identity rhetoric, but Russia is too closely associated with the Soviet Union, too xenophobic, and too paternalistic about the Russian minorities within its neighbors' boundaries. Its goals of Russian lan-guage use and shared culture clash with nation building. To the extent that Russia appears as a counterweight to China, it can make some headway, but this is limited by China.

Claiming only to be defending Russia's national interests, Russians increasingly revived a dichotomous view of two blocs, opposition to the West, and equation of Russia with the Soviet Union.[34] Despite aban-donment of the goal of forging a communist future, the quest resumed for an international mission comparable to that of the Soviet Union. The West refuses to recognize Russia as an equal, denying its sphere of influence, unlike the response to Soviet power in the Cold War, and encouraging demonstrations against the way power is wielded that in 2011–12 stimulated a democratic opposition in Russia. The result-ing zero-sum logic linked horizontal and vertical identity. The strug-gle between two blocs was seen as playing out inside Russia through international organizations providing financial assistance for purposes such as free elections and a free press. Demonizing these NGOs and all who took their money echoed xenophobic campaigns in Soviet times. It proved useful to posit the arrival of a new world order, based on emerging powers more than established ones. In this way, the West gets its comeuppance, and Russia rides a wave of global transformation to regain its pride oblivious to China's rise.[35]

What in the 1980s became a struggle among four approaches to national identity has narrowed into a contest between two dominant approaches, which Russians often simplistically lump together, and two marginal approaches within the community of international relations specialists, even if they are criticized as if they have more impact. The dominant approaches are multipolarity and a new cold war, while the marginal ones are international community and xenophobia. To appreciate the character of Russian debates on China, all four approaches should be taken into account. Complicating moves to differentiate the dominant views is the difficulty of separating identity as a separate civilization serving as pole in the global system and as a non-Western civilization joining in opposition to the alleged US drive to impose a single, hegemonic global civilization.

With China the focus, the four approaches have been voiced by specialists and politicians alike. The international community's viewpoint is rare for China hands. Others—such as I. Chubais, D. Trenin, and V. Mikheev—advocate it, often with more resonance among foreign audiences. Primorskii Krai governor E. Nazdratenko took a xenophobic approach when it was popular in the media in the 1990s, but there is no standard bearer of note among today's politicians who are focusing on Asia. Arguments for a new cold war are widely heard in the State Duma and are reinforced by China specialists such as M. Titorenko and others at the Institute of the Far East. Yet the case for multipolarity is no less common, especially among such China specialists as E. Bazhanov and A. Lukin. The myth that the multipolar and cold war approaches are the same leads to complacency about China, while the case that multipolarity is better realized by the international community—which would lead to priority for Japan, South Korea, India, and the Association of Southeast Asian Nations (ASEAN) as well as more seriousness about a strategic triangle balancing China and the United States—is rarely found in Russian sources.

THE INTENSITY DIMENSION

In the Soviet period, national identity was shifting from the center of revolution to the defender of sovereignty, reducing the role of conflict at home in favor of harmony in a shared undertaking. Yet demonization of the West did not fade; it was convenient for regime legitimacy rooted in lies and coercion. The post-Soviet era started with assertive aims to overturn the old order, but soon shifted to urgent demands to achieve coherence in pursuit of an undertaking quite similar to that of the later Soviet era. Again, it was decided that state guidance would preempt collective identities, and the struggle against the West had few limitations. Despite more tolerance for capitalist market forces and the global business world, the focus returned to a strong, unfettered state that preferred to rely more on a carefully managed national identity than on the forces of coercion.[36] Putin was committed to intensifying national identity, doing so during his first two terms as the president of Russia and again as he reclaimed the top spot in presidential elections. The low intensity of identity in the early 1990s was changing under Putin, more so starting in 2012.

The softening of national identity rhetoric for a few years under Medvedev in the aftermath of an upsurge in intensity during Putin's second term may have been due to the world financial crisis even more than Medvedev's own style. The model of development based on high commodity prices seemed to be in trouble. If investment from the West was needed in order to forge a new economic base, then a different tone was desirable. Yet in 2011 the West, especially the states of the EU, were facing new economic and political difficulties, and Russia's economy had recovered with higher commodity prices driven by demand in China, above all. Meanwhile, social upheaval spread in the Arab states, with the possibility that it would be contagious. Putin dispensed with Medvedev's facade. The intensity of Russian national identity was climbing to a level not strikingly inferior to that during the Cold War era.

When a nation's identity is threatened, especially at a time of loss of international status and great economic instability, people are prone to blame their fate on scapegoats. Demagogues exaggerate threats and stir intolerant responses, suggesting that solutions are readily available. Such alarmism fuels identity cohesion around some in-groups in opposition to specific out-groups.[37] Immigrants make a convenient target for economic anxieties and fear of cultural vulnerability. In Russia, xenophobia centers on them. Yet insecurity also has an international dimension, given that people are fearful that weakened state capacity leaves them exposed to the machinations of other states. Thus national security is in doubt, resulting in an obsession with reestablishing power. Putin played on this.

On Russia Day, June 12, 2013 (which commemorates the independence of the Russian Federation in 1992), Putin spoke ominously about peace slipping away in a world of growing competition. Denigrating the United States for its history of "genocide" toward Native Americans, slavery, racial segregation, and the atomic bombing of Japan, which he doubted Stalin would have done to Germany if the Soviet Union had had the bomb and victory was assured, Putin argued that US leaders are worse than Stalin. In a comparison of identity, Putin focused on Russian collectivism, eternally and directed connected to God, versus US individualism, pragmatic but making it hard to understand each other. In dealing with Iran and Syria, the United States was accused of imperialism.[38] This echoed the extreme rhetoric of Brezhnev's days, carrying identity to an extreme.

CONCLUSION

Historical memory trumped idealism for the future. Whatever the arguments for democracy, human rights, and free market competition, they hinged on trust in fellow citizens and officials to allow these processes to go forward. Such trust was absent in Russia. People rightly assumed that officials would abuse their power and that voters would fall under the sway of demagogues or others without respect for ideals. Losing a sense of normalcy and self-esteem, people grasped for symbols of the revival of national pride. This put a premium on manipulating the public to react with strong emotions against the targets supposedly standing in the way.

Conditions were ripe to succumb to such appeals at a time when there were few signs of hope, but stale messages may again ring hollow.

The tensions associated with conflicting identities were pronounced in the 1990s. Despite greater economic decentralization, China prevented any similar challenges after the shock of mass protests in the spring of 1989. The vacuum at the top in Russia was a factor, as was the opportunity for ethnic identities to flourish in the relaxed days of the 1990s, while China's oppression of the Uighurs and others drove such reactions underground. Yet the reestablishment of a single all-Russian identity proved easier than many had expected, testimony to the enduring legacy of communist identity. Once clear, strong leadership came from Moscow, local leaders fell in line. The fragility of localism was exposed as national political identity revived.[39] In its wake came the intensification of the national identity narrative along each of the dimensions identified in this book.

Russians lost self-esteem as their identity was repeatedly questioned under first Gorbachev and then Yeltsin. Much of the earlier identity appears artificial: equality as a superpower with the United States, heroic workers favored as a class, and a model society living in harmony and mastering scientific development. Far uglier was new evidence of intolerance of others perceived as different, receptivity to manipulative symbols of what the in-group has in common, and a virtual absence of sources of self-esteem in daily life. The Soviet legacy relied on scapegoating—whether of class enemies, international spies, or foreign antagonists. It deflected criticism by hurling accusations. The need to do this only increased in the 1990s. Ethnic scapegoating became popular. Ideas of imperialism resurfaced with charges that the West wants to colonize Russia. Fear of loss of identity combined with a sense of entitlement from the old order were framed in a zero-sum prism.[40]

Just as Japanese politicians and writers kept insisting that the reconstruction of Japan's national identity is nothing more than a quest for normalcy, so too did Russians. The nation had lost its bearings, falling from a high pedestal of belief in its special nature. To regain normalcy required social cohesion, renewed belief in the motherland, and a symbolic confirmation of the cultural and political order. This could not occur if a nihilistic view of one's own history was not overcome, many argued. Yet the proposed solution proved to be nothing short of nostalgia for a bygone world of oppression and intolerance. In Russia, the idea of *sobornost'* revived ostracism of boosters of individualism opposed to arbitrary state power. A search for cohesion, legitimacy, and esteem courtesy of a strong state defending supposed cultural uniqueness is only an illusion of normalcy, as Marlene Laruelle argues.[41] The quest for normalcy turned into a drive to marginalize those who are sympathetic to a different sort of normalcy, joining the international community by forsaking emotionalism about uniqueness despite the backlash against national decline.

Aleksandr Lukin attributes Putin's popularity to support for a paternalistic state able to achieve developmentalism. Noting that Inkeles and Bauer in the 1950s and the Soviet interview project of the early 1980s had Soviet public opinion centered not on anticommunism but on state paternalism, he credited Putin with satisfying those aspirations. Gorbachev had fallen victim to his own reforms, which diminished the state, revealing its inability to provide order and welfare. Lukin found Putin boosting his popularity after the US invasion of Iraq by becoming more critical of the West, in line with the thinking of the Russian people. Giving people order, welfare, and pride in the state's international status, Putin found a receptive audience. As liberals focused on economic policy, he sees Putin satisfying the power bloc's foreign policy goals and the statist group's call for order.[42]

The Russian literature in the 2010s on Russian national identity keeps expanding without bringing clarity to how this concept can be used to study state policies. Denying a monopoly to those who would embed this concept in its communist and tsarist legacies, a few voices recall the reformist path of officials such as Sergei Witte and Peter Stolypin as they rejected the communist course in its entirety. Igor Chubais stands in the forefront of this group with a 2012 book on the Russian idea, insisting that ninety years have been lost, not only from communism but also from its aftermath.[43] From this standpoint, China serves as a reminder of what stands in the way of Russian identity, a contaminating force, as opposed to the West with its inspirational impact. This is decidedly a minority view.

If communism is no longer invoked, this does not mean that Russians have stopped insisting on being distinct from the West, and thus demonstrating their nation's exceptionalism. From about the time Putin took office, this differentiation intensified, rooted in arguments about Russia being culturally unique as well as requiring autonomy as the sole defense of sovereignty. Collective identity bolstered claims of this sort, drawing sharp contrasts with the West, which loomed as the prime threat. Culture drove political contrasts without need of an ideology of communism, but reliant on its legacy of identity along many dimensions.

One view of continuity in national identity is that communism is essentially an outgrowth of Russian political culture. Authoritarianism is assumed to be deeply embedded, the collective will is treated as something that continued to override any upsurge in individualism, and the Mongol occupation is considered more formative than the following four centuries of increased ties to other European countries. To those who make these linkages, Putin appears to be a return to tradition, denying the deep impact of the break from it under Gorbachev and Yeltsin. Critics in Russia argue that Russian history was not so distant from that of the West and that Putin's impact is part of a complex transition, in which authoritarianism is uncertain and the revival of attachment to "holy Russia" is proceeding without denying its European nature.[44] To them, communism imposed something new, which will be further contested ahead.

Many focus on unifying symbols that resonate in today's society, such as Russia's victory in the Great Fatherland (Patriotic) War—the eastern front of World War II. Yet they cannot avoid drawing attention to barriers from the past, for example, Russian (*Russkaia*) ethnic nationalism, in the way of Russian (*Rossiiskaia*) civic nationalism.[45] Beyond this, there is the difficulty of separating religious and secular nationalism in defining a "civilizing mission." Reflecting on the debate over Eurasianism as the essence of this mission, V. A. Tishkov finds its roots deep in Russia's past, warning that frantic energy to philosophize about an abstraction that arouses such controversy has left readers no closer to knowing what is meant and how leaders justify applying it.[46]

The core of Soviet national identity survived as great power identity, cultural exclusivity, and a resistance to the Western identity threat. Once communists acceded to Russianness, they could help to steer the transition, demonizing the United States and assuming that Russian power is greater than it really is, subordinating reality to identity. In contrast, the liberals faded into a small minority, unable to win much support at the ballot box and stifled in conveying their message to the public. When in 2012 they turned to demonstrations in Moscow, where support was greatest, they relied on the xenophobic right to bolster their numbers before a reenergized Putin pushed harsher laws through the Duma to make demonstrations and foreign funding of NGOs difficult. These measures were framed in the identity narrative as a further response to the external threat to weaken the Russian state by undermining the coherence needed to defend a beleaguered nation. In Putin's reconstruction of identity, the Communist Great Power (T1) National Identity Syndrome (CGP (T1) NIS) is unmistakably advancing with close parallels to China, as seen in chapter 4 and then in the comparative conclusions of chapter 5. By carrying this legacy to an extreme, however, Putin may be sowing the seeds for another transition. Overreaching plus stagnation in the Brezhnev era turned what many treated as a settled national identity into a farce that was unviable in the rapidly transforming world of the 1980s; and Putin's efforts to turn the clock back, however much they were made possible by the legacy of communism, pale before the flexibility that even Medvedev showed, and may be exposed as out of touch with the times in an impending economic downturn.

CHAPTER 4

CHINESE NATIONAL IDENTITY FROM THE 1990s TO THE 2010s

Given the presence of a chapter on Chinese national identity, differentiated into six dimensions, in the 2012 book *East Asian National Identities*, I cover the topic in a shortened presentation here, with emphasis on themes relevant to the Communist Great Power (Transition 1) National Identity Syndrome, or CGP (T1) NIS, and to comparisons with coverage of Russia that will be raised in chapter 5. At the start, this chapter briefly reviews the 1990s, then the period 2000–2008, and finally the period 2009–13, downplaying the impact of leadership changes in 2002 and 2012. Those looking to the 1980s for clues to an alternative path to national identity will not find that here. The sprouts of that decade are absent in recent, censored sources. China's rise was punctuated in 2000–2001 by a more confident approach to national identity, and even more in 2009–10 by an intensification in assertiveness that did not subside. Unlike Russia's change of direction after the early 1990s, China's path is continuous, if anticipated inadequately as it obscured national identity at a time it was keeping a low profile. Xi Jinping's impact in 2012–13 is important less as a change of course than as a more assertive, definitive articulation of themes earlier gaining momentum.

In the earlier coverage of six dimensions of Chinese national identity, I noted the presence of an East Asian National Identity Syndrome (EANIS), while pointing to indications of Chinese exceptionalism. In the roots of their identities and the manner in which these identities spiked—that is, became intensified—in the aftermath of "economic miracles," I specified striking similarities between China, Japan, and South Korea. Yet, in the scale of its spike and the special features of each dimension, I discussed factors that make China unique. Coverage of the evolution of national identities paid attention to the distinctive character of premodern China. In this book, the emphasis is on how communism shaped the identity of China, treated to a degree in this chapter and more systemically through the following comparisons with Russia. In the years 2012–13, the two were drawing closer as their national identities found a surprising degree of common ground, despite the potential clash ahead due to exclusive orientations that do not point to any accord.

THE DECADE OF THE 1990s

The expression of Chinese national identity is a function of national power as well as the Chinese Communist Party's combination of confidence and vulnerability. In the first half of the 1990s, power was low and vulnerability was high, contrasting with the reverse conditions two decades later. Leaders rankled at pressure by the West, using the human rights question, but acknowledged that China lacked the ability to play the role they desired in forging a new international order. They were also aware that China's culture could not display its competitiveness due to the backwardness of the country's economy and technology.[1] This left China heavily exposed to the penetration of Western culture, which threatened to erode the country's culture and political system. The implication is that China must bide its time, overcoming a gap of at least ten to fifteen years before it could assume the leading role it deserves. In these years of restraint, the way to widen the identity gap with the West, which had narrowed disturbingly by 1989, was to paint the United States in a more negative light. And by accomplishing this primarily through accusations about America's designs on a weakened Russia and its plans to keep China weak, the Chinese stressed the threat of Western values, cloaked in calls for universal human rights and democracy, as the leading edge of neoimperialism.

National identity in the 1990s was narrowly focused and moderately intense. The theme of socialism was kept low key for those outside inner–Communist Party circles. Pride in Confucianism was only gradually becoming acceptable as an identity theme. Past history seemed geared more toward patriotism, as in the war against Japan's aggression, than toward a defense of socialism. The tendency was to allow more open debate in academic circles, such as on the Korean War, rather than to reassert the glory of this endeavor and others during the Cold War. Although great power identity was vigorously claimed, it was with an anticipation of multipolarity, not draped in Sinocentrism. The United States' intentions were treated with suspicion without demonizing its identity, the nature of its alliances, and Western civilization. Observers found reason to conclude that China accepted the international community and was a status quo power, although closer examination of the way national identity was depicted contradicted such optimism.

In 1992, as the world was in flux, one theme that was highlighted was "East versus West." Culture was in the forefront in arguments that Western culture predominated and both Westerners and Easterners underappreciated Eastern culture, but a new stage of history was predicted with the rise of the East.[2] This fit a new strategy of Asian good-neighborly relations to buttress a focus on great power multipolar relations.

The main indicators in downplaying the intensity of national identity through 1999 were limited arrogance about Chinese superiority and cautious accusations against the international community and especially regional partners. A more fiery tone could be found in Chinese writings on Russia, how it had been victimized by the West, and what additionally was sought to keep Russia weak, divided, and unable to resurrect its identity. It was understood that this was also the fate planned for China. Reconstructing national identity to forestall this outcome was a driving force in this decade.

The Chinese national identity reaction to developments in the years 1996–97 was to see the US presence in East Asia as incompatible with China's rise. With Taiwan in the forefront, the conclusion was that the US presence only slows reunification. The United States' alliances with Japan and South Korea were no longer seen as stabilizing the region, constraining Japanese militarism and North Korean provocations, but as containing China. Although this conclusion was tempered by the Jiang-Clinton summits and the regional balance-of-power arguments from specialists who warned that China was still too weak to challenge US power, it gained increasing traction. Hiding behind the image of China's limitations as a great power proved convenient, even as views were gravitating toward the urgency of expressing China's identity more assertively. Hostility toward US "Cold War" thinking shifted toward a critique of US efforts to blend regional integration into global integration, due to America's attempts to persuade Asian countries to establish an international community following US principles.[3]

By the end of the decade, the trend for China was unmistakably rising assertiveness toward both its neighbors and the United States. Japan's negative responses in 1995–96 to China's nuclear tests and show of force in the Taiwan Strait drew a rebuke against the notion that Japan's past disqualified it from invoking values against China and gaining a leadership role or even a strategic partnership with the United States in a regional context. In the Kosovo war, China made clear that it rejected "humanitarian intervention" and any notion that this would be suitable for the international community. If national identity remained clouded, it was already growing more combative in what China opposes. Efforts to keep the national identity gaps with the United States and Japan from widening beyond what seemed prudent at the time were required with increased frequency, but to limited avail.

THE PERIOD 2000–2008

Whereas in the early 1990s China appeared isolated with little power to alter the triumphal path of US unilateralism, a decade later it had a leading role in East Asian regionalism and growing soft and hard power, including economic clout that enabled it to influence its neighbors. It claimed the mantle of multilateralism, especially as the United States, under the impact of neoconservatism, appeared to be relinquishing it. There was no letup in criticizing the United States, but in addition to the optimism of the 1990s about the emergence of the multipolarity that would constrain America, there was much talk about the decline of US hegemonism in East Asia that was being handled, at least in the short term, by cooperation more than competition. This overall theme allayed some concerns, even as it barely concealed growing accusations concerning US behavior that was aimed at sustaining hegemonism and containing China's rise.

Among those who insisted that China is biding its time until the mid-twenty-first century—focusing on becoming an economic great power while continuing to identify with the developing world—attention was given to the need for the world to recognize its increased status. Its "peaceful development" orientation was credited as a source warranting this higher status.[4] Highlighted in the mid-2000s, this approach praised its internationalism, but there was considerable evidence that this mantle did not fit China's actual thinking.

James Reilly captures the revival of the "propaganda state" in manipulating public opinion toward Japan and responding to it for strategic advantage.[5] Showing in 2006–7 an upbeat, top-down image, which was carried forward in public opinion even into 2010, Reilly assumes the presence of a moderate stance that could manage angry public flare-ups, but developments beginning in 2010 clearly demonstrated a different role for Japan in China's identity and strategic thought. Pretenses over many years did not assuage the public ire being aroused, and leaders then fed this ire with a harsher tone toward not only Japan but also the United States, South Korea, and others who defied its strategy.

The tone of accusations had grown more strident as pride in China's past and present achievements kept mounting. When criticism of the United States intensified with regard to unilateralism and hegemonism, many misunderstood this criticism as a response to the policies and rhetoric of the George W. Bush administration, which would subside when a new US president reemphasized multilateralism and turned to China for a kind of Group of Two partnership to resolve global problems. When Bush shifted direction in Asia, especially in the case of the Six-Party Talks on North Korea's nuclear program in 2006–7, China stressed the positive state of relations, which seemed to confirm the temporary nature of criticisms. Yet the way in which the 2008 Beijing Olympics were managed (the sacred torch parades, the opening ceremony, the handling of public dissent, and the wounded pride found increasingly in Chinese rhetoric) indicated that a turning point was approaching. Although US diplomats called on China to set aside its passivity in order to work together more closely as a "responsible stakeholder," calls for it to shed its "low profile" misjudged what would happen as an assertive antagonist emerged, empowered to express its national identity more fully and widen existing gaps with states active in East Asia.

In the spring of 2008, before the global financial crisis erupted, a debate was raging in China over whether the time had come to abandon passivity. Hard-liners focused on Taiwan's push for independence, the recent instability in Tibet, and global tensions over China's pre-Olympics torch parades. Intensifying their charges against the United States' "peaceful evolution" despite recent US pragmatism and optimism about Sino-American relations, they disagreed with others who still put a priority on development, insisting instead that sovereignty and security are the foremost concerns. Reemphasizing socialism as a word that needs to be highlighted, despite its divisive impact, they were focused on national identity. Ideology was making a comeback, linked to cultural identity. An indicator of this was the fact that debates about Gorbachev and the Soviet collapse due to a US plot and spiritual pollution continued to rage under China's leadership. Ideologues focused on socialism kept vigil against those who would blame the authoritarian Soviet political system, as China turned from avoiding confrontation to a new assertiveness. This shift can be observed in writings on South Korea and the handling of the territorial dispute with Japan in the East China Sea.[6] It became pronounced from 2009 to 2010.[7]

THE PERIOD 2009–12

Wang Jisi notes that in July 2009, China redefined the aims of its international relations to "safeguard the interests of sovereignty, security, and development," and he added that in December 2010, State Councillor Dai Bingguo specified China's core interests as, first, the political stability of the leadership of the Chinese Communist Party and the country's social system; second, sovereign security, territorial integrity, and national unification; and third, sustainable economic and social development. Aware that these core interests are contradictory, he notes that many in China favor a tougher foreign policy. Although he makes an appeal for improving China's image and raising its cultural soft power, drawing on common values, this is not the thrust of newly redefined priorities and identity.[8]

In 2010, the Chinese raised the intensity of national identity by highlighting its symbols—Taiwan arms sales that violated China's sovereignty; the meeting of Obama and the Dalai Lama, which encouraged separatism; US aerial surveillance along the borders of China, which serves containment; and the like. Such symbols could be invoked almost at will, allowing for the widening of identity gaps whenever China's leaders desired.

On all dimensions of national identity, Chinese publications unreservedly widened the gap with others states, especially the United States and its allies, starting in 2009. The global financial crisis emboldened writers to contrast a booming China to a declining West. The transition from Bush to Obama elicited comments not about the growing US interest in multilateralism but about the dangerous expansion of containment toward China resulting from the US "return to Asia." The differentiation of Eastern and Western civilizations intensified, faulting the West historically and even today for its cultural imperialism and other shortcomings while putting China at the center of the East.[9] Some may see growing fears of vulnerability from small-scale demonstrations scattered across China or uncertainty about the future of the model of economic growth being used, exacerbated by the demonstration effect from the 2011–12 Arab Spring, but Chinese sources pointed instead to rising confidence. In the earlier books in this series and articles I have written, these points are developed at length.

Chinese leaders and their boosters were particularly prone to triumphalism. Intoxicated claims in 2009–13 expressed pent-up frustrations after two prior eras of unmitigated pride had ended in disappointment.

Imperial China's Confucianism was sharply contrasted with uncivilized barbarians. Maoist China's communism was no less sharply differentiated from a caricature of capitalism interminably beset by class conflict. After having suffered for three decades starting in the 1980s from criticisms of the backwardness of communism, its adherents could at last turn the tables. China not only had emerged as a first-class global power and a state deserving of equality with the United States; it had also won praise as the savior of the global economy. Yet the more the Chinese were trumpeting their pride, the more distrust they were sowing. This led to cautionary moves in 2011, but no real retreat from the assertive identity of 2010. By 2012, the intensity of national identity had clearly resumed the trajectory evident earlier as a leadership transition in China left no doubt of a concerted, top-down inculcation drive.

Whatever the cause one chooses for the spike intensifying all dimensions of Chinese national identity, there is no reason to expect a retreat from the widening gap of recent years. The desire of the Chinese Communist Party to retain power and strengthen its legitimacy would lead it to rely even more on the diversion of identity gap widening if the economy were to slow. The rising clout of the military and security services is bound to continue, if national power expands and identity symbols lead to a downward spiral in bilateral relations. The US tendency to take countermeasures and respond to demonization with talk of a China threat is unlikely to be reversed. The limited pause in 2011 suggests that setbacks to Chinese foreign policy can have a temporary impact, not be a cause for a turnabout. Xi Jinping's greater concentration of power is accompanied by more intolerance of those who would stand in the way of galvanizing public opinion around themes of national pride.

To mobilize public opinion, China stirs feelings of victimization, feigning it even in the halcyon days of 2009–13, when world opinion was marveling at China's success. In warning of a new cold war instigated by those intent on containing China, the Chinese depict a beleaguered country. Charging a surge in containment behavior, they view China's "core interests" under threat. It did not matter that developments in recent years were overwhelmingly favoring China. The unrelenting message was that China was being denied its due. This led to a growing gap between expectations and realities. The Chinese spike in national identity comes with efforts to widen the gap with the United States and its allies in Asia on each of the dimensions of identity.

The themes that suggested moderation lost ground. Observers who had seen China becoming a "responsible great power" awakened to charges that the United States is an "irresponsible power." Hopes for joint support of "global governance" faded as the Chinese disavowed this concept. Rather than agree to joint restructuring of a troubled world economy, China openly distinguished its superior economic model. Instead of focusing on coordination of a new power joining an established power, the Chinese saw a declining power refusing to yield to a rising power. Earlier notions of soft power gave way to sharp warnings about how China could use its hard power. Yet there were also ambiguous terms—notably, in 2013, calls for a "new type of great power relations," which suggested a path toward narrowing the gap with the United States without indicating what China would do to enable this or endorse it through national identity.

National identity intensified. As Premier Wen Jiabao struggled to refocus on China as a problem-ridden country in need of political reform and even attuned to universal values, Political Standing Committee aspirant Bo Xilai and supporters after his downfall made "sing red, strike black," a slogan for reviving Maoist songs and identity themes and going against "criminal" elements with campaign methods, paying no heed to legal niceties. In the divisive run-up to the Eighteenth Party Congress, social stability was prized through consolidation of the "harmonious society."[10] This facade of order came amid efforts to boost identity, especially through targeting Japan over an island dispute in the East China Sea. In the fall of 2012, the handling of territorial disputes, putting the blame on both the United States and neighbors, deepened strategic or identity distrust even more.[11] Xi Jinping further pressed identity issues, even the legacy of Mao, in his consolidation of power after becoming party leader in 2012.

THE IDEOLOGICAL DIMENSION

China downplayed ideology from the start of the Deng era without rejecting it. Proclaiming the four fundamental principles in 1979, Deng made clear that there would continue to be a place for communist ideology, however tenuously its themes might be associated with the specifics set forth by Mao or other venerated figures. In various campaigns, conservative leaders won support to draw the line on ideas seen as harmful to the ideology. In 1989, a decade of debate was ended, narrowing what was permissible to discuss. Although many assumed that pragmatism had prevailed so that ideology would gradually fade away, Jiang Zemin reasserted anti-imperialism, which had never been dropped in textbooks of the 1980s, and Hu Jintao's leadership saw a broader ideological amalgam gaining momentum. Xi Jinping introduced the "China Dream," upping the intensity of the identity narrative. Compared with the emphasis on ideology in Russia, there was more continuity and a more vigorous revival in China.

The ideological mix in China resembles that in Russia, but it has deeper roots. Whereas Russia had cobbled together statism on the ashes of socialism, China has kept alive the traditional theme. Although Russia has revived anti-hegemonism after a short interlude, China has intensified charges that this is the essence of Western or US dealings with the world from time immemorial. Sinocentrism also trumps the reemergence of Russocentrism. After all, it is not attenuated by a Eurocentric view and did not experience the ambiguity of Soviet-versus-Russian identity claims. Neither state has an unfettered path to bringing ideology back to center stage, but both see serious challenges to their national identities that lead them to try harder. China's leadership was emboldened after the world financial crisis to refocus on socialism's superiority to capitalism as it demoted multilateralism while pursuing Sinocentrism.

In the mid-1990s, China's leaders warned of an imbalance between economic identity and ideological apathy, which was allowing Western culture to spread. To strengthen the building of a "socialist spiritual civilization," they incorporated some Confucian norms, strengthened propaganda institutions, and redoubled education about patriotism, collectivism, and socialism.[12] With this, ideology was reviving.

Chinese authors charge that the United States is ideologically driven, seeing the collapse of the Soviet Union as the "victory of US values" and driven ever since to extend its Cold War containment of communist expansion to both the containment of China and the prevention of East Asian integration.[13] This narrative assumes a Cold War–style conflict, intensifying under Obama, between China and the United States due to ideology, in which Russia and North Korea have remained targets since the 1990s.[14]

Anne-Marie Brady refers to the officially sanctioned, Confucianized national identity in China and links it to Sinicizing Marxism. She notes the "Chinese studies fever" of the 1990s, suggests that the Chinese Communist Party was turning into the "Chinese Confucian Party," and emphasizes the goal of combining socialist and Confucian ideas in a way that stimulates popular interest.[15] Tensions persist over the threat to party control from endorsing Confucianism unambiguously, but it now has a place in ideology.

Confucianism and traditional communism both represent rule by ideology. Although Deng Xiaoping was noted for eschewing this in favor of pragmatism, there was a duality to his approach that many observers ignored, as they fixated on his economic reform thinking and open door to foreign exchanges without paying much attention to his political thought and stage theory, treating the preliminary stage of socialism as temporary. By the end of the 1990s, some saw "re-ideologization" as under way.[16] This became more pronounced, especially with the intensification of national identity starting in 2008.

Much of the discussion about socialism revolved around interpretations of why the Soviet Union collapsed. Whereas many minimized the impact of the crux of Marxist-Leninist ideology and even of Stalinism, a few assailed the Stalin model as not only standing in the way of economic reform but also preventing any spirit of political reform. This means concluding that the reason Khrushchev's reforms failed was not because they criticized Stalin's cult of personality, or that Yeltsin's reforms did not fail because of shock therapy, denying that both leaders were led astray by accepting Western models. Yet this minority view mattered little in ideology.[17] It was not in favor, losing ground in a charged atmosphere after the Beijing Olympics.

In June 2012, Xi Jinping, expected in a matter of months to take the top post in the leadership, called for giving the Communist Party a larger role in universities and doing more to "guide faculties and students to grasp the Marxist worldview and methodology and build up confidence for socialism with Chinese characteristics."[18] This represented an upgrading of the role of ideology for the best-educated citizens. The period when ideology was deemphasized has past. This resembles the switch in the Brezhnev era to reemphasizing ideology after it had been waning, also stressing anti-imperialism as one core of ideological thought, while striving, albeit in a rather more limited way in China, to reassert the contemporary relevance of socialism.

China's ideological amalgam is unstable. Socialism takes precedence, as some in the leadership seek to revive more of its old ideals while resenting Confucianism. Even recent hostility to Westernization is not sufficient for some who would dwell on this with renewed intensity. The hollowness of identity claims is leading officials to press for an intensification of propaganda, even if there are others who would prefer a cautious rhetoric capable of reducing cynicism and stimulating more belief in values. The Soviet Union lost the battle with cynicism under Brezhnev, and China may indeed lose it eventually, but in the 2010s it is striving to prevent that outcome. To China's advantage is the determination of its leaders to pursue economic reforms with pragmatism in the forefront, as seen at the Third Plenum of the Eighteenth Party Congress in November 2013.

THE TEMPORAL DIMENSION

Zheng Wang argues that the most important factor in overcoming the decline in ideological identity and the spiritual crisis of the 1980s was historical consciousness, which had long been central to China's identity and resurgent in the "patriotic education movement." By channeling memories to the "century of humiliation" and concentrating on novel ways of "upbringing," including demonstration bases and entertainment as well as an intense use of the educational system, starting in 1994 China embarked on a long-term, sophisticated propaganda exercise centered not on tired ideological quotations but on boosting self-esteem linked to national cohesion. Instead of people directing their frustrations toward the Communist Party, they targeted, to a startling extent, those charged with victimizing China. In contrast to Mao, who had suppressed the national humiliation narrative, leaders forgot class divisions in order to stir people, at last, to wipe clean the slate of national humiliation. This focus on the temporal dimension aimed primarily at legitimizing the party reverberated in horizontal identity, notably toward Japan.[19] Wang concludes that not only is historical memory the key element in Chinese national identity, aimed not at the realization of communism but at the great rejuvenation of the Chinese nation, but also that people need to be liberated from official statements in order to realize mass mobilization on the basis of traumatic myths in a master historical narrative.[20]

History is at the essence of Confucianism and communism, presenting a clear chronology of success and failure equated with good and evil. If the narrative in the Mao era contrasted the communist movement and rule with the evil of class rule in imperial times and under capitalism, later there was confusion after an abrupt shift regarding the role of class struggle. The topic of Soviet revisionism left a residue of doubt, talk of joint Soviet and US responsibility for the Cold War muddied the narrative, and a lack of clarity about where China was heading by borrowing heavily from the most advanced capitalist countries added to the uncertainty. The picture changed by 2010 to differentiate the harmony of Chinese civilization from the warmongering of Western civilization, and the relative innocence of the Soviet Union, North Korea, and other socialist countries during the Cold War from obsessive anticommunism in the United States. The temporal dimension figured in widening the identity gap with the West and its allies with regard to successive periods, ranging from early history to the post–Cold War era.

Premodern history has been turned on its head by eliminating the theme of class struggle and fixating on unification, harmonious society, harmonious world, and state cohesion. Great pride is taken in the very history that under Mao incited harsh criticism for standing in the way of peasant rebellions that bring progress. A model compared with the rest of the world, imperial China serves as proof for what China is now accomplishing: satisfying the interests of China's ethnic minorities, demonstrating to other countries that Chinese power does not bring hegemony or instability, and proving that Chinese civilization is fundamentally different from Western civilization with positive consequences for the social order. Although for roughly a century, China lost some of the strengths of this legacy through its semicolonial position, it recovered the legacy in stages after 1949, suggesting continuity where the communists had previously found discontinuity. Yet discourse on the century of humiliation still retains much of the tone of the Maoist era. Victimization by the Western powers and Japan helps to drive home the contrast between their traditions and China's legacy.

With class struggle denied, the primary criterion for evaluating the period up through 1949 is resistance to imperialism. This has led to some adjustment in evaluations of the Chinese Nationalists, who fought the Japanese, albeit not with the same devotion as the Chinese communists. The identity objective is to focus on commonalities of Chinese on the mainland and in Taiwan, making the case for reunification. To show that Chiang Kai-shek supported an independent and united China serves this goal.

To repudiate Mao, no matter how heinous his crimes, would vitiate identity claims for Chinese communism. It is hard to imagine that the Communist Party would maintain its hold on power. Parallel to the Brezhnev manner of handling Stalin's legacy, the approach chosen was to acknowledge some mistakes but to conceal their scope at the same time as the period from the time of the Revolution to the present elicits heavy praise in a selectively censored narrative. Avoiding the ups and downs of the Soviet treatment of Stalin over several decades, China had realized consistency, and today's Mao nostalgia capitalizes on past silence about Mao's extremism and makes possible top-down campaigns on his behalf even amid uncertainty, as during the Brezhnev era, about which way the historical winds will next blow. Despite this shadow, the leadership has plunged ahead with an assertive identity narrative in which the periods of the 1920s–40s and the 1950s–70s have an indispensable supporting role.

Although, in the 1970s and 1980s, China accepted some overlap with the United States on the horizontal dimension, the gap on the temporal dimension narrowed less. It proved impossible to discuss the Korean War, which was the province of the People's Liberation Army, and barely possible to assess matters critical to the Communist Party's history, but imperialism was still a staple. During the 1990s and 2000s, the gap widened. In October 2010, when Xi Jinping repeated long-prevalent Chinese myths about the Korean War—for instance, that the war was caused by South Korea, and that the United States had used weapons of mass destruction—hopes were dashed that, with time, history would become less sensitive. On the contrary, in explaining identity gaps with other countries, including both South Korea and Japan, attention has shifted to the roots of these differences that can be traced to their early history. These sources, cited in the second book of this series, consider that they exert a decisive impact on the contemporary conduct of nations, a kind of civilizational determinism.

As with Russia, China's current identity widening toward the United States leads to a more negative view of the United States during the Cold War than was prevalent under Gorbachev and Deng. Doubts about two lost decades starting in the late 1950s and the balanced critique of the two superpowers have been replaced by overall praise for building socialism in China and one-sided disapproval of US policies during this period.

China is not as negative about its leadership in the transition of the 1980s and 1990s as Russia is about Gorbachev and Yeltsin. Indeed, in the entire history of socialism, no leaders are subject to as much scorn as Gorbachev, in Russia or China. His grievous mistake was to undermine vertical national identity, which for the Chinese is tied to the legitimacy of Communist Party rule. As the de-Stalinization speech of 1956 had this impact on China as well as the Soviet Union, so too did the

1986 arrival of glasnost. China's notion of reform socialism was in sharp contrast to these chinks in the identity armor. It anticipated a lengthy process of catching up, protecting national identity from the vulnerabilities created in the interim. The shock from Soviet foreign policy, ideological deviations, and even collapse after the Communist Party lost its hold on power led China's leaders to stay the course on an extended transition, in which identity had to be carefully protected.

In opposing the Soviet Union, then keeping a distance from the West, and later asserting global leadership, China categorized itself as a developing country. This proved convenient in making the argument that China trails so far behind that any talk of a China threat is far-fetched. It was concentrating on narrowing a vast distance and addressing a paralyzing array of problems, suggesting a long time frame ahead. Yet this frame kept shortening and often seemed to be merely an argument being used by reformers to deflect the rising clamor of those making the identity arguments for action, delaying their new temporal identity.

Communist thought is steeped in stages, conditioning policies in accord with the forces of production and other factors indicative of the current stage. A breakthrough in the 1980s was China's decision that it was only at the initial stage of socialism. No less important was the calculus of how far back China remained, requiring cooperative ties to the United States and others. Rather than the lexicon of socialist stages, premised on the changing balance of social classes, a version of modernization theory, coupled with data ranking states by comprehensive national power, was used to guide leaders on how long China should bide its time and be relatively passive. In the mid-1980s, a half century was the estimate. In the mid-1990s, as China's economy was booming, one heard estimates of a quarter century. As the 2000s progressed, confidence mounted; calls for patience were shortened to a decade or so. By the end of the decade, the debate was intensifying over whether the time was fast approaching. At stake was the issue of whether both to challenge the world order centered on the West and to press forward with designs for a new regional order.

Whereas Russia starting in 1992 recognized a new era, China was more hesitant. In 2010, it was intent on erasing the memory of the events of 1989–91 with a new periodization, in which the Cold War or something close to it persisted through the United States' unilateralism and anticommunist mentality until China's rise and that of other powers resulted in a balanced world order. Anticipation of a new type of international community laced Chinese writings, and it was echoed in Russia as Putin rekindled identity rhetoric, downplaying earlier views of how the events of 1989–91 had changed the world.

THE SECTORAL DIMENSION

China's economic identity suffered a severe blow with the abrupt about-face of 1978. Its political identity reeled under the weight of uncertainty about the post-Mao direction China would take. Even its cultural identity suffered, given the dead end of the Cultural Revolution. Similar to Japan's vacuum after 1945 and Russia's after the collapse of the Soviet Union, China faced an uphill fight to restore a sense of its cultural superiority. As in the other two cases, culture was the key to rebuilding pride. It took more than a decade for cultural identity to recover a high plateau, soon accompanied by a spurt in economic national identity, rooted not only in repetitive high growth rates but also in China's claims, after joining the World Trade Organization, to have mastered the art of economic globalization in a new era of integration of the world economy, as political identity also was climbing to fresh heights. By 2010, all of sectoral identity was ascendant.

As economic national identity intensified in China, it pulled along cultural and political identity—the entire sectoral dimension. Similar to two decades earlier in Japan, the Chinese were amenable to claims that an "economic miracle" also means cultural and political superiority. Recognition of China's success came as early as 1993. Competing economies were dismissed as inferior, one after the other—Russia, then Japan and South Korea, and finally the United States. The case against the West greatly strengthened in 2008 through the differential impact of the global financial crisis, and in 2012 by the euro crisis and the dysfunctional economic role of the US Congress.

China's failure in the nineteenth century is attributed to cultural narrowness that failed to refocus on the competition for comprehensive national power, based on modernization and economic openness. Yet the danger of being too closed is not seen as a reason to succumb to the danger of becoming too dependent. Culture must avoid both extremes. Globalization is welcome in certain economic respects, but it is anathema as a geopolitical or cultural goal. Juggling these two conflicting notions of international relations means greater economic integration to make other countries more dependent on China than it is on them, and greater self-reliance to make it easy for China to assert itself without fear of public resistance, military opposition, and economic and energy sanctions. The identity narrative serves these dual objectives.

Chinese leaders were obsessed with culture in attacks on Khrushchev's shift to humanism and later warnings against humanism linked to spiritual pollution through the 1980s. In early 1992, the same conclusion was drawn about the collapse of the Soviet Union and the defeat of socialism abroad.[21] Although this linkage of Gorbachev to his reform predecessor for causing a "crisis of culture" and succumbing to "complete Westernization" was put on hold, it showed the dominant strain in identity rhetoric and was a harbinger of the narrative that took center stage by the end of the 2000s.

Advocates of universal values face an uphill battle reconstructing identity. Even when backers of the traditional communist national identity lost ground in the 1980s, they had many ways to shape identity formation. As economic reformers battled orthodox thinking, the outcome seemed favorable to them and their valued technocratic expertise, but space opened too for those who framed identity to keep their ideas in check. Starting in 1992, China claimed that as much as it encouraged market forces, it would remain a hybrid "socialist market economy." The state's role and the role of state-owned enterprises would differ significantly from what existed in capitalist countries. With the 2008–9 global financial crisis, assertions of difference acquired a more assertive tone. Growing confidence in the continuation of China's "economic miracle" turned a defensive claim into an arrogant identity gap, despite some warnings that the model of growth could not be sustained without reforms, attenuating claims of superiority through state guidance.

Whereas China's leaders feared economic vulnerability, as seen in the failure of the Soviet Union, and military vulnerability, brought home by the Persian Gulf War, their most persistent worry has been cultural vulnerability, which is regarded as the primary cause for the failure of communism in the Soviet Union. In response, they go on the defensive by warning against the cultural threat from the West while striving through censorship and manipulation of the Internet to limit discussion of sensitive themes. Also, Chinese leaders take the offensive through a full-fledged effort to boost *minzu yishi* (national consciousness) and a sense of cultural sovereignty. In contrast to the crude reliance on ideology under Mao, political identity is reinforced by *wenhua yishi* (cultural consciousness), interpreted to center on the state and the party, not to rest in some embodiment of the public capable of gaining a separate identity.

Cultural identity is a threat to socialist identity. To make the link inseparable, Chinese sources refrain from using *wenhua rentong* (cultural identity) as a label, insisting on *guojia rentong* (state identity), and then referring to socialism as essential to the state and its major functions. They have hesitated to repeat the sort of excessive claims for socialism that were heard in the Mao era or even in the Soviet Union, refining political education with an emphasis on the Communist Party's role in economic development and political stability. Yet avoiding the old slogans does not prevent rigidity alien to the preferences of today. Entertainment diverts attention from national identity goals, and the fall 2011 crackdown on television entertainment revealed the real priority.

Promoting "socialist culture" serves multiple purposes. It puts socialism back in the forefront, as if it is the essence of culture rather than Confucianism. Moreover, it opposes universal values, replacing the dichotomy with capitalism with a contrast with Western culture. Attacks on "recolonization" through an imposing of Western culture raise charges of looking down on the Chinese nation, confusing Communist Party policies on human rights with the essence of Chinese civilization. Charges that the West had used culture to cause the collapse of the Soviet Union (including Communist Party rule) are taken as warnings that similar plots are being prepared against China. The principal battleground is culture based on a simple dichotomy: either complete Westernization or a defense of Chinese civilization by the Communist Party.

Similar to the Brezhnev era, Chinese leaders appeal for cultural superiority mixed with ideological correctness, producing a sterile outpouring of empty rhetoric filled with platitudes. The more confident China grows in its hard power, including its economic leverage, the more counterproductive is its advocacy of soft power. Culture is seen as the key to national cohesion and comprehensive national power competitiveness; however, because culture is considered to be lagging behind economic development, culture is understood to need to make a greater effort to shape people's thinking. The old staple of serving society is trotted out, along with repeated linkages between socialism and culture. In contrast to the retreat from exporting Chinese socialism in previous decades, talk has resumed of turning it into global leading thought (*quanqiu zhidao sixiang*). As in the case of the Brezhnev era, the more doubtful the reform process, the greater the claims for scientific development (*kexue fazhan*)—as if that slogan could mask a loss of reform momentum, at least under Hu Jintao, before the reform process resumed under Xi Jinping. The sorts of slogans and platitudes typical of Soviet and Chinese communist history insistently repeat the idea that socialism satisfies the people's cultural quest. Instead of moving away from socialism as the crux of national identity, socialism is being reframed in cultural terms. Communist Party discourse allows no room for Confucianism to be mentioned, but the term "culture" alludes to it.

In the pervasive Chinese literature that directly or indirectly draws lessons from the failure of the Soviet Union, one unquestioned conclusion is that Soviet leaders mishandled national identity. This applies particularly to the combination of state and ethnic national identity, that is, the nationality question. The handling of ethnic minorities—a critical part of what I am calling the vertical dimension—is viewed as prone to arousing confusion that leaves national identity in shambles. Chinese leaders are insistent on addressing both ends of the relationship, suppressing any sense of minorities as an entity entitled to a national identity while orchestrating a comprehensive state identity that is intended to fill the space that ethnic identities normally occupy. Both China and Russia glorify the country as a whole, downplaying ethnic diversity as a basis of identity. This means combining the communist and precommunist periods into one tradition, opposed to both the West and the autonomy of the minority ethnic nationalities within today's national borders. History mixes with literature and philosophy into a clear narrative of the nation (*guoxue*) that culminates in contemporary cultural identity.[22]

China is going to extraordinary lengths to establish an intense and effective cultural identity, reforming its cultural system to uphold the grip of the Communist Party and strengthen cultural security.[23] For a quarter century, China's national identity was colored by claims that it was preoccupied with peace and development due to the overwhelming challenges of sustaining economic growth and social stability. Given these priorities, it had embraced globalization, cooperation with the great powers, good-neighborly relations, and even the image of a status quo power. Even when its comprehensive national power rose precipitously, the facade of this benign national identity allayed concerns. The principal spokespersons for these reassuring images were respected scholars attuned to popular social science theories in the West, who could couch China's image as a source of stability in the most favorable light. It was possible to highlight shared national interests and, with some credibility, to suggest that the United States' hesitation to accept China's rise was a primary source of distrust. Yet the reasoning of these international figures and reassurances from the Foreign Ministry were repeatedly contradicted by a large number of Chinese sources, while slogans about cooperation were subject to contradictory interpretations. The cultural push in 2012–13 was proof that insistence on a divided world trumps earlier themes.

Chinese sources depict a struggle between Western and Asian culture. This is a major component in imperialism and hegemonism, alongside the loss of territorial sovereignty. It is a state of mind, demeaning Asian nations (*Yazhou minzu*) as inferior. Only by recovering pride in the superiority of their own cultures will they cast off the impact of humiliation. Implicit in this outlook are views of the West as relatively homogeneous and of Asia as sharing both past and future traditions, which are simplistically equated with Chinese civilization. A shared civilizational identity is deemed to be within reach, starting with the state as the unit (*guojiazhuyi*) and focused on the rejection of Western cultural claims. To make this case, tensions between the Manchus and Han Chinese in the Qing era are minimized, the cultures of ethnic minorities are treated as exotic rather than as salient for national identity, and the dichotomy of East/West proves convenient. As the focus on China's identity has come to the forefront, leaders have pressed harder to remove ideas that are suggestive of shared values with the West. Suggestions that socialism will converge with capitalism were removed in 1987. Modernization theory and its language denoting convergence were decisively rejected in 1989. More recently, global governance has been excised from discussions. Theories in areas as diverse as culture, history, and international relations have all been cleansed in this fashion on behalf of identity.

THE VERTICAL DIMENSION

Refusal to criticize Mao severely and insistence on censorship to limit further criticism were not merely an effort to maintain stability. They proved to be a holding operation before a more positive assessment of Mao could be pushed. Rejection of Western theories that suggested convergence ahead was not just a way to constrain thinking detrimental to regime legitimacy. It laid a foundation, as in the case of modernization theory, for assertive Chinese theorizing that made the case for Chinese superiority. Cultural distinctiveness became an obsession, convenient both for rationalizing the Communist Party's authoritarianism and for reconstructing China's identity.

Globalization is divided in Chinese thinking. At least since 1992, economics and geopolitics have been treated as separate, and culture has been increasingly joining geopolitics as problematic. As was noted in one report, "If economic globalization has brought more opportunities than challenges, then cultural globalization has brought more challenges than opportunities." Interpreting this statement, Peter Mattis observes that after the fall of the Soviet Union, China saw itself as the target of the West, which redirected its cultural propaganda in order to undermine its party-state nexus.[24] Thus, a focus on strengthening cultural autonomy versus Western values is needed.

The process of privatization overshadows the responsibility system in agriculture and the direct establishment of foreign firms across China as the key to understanding changes in the state's role in the economy. It combines insider, management collusion with the local or central government to seize ownership, tight Communist Party control over personnel decisions rooted in the old *nomenklatura* system, and renewed favoritism for both state-owned enterprises and firms closely linked to political authority—with much of the wealth flowing into the coffers of the party elite. This has helped to reassert state-centered economic identity, not civil society identity.

Chinese thinkers portrayed Westernization as synonymous with cultural imperialism, linking it to splittism, disunity in China, and even regime change. In contrast, starting in 2008 the field of Chinese national studies (*guoxue*) galvanized around the theory of a distinctive and superior Chinese culture (*Zhongguo wenhua teshulun*). Ignoring the distinction between the Han and non-Han ethnic groups, it celebrated the single Chinese nation (*Zhonghua minzu*). Gala events, such as the Beijing Olympics and the Shanghai Exposition, were occasions for glorification, invoking the national spirit (*minzu jingshen*). Comparative analysis threatened efforts to heighten pride. It was stifled in 1987, when the dangers of comparative socialism became clear. By 2010, simplistic dichotomies were preferred, in what masqueraded as the study of comparative civilizations. After all, what was at stake was cultural security (*wenhua anquanlun*), a growing concern in the 2010s.

At the Sixth Plenary Session of the Seventeenth Party Congress in October 2011, the focus was reform of the cultural system. Already a theme at the Sixteenth Party Congress in 2002 and prioritized again at the Seventeenth Party Congress in 2007, the goal of fostering a strong sense of self-respect and building a cultural strong power was linked to alarm that socialist core values are endangered by three forces: the worship of money, a loss of normal morality, and the individual values that lie at the core of Western democracy. If Bo Xilai took this perspective as a green light for reviving Mao Zedong thought, others directed their attack against the United States, not hesitating to also belabor Japan's cultural evils.[25]

The vitriolic tone of Chinese publications in 2012 contrasted China's natural "top-down" approach to the "bottom-up" designs of the West, which are considered to be an alien model of liberal democracy. Recalling the nefarious targets during the Cultural Revolution, Chinese netizens labeled the five evil forces—rights' lawyers, underground religion, dissidents, Internet heroes, and disadvantaged social groups—as listed in *People's Daily*, as the "five black categories," recalling Mao's campaigns. Introducing the idea of "military cultural security" (*junshi wenhua anquan*), sources in July 2012 raised the stakes further.[26] In June of that year, *People's Daily* had accentuated the salience of culture as a "guide for thinking," a "conceptual pilot," and the "lifeblood of the nation." Referring to "*minzu*" (the nation), this approach brought identity even more to the fore. Apart from new attention given to civil-military relations as the prominence of the People's Liberation Army kept growing, this followed warnings that the danger of cultural infiltration was now a kind of "war."

China's *guanxi* relations are indicative of a network society with few binding solidarities. Investing in close ties with immediate kin and instrumental friends, the typical Chinese has little basis for collective identities at the intermediate level. With a priority on treating high-status people with appropriate "face," networks separate from authority are suspect. Although grievances are numerous and give rise to feelings of commonality in facing local authorities, leaders are intent through control over information and organization on blocking coalescing identities. This inhibits a "single solitary community," reshaping the vertical dimension.[27]

One of the preoccupations of the effort to construct a specific national identity is the issue of ethnic nationalism. Devoting great attention to this issue, writers claim to have found answers for this problem, which contributed to the unraveling of the Soviet Union. I do not dwell on their views because they can be summarized rather briefly as a matter of strengthening state identity as a shared worldview. Given the focus here on state identity, it suffices to refer to manipulating ethnic identities within the Chinese state. Sinocentrism begins inside China's boundaries with the way the Tibetans and the Muslim minorities are treated, along with the tight restrictions on the Mongolians of Inner Mongolia, the Korean minority in Jilin Province, and other ethnic groups. The Dalai Lama most clearly symbolizes the narrow tolerance of both cultural and political autonomy. Because they are fearful of political unrest, the Chinese focus on the cultural roots of social control, pointing to the collapse of the Soviet Union for what could go wrong. The vertical and horizontal dimensions are linked by the external threat to stirring up ethnic identities.

THE HORIZONTAL DIMENSION

In 2010, China's national identity intensified as a result of popular and elite perceptions that the power gap with the United States had closed. Yet this intensification's main elements were the top-down rhetoric that inflamed the public and the bullying tone of officials belittling other nations, along with mounting pressures on moderates from the leadership and the public to silence their voices. At a time of intense jockeying for positions in the leadership to emerge in 2012, any indication of weakness could be used against one's faction. In 2011, a backlash against the impact of assertive policies led to a revival of debate on whether China should keep a low profile, downplaying any shift in its strategy and its national identity, but this was more about fine-tuning the timing of expressing and acting on national identity concerns than about their contents. The emotions of 2010 were rekindled in 2012, especially in criticisms of Japan. They were repackaged under Xi Jinping in 2013, with more subtlety toward the United States, ASEAN, and South Korea but no major shift.

The Chinese tempered their national identity claims with cautionary comments about relative national power. In the early 1990s, strident opposition to the United States' new world order was toned down as

Deng prioritized cooperation and China built its economy and power. In 2003, calculations were made that China could not stop cooperating with the United States and had to remain quiet in the face of the US war in Iraq and other intensifying hegemonic ambitions. One important internal source acknowledged that restraint was hard on China but found hope in the first major change in great power relations since the Cold War, opening the door to greater resistance to US hegemonism.[28] Hu Jintao had to keep US ties stable, but by stressing great power relations with Russia, good-neighborly relations, and regionalism, he could begin to seize the opportunity. Talk of China's "peaceful development" and soft power spread in this opportunistic environment. The image was of a national identity kept under wraps.

In the aftermath of the collapse of the Soviet Union, the Chinese observed that the world, and especially the United Nations, would not support the United States' ambitions to extend its hegemony, forging a "new world order." Appealing to the notion of the international community in which Japan, Germany, and other states would desert the United States as their perceptions of a Soviet threat subsided, many authors insisted on the limits of US unilateralism under Bill Clinton. This association with world opposition to the United States gained a new lease on life with George W. Bush's neoconservatism, but it had faded by 2008.

The concept of "harmonious world" is the embryo of a China-centered order, which breaks from Deng's legacy of lying low. William Callahan traces the transition to 2005, when a more assertive international posture was seen. Celebrations presenting China to the world and refocusing public opinion in 2008 and 2010 saw an internationalization of Chinese norms, linking premodern ideals to global transformation not dominated by the West. Callahan describes this change as the "romanticization of a particular national culture into 'universally desirable values.'"[29] This was clearly occurring in the period 2010–13. In 2008, many Chinese wrote proudly of their state's role in the Six-Party Talks as proof of a new approach to international relations in pursuit of a "harmonious Asia" and a "harmonious world." This activity, which was based on China's culture and confidence as well as its rising power, was supposedly proof of its fitting into the existing international order in support of common interests.[30] It was also a means to build mutual trust with the United States as part of the objective of energetically developing relations with the developed states and deepening good-neighborly relations with nearby states. However, if the stress on cooperation over North Korea was at its peak in 2008, the situation abruptly changed to China's losing the trust of other states on this issue and then being seen as abetting behavior that destabilized the region, casting a shadow on its "harmonious" claims. The shift signaled revised thinking in support of Sinocentrism, twisting the meaning of "harmony" in line with China's past.

Numerous authors seemed to be under the illusion that China could readily convert its rising economic power into soft power, leading steadily to its acceptance as the region's political leader, especially in Southeast Asia. This was a faulty reading of what is needed for soft power and how trust is built between states. The fallout from arrogance about one's economic power is in fact harmful to soft power, as China discovered in 2010. Rather than admit the setback, blame was placed above all on the United States, but also on neighboring states falling under the sway of the West.

The case for Sinocentrism was trumpeted starting in 2009. If the Asia-Pacific region will lead international relations in this century and East Asia is its nucleus, and China is at the center of East Asia and the force pulling it forward, then it follows that China is the emerging world geopolitical center. Yet the West, steeped in Christian ideas about an insurmountable divide between good and evil, will not accept the Chinese tradition of cultural coexistence and fusion.[31] Although China stands for a harmonious world, the West perceives a threat. This leads to a clash, which is not caused by China's own actions. It follows that China must reject being incorporated into the existing world system, which locks in the unfair gains and Western values from the age of imperialism and would oblige China to abandon its values and political system.[32]

The Tianxia system is the key to China's ideal world order. It may be depicted as an attempt to revive a distinct regional order, but it was historically premised on the notion that there is one all-inclusive order, albeit with more stringent demands on populations the closer one is to the center of this order. This concept puts primary stress on harmony and order, not freedom. Nation-states under the impact of Western principles that highlight competitiveness gave rise to imperialism. The revival of Tianxia in a modern veneer suggests a postimperialist environment in which civilizational ideals are largely shared and reduce the role of coercion and exploitation in guaranteeing order. This could easily lend itself to a league of autocracies hierarchically grouped under coercively shaped "harmonious societies" following China's principles.[33]

Chinese identity is rooted in deep-seated distrust of the United States, which is increasing not because of growing vulnerability but due to new empowerment as China's power expands and that of the United States is seen as declining.[34] Already in the early 1990s, Chinese sources had anticipated a new world order opposed to Western values, ideology, and hegemonism. China championed sovereignty as the first line of defense. Distrust grew as Chinese leaders increased their aspirations, making issues previously seen as amenable to cooperation without serious national identity consequences tests of irreconcilable identities. Although a rising power may change its thinking as expectations grow, a separate factor is the Communist Party's quest for legitimation, assuming a zero-sum situation and pretending that it is the United States, still under the sway of anticommunism, that cannot tolerate China's rise.

THE INTENSITY DIMENSION

The Chinese are specific about the importance of raising national identity (*tisheng guojia rentong*), treating it as having historical importance and being the nucleus of nation building. Until 1911, China was a dynastic state in which dynastic identity superseded national identity, but this gradually changed until Japanese imperialism provoked an upsurge in modern identity fusion focused on the state. Claiming that national identity gained a huge boost from the liberation movement led by the Chinese Communist Party, which established a sovereign people's democracy, various authors argue that a fusion of *minzu* (ethnic nationalist) and *guomin* (state nationalist) identities was the critical turning point starting in 1949, with tremendous importance given to the Chinese people's consciousness of identity and their political culture. Yet they add that the task ahead remains formidable. One problem is the multiple identities of nationalities, although the dynastic unifications of the past had overcome many local identities and made possible economic and cultural fusion resulting in a single *Zhonghua minzu* (Chinese nation). Warning that a weak national identity could lead to ethnic separatism, unstable borders, and foreign threats to security, many argue that forging a single, strong identity is essential.[35]

China's leaders adopted a bifurcated approach toward horizontal identity, by arguing that relations with other great powers were cooperative and by strengthening and reinvigorating charges against the United States and its allies that they were plotting to subvert China's identity. Reform-oriented writers tried to turn attention away from "bourgeois peaceful evolution" to other causes for the Soviet downfall, with implications for China to become more equal, open, and democratic. They flailed against censorship bent on turning the Soviet downfall to the advantage of China's leadership, but the anti-Gorbachev obsession in the leadership never faded. Revitalizing ideology focused on themes with an ambiguous meaning, such as "socialist harmonious society." David Shambaugh is correct to argue that there was a considerable effort to find reform meaning in slogans, as China was building its soft power and capitalizing on public pride over its remarkable economic growth and stability, but the most creative ideas for adaptation were actually cries in the wilderness, struggling against great odds.[36]

China's national identity for a quarter century was colored by claims that it was preoccupied with peace and development, owing to the overwhelming challenges of sustaining economic growth and social stability. Given these priorities, many said that it had embraced globalization, prioritized cooperation with the great powers as well as good-neighborly relations, and even welcomed the image of a status quo power. Even as its comprehensive national power rose precipitously, the facade of this benign national identity allayed concerns. Principal spokespersons for these reassuring images included respected scholars attuned to popular social science theories in the West, who could couch China's image as a source of stability in the most favorable light. It was possible to highlight shared national interests and, with some credibility, to suggest that the United States' hesitation to accept China's rise was a primary source of distrust. Yet many Chinese sources repeatedly contradicted the reasoning of these visible figures and the reassurances of the Foreign Ministry, while the content of many publications contradicted the slogans about cooperation. This discrepancy has faded appreciably in recent years as disclaimers about China's real intentions have been greatly overshadowed by its assertiveness in having its voice heard. This intensification of identity occurred during the 2008 Beijing Olympics, in 2009–10 as caution was further set aside, and even more under Xi Jinping's strong direction in 2012–13.

CONCLUSION

The Chinese reconcile the contradiction between the realities that their history is glorious and that only the revolution led by Mao saved China from a dire fate. The explanation is that China, battered by imperialism, could not rise up without the communists taking power. Both the kind of capitalism that had begun before 1949 and any shift to capitalism today would leave China dependent and weak without a national identity to defend itself. Without the vertical identity sustained by communist rule, horizontal identity would be devoid of pride. Thus, anti-Western views permeate ideology (anti-imperialism), the temporal dimension (China's past humiliations and current attempts to prevent future humiliation), the sectoral dimension (Chinese civilization is at stake), the vertical dimension (only communist rule under an authoritarian state impedes interference destructive of China's national identity), and the horizontal dimension (narrow cooperation may still go forward, but a United States–led international community is posing a grievous threat).

In 2009–10, the Chinese were presenting a new approach to regionalism and the wider world. One presumption was that it would not be similar to the Western approaches of the past. Another was that it would confirm China as the nucleus of the East Asian circle. A third starting point was that this approach would go beyond economic integration to signify the rise of Eastern civilization and, consistent with the notion of harmony, would accept cultural differences without trying to eradicate or to reform them.[37] With culture in the forefront, the tone in Chinese sources changed appreciably. In the *Washington Post* in January 2010, John Pomfret reported on "a new triumphalist attitude from Beijing that is worrying governments and analysts across the globe. . . . China observers have noticed a tough tone emanating from its government, its representatives and influential analysts from its state-funded think tanks." Pomfret found evidence of this in the views of Europe, the United States, and India, suggesting policy consequences before the 2010 conflicts.[38] This proved correct when aggressive actions soon followed.

On October 18, 2011, at the Sixth Plenary Session of the Seventeenth Communist Party Central Committee, Hu Jintao issued a statement on strengthening socialist culture, arguing that without cultural security there is no national security.[39] Insisting that confrontational forces are on the rise in the international arena, Hu drew a zero-sum picture in which Westernization is equated with separatism and is based on long-term penetration in the cultural sphere. This puts a premium on the struggle over ideology and culture under party leadership. Strengthening socialist culture with Chinese characteristics (*Zhongguo tese shehuizhuyi wenhua*) is a theme that appeared often in Hu's exhortations. Assuming that the world faces a great turning point, he viewed the function of culture as increasingly critical in international competition over comprehensive national power. Arguing that enemies are plotting to penetrate China through the sphere of thought culture, Hu prioritized consciousness, making the case for national identity intensification and the widening of key identity gaps.

Xi Jinping took office in late 2012, trumpeting the great revival of the Chinese nation, a theme known as the "China Dream." Although his words hinted at a new vision, they actually serve as a more forthright acknowledgment of the Sinocentrism at the core of Chinese identity, as more strident views were spreading. While adding the ambiguous concept of a "new type of great power relations" focused on US ties, he led in intensifying national identity rhetoric.

On June 27, 2013, Foreign Minister Wang Yi gave a speech explaining the concept of "great power diplomacy with Chinese characteristics," which had already been practiced in relations with Russia. The themes were familiar: Oppose hegemony, reject interference in the internal affairs of other countries, respect sovereignty, build a harmonious world, support developing nations, and so on. Wang also brought Xi Jinping's China Dream into foreign policy, calling for the protection of Chinese abroad. Omitting the East Asian Summit from a list of organizations to which China will pay greater attention—while including the Shanghai Cooperation Organization, the BRICS (Brazil, Russia, India, China, and South Africa), and the Asia-Pacific Economic Cooperation (APEC) forum—Wang demonstrated China's shift away from the regionalism led by ASEAN, as it drifts away from exclusive regionalism minus the United States.[40] His speech is a sign of a more "active" foreign policy, a word he often used, explaining that the international system needs reform.

On August 1, 2013, Xinhua carried an editorial warning that an upheaval in China linked to democracy and sought by the West would cause more chaos than it had in the Soviet Union in the 1990s, backed by instructions that all Web sites must prominently display the editorial. This combines the vertical dimension, which is threatened, with the horizontal dimension, which poses great danger. The discussion is framed as socialism versus capitalism, bringing the ideological dimension back to prominence.[41] And it came at about the time of Document No. 9, described in the introduction to this book as a stark, if secret, assertion of national identity on all dimensions in contrast to identities in the West. Xi Jinping's intensification of national identity was still gathering steam.

CHAPTER 5

THE COMMUNIST GREAT POWER (TRANSITION 1) NATIONAL IDENTITY SYNDROME

Traditional communism was left in tatters in the second half of the 1980s. Its favorite theme of class struggle had been relegated to the dustbin of history, and calls for economic integration into the global community and security cooperation with the United States cast doubt on the "sacred," revolutionary narrative about a world inescapably split between two blocs. Reform voices were emboldened, questioning major events in the history of communism. Yet, as analysts were looking ahead to the eclipse of communist identities in China and what became Russia after the dissolution of the Soviet Union, many assumed a prism of communism versus democratic capitalism without noticing the staying power of various dimensions of the preceding national identity. Following some uncertainty, traditional communism was superseded in both China and Russia by an identity heavily rooted in the past. I label this identity the Communist Great Power (Transition 1) National Identity Syndrome, or CGP (T1) NIS, drawing on evidence in prior chapters and, for China, in the two previous books in this series.

East Asian National Identities: Common Roots and Chinese Exceptionalism, the first book in the series, depicts the East Asian National Identity Syndrome (EANIS) as parallel developments in three nation-states, despite Chinese exceptionalism. *National Identities and Bilateral Relations: Widening Gaps in East Asia and Chinese Demonization of the United States,* the second book, analyzes national identity gaps between pairs of countries, which for the most part have not been narrowing, in spite of rapid mutual economic integration. The CGP (T1) NIS showcases both similar and different effects; similar in accounting for parallels between countries, and different in contributing to narrowing the identity gap rather than widening it, although the potential for widening remains. The two syndromes are distinctive. The EANIS is rooted in premodern Confucianism, transitional humiliation, and similar economic miracles with attendant effects. The CGP (T1) NIS is centered on more recent communism, the legacy in the ideological and the vertical dimensions of an elite steeped in communism, and sustained fear that the United States and the West threaten regime legitimacy and national identity. Parallels exist between the two communist great powers—direct continuities and powerful, shared effects from their decades spent in traditional communism. As will be seen in chapter 7, recovery from the Sino-Soviet split was made considerably easier by complementarity in the evolution of their two national identities.

The popular argument for sharp discontinuity in national identity starts with thinking that communism is a cancer on society, imposed ruthlessly by dictators on a populace that is desperate to restore a combination of its earlier national identity and elements of the universal identity that comes with freedom and integration into the world community. If the floodgates are open through market economies, Internet communications, and the end of authoritarian controls, it is assumed that the people will throw off this alien worldview. The CGP (T1) NIS makes a different argument. First, national identity is more complex and subject to greater manipulation than the dichotomous logic used to predict a sudden, drastic transformation. Second, communism can be disaggregated, opening the way for hybrid forms of identity, many of which survive even without retention of former pillars of the ideology. Third, adoption of various so-called universal elements of identity poses challenges everywhere, especially in countries furthest removed from them, as people find it hard to reconcile enduring features of their prior identity with anticipated elements of a new one. Positing this syndrome draws attention to continuities in identity.

Communism prioritizes consciousness, particularly after Lenin railed against false consciousness and established a propaganda apparatus dedicated to inculcating a shared identity that would displace nearly all other identities. Stalin and Mao refined the notion of communist or socialist identity, ruthlessly employing virtually all means possible to eradicate other identities deemed to be blocking its complete penetration. The starting point of the syndrome, then, is the sweeping campaigns over decades to replace identities of all sorts with a single, comprehensive identity focused on the party–state and its leader. This identity centers on ideology, but it is not limited to ideology and can refocus on other levers. In its first decades as a ruling worldview, communism grew ever more radical in trying to sweep away old identities to implant a new one.

Leaders who followed Stalin and Mao opted for more identity diversity. Totalitarianism was found wanting, and ideology stood in the way of essential reforms. Ties to the outside world were too limited to meet economic development needs. The Soviet Union spent three decades in limbo, more fearful of a legitimacy crisis due to identity confusion than of a lack of dynamism from identity stagnation. At least four reasons can account for this outcome. First, the degree of elite continuity from the 1950s to the 1970s favored identity stagnation. The upwardly mobile officials of the traumatic 1930s who survived the purges and World War II were well ensconced in the high rungs of the *nomenklatura*, giving rise to the gerontocracy that survived through the 1970s. Second, Soviet ideology early on shifted away from class struggle that was disruptive to stability and toward hypercentralization centering on state identity. Victory in the war and the prioritization of economic growth based on command methods favored this shift. Third, a superpower, postwar identity served to refocus many dimensions of identity rhetoric. The result was to camouflage some of the problems of transition from the Stalinist narrative. Fourth, the Soviet Union relaxed identity controls sufficiently to accommodate alternative orientations; thus, ethnic, religious, humanist, and family identities all were given limited scope. Ideology reigned supreme in national identity despite these modest adjustments that helped communism to endure.

China's identity disconnect after Mao's death lacked an environment favorable for these conditions to arise. The threat to national identity appeared to be greater for at least five reasons. First, the record of the past two decades had produced little that could be construed as success—no great patriotic war victory, stagnant industrialization, and no massive upward mobility—so failure had to be acknowledged. Second, instead of vying with the United States as a recognized superpower, China was cooperating with the state regarded as most threatening to its national identity and opening its door wide to exchanges. Third, a vacuum existed, necessitating the rapid rise of a new elite at a time when prior formulations of national identity seemed to be spiritually bankrupt and unlikely to find adherents. Fourth, Taiwan and Hong Kong provided alternative identities based on Chinese tradition, which could seem appealing in comparison with China. Fifth, with Japan and South Korea in the lead, East Asian national identities with wider appeal were poised to develop a kind of regional identity, with powerful implications for China's path.

Despite differences between China and the Soviet Union in conditions for transitioning away from traditional communist identities, the fact that their identities overlapped heavily meant that they experienced many parallels starting in the 1980s in the challenges they faced. What had long held the Soviet Union back shaped its turbulent course, while the difficulties that threatened China actually stimulated decisions that eased control over the identity transition. Comparisons of the 1980s and early 1990s show these contrasts as well as a shared syndrome.

The transformation of Chinese identity in the period 1978–85 and Soviet identity in the period 1986–89 altered thinking along all dimensions. Deng Xiaoping's four cardinal principles set limits on change, and they kept being tested from both the right and the left. When Mikhail Gorbachev introduced glasnost, however, he opened the door wide to the right and kept the left on the defensive without much chance to resist identity shifts. Given blatant lies at the root of traditional socialist identity, it was vulnerable, particularly as corrections appeared one after the other. Starting in 1980, constraining criticism of Mao was the finger in the dike that held back the deluge, while encouraging attacks against Stalin and acquiescing to more against Lenin allowed torrents of criticism to swamp public opinion. Enough information reached urban Chinese to give rise to the massive demonstrations that led to the June 4, 1989 repression; so national identity was unsettled. When leaders later reinforced a top-down identity, they could not be sure how much they had silenced the critics or convinced them. For Russian leaders, the problem by the mid-1990s was uncertainty about how lasting the public's recent transformation of worldview would be, because "old thinking" was making a strong comeback.

Assuming that a sharp break was needed with an identity that had stood firmly in the path of reform, Russian leadership for a time and foreign advisers for longer were inattentive to the power of the backlash from an identity disconnect. Chinese leaders chose a path rooted in the past, assuming correctly that economic success did not depend on the kind of national identity transformation favored by reformers and foreigners. Soviet leaders were fixated on the superpower competition and nuclear standoff, while Chinese leaders refocused on economics.

The Soviet Union and China each faced a national identity dilemma in the second half of the 1980s after the Stalinist and Maoist legacies had been exposed as way out of touch with the requirements of the times, leading to groping for a way of reconstructing identity. If some exposure had occurred earlier, censorship stymied serious debate until 1984, when Konstantin Chernenko's last-gasp crackdown on dissenting voices and China's anti-spiritual pollution campaign shut the lid on reform rhetoric. This situation changed with Hu Yaobang's 1985–86 intensification of theory reassessment, which was rekindled in the years 1987–89 with Zhao Ziyang's encouragement and allowed under the watchful eye of Deng, and the inception in 1986 of Gorbachev's glasnost, new thinking, and a general rejection of the stultifying impact of the prevailing dogma. Ideology stayed in the forefront in the two countries in this quest for change.

In 1989, China suffered a blow to reconstructing its national identity, and by 1992 Russia had sustained a crushing loss as the heir to a failed state. China's leaders succeeded quickly in strengthening the authority of the ruling elite under the Communist Party, in raising China's international standing, and in instilling pride in an "economic miracle." The experience of 1989 and other shocks through 1991 solidified support for a new strategy in forging national identity, which had taken shape in 1992. Russian leaders struggled longer. Having less to celebrate, they had greater need to find a positive message in the past, while blaming those leaders who had squandered it. There was no villain in China comparable to Gorbachev and, for many, Boris Yeltsin as well, in this process of finding a way forward. The flawed strategy that reached its peak in 1992 was gradually replaced over a decade of uncertainty prior to Putin's synthesis.

By 1978 in China and by 1985 in the Soviet Union, the reconstruction of national identity was under way. For at least a decade, each country was convulsed by debate, struggle, and a reassertion of top-down orthodoxy. China's reassertion was more definite, but there was some tentativeness due to Deng's admonition to be patient until China had much greater power. In Putin's hands, Russia's path became clearer, and by 2005 it was also growing assertive. Although Dmitry Medvedev voiced different notions of Russia's future when he served as president, Putin's return to the top post sustained the clarification of Russian national identity that he had provided in his earlier terms in power. Putin succeeded in clearing up much of the confusion about national identity during the Yeltsin era, and the synthesis he championed drew heavily on Soviet national identity, paralleling in its rejection of many currents popular in the 1980s the revival in China of the identity thrust of communism. The global financial crisis of 2008–9 turned confidence to arrogance in China. In 2012, Putin revived identity rhetoric in a more extreme version, as Xi Jinping was intensifying China's identity. The result in 2013 was an overlapping spike in identity, gathering in intensity, separating the two nations from the outside and, at least for the time being, boosting their ties.

THE IDEOLOGICAL DIMENSION

In both the Soviet Union and China, the 1980s saw the end of rigid deductions defended by definitive quotations. This fundamentalist approach, akin to religious reasoning in which faith is given preference over science, fared poorly after the personality cults of Stalin and Mao gave way to pressure to deemphasize the omniscience of the leader. Yet ideology was more than quotations from the classics and from the top leader. It rebounded in China, where censorship prevented exposés of the erroneous nature and harmful effects of the old way, and in Russia, to a lesser extent, where criticisms of Putin were becoming marginalized. A new set of truths became sacrosanct, incorporating some of the earlier "truths" in a shifting, rarely challenged, amalgam.

Ideology long trumped the social sciences, leaving trust in them in doubt. The internationalist facade starting in the 1980s hid a base distrustful of the outside world, which drew on the paranoid atmosphere inculcated by Stalin and Mao in the generation they had nurtured, reinforcing prejudices and adding a strong dose of regime propaganda to demonize the West.[1] Despite the thaw after Stalin and Mao, the older, conservative elite had the edge, as the seeds were planted for further contestation over identity. Optimism was heightened over economic growth, as the view spread that combining communism and precommunist identity reduces the need to borrow from outside. In decline, the West would be overtaken, as one's country becomes a leader in the new order. The members of a growing middle class fixated instead on their own state's serious problems and the need for more convergence. China managed this transitional period by integrating more into the global economy and encouraging market forces, but it also had more confidence that it could avoid being drawn into Western civilization and could keep core elements of communist thought as ideology was reinvigorated.

Liberals in China and Russia shared much in common. They were obsessed with de-Stalinization or de-Maoization, starting with a full revelation of the heinous crimes and disastrous policies of the leader indelibly associated with communist identity in their country. Whenever ideology was subject to debate, although it was not disavowed, they assailed it to the extent possible. However much they felt obliged to couch their arguments in a framework of reforming socialism, their usual preoccupation was with convergence with the outside world, eliminating all arrangements that put Reds above experts. For a time, China and Russia fueled each other's aspirations: Deng served as an example, despite tight Soviet censorship until 1986 and the pretense that Chinese reform was meager or unsuccessful; and Gorbachev seized the mantle of reformer for many Chinese starting in 1986, even in the face of severe censorship, especially after June 4, 1989. The heyday of de-ideologization lasted less than a decade.

Communist regimes fight a running battle with truth. De-Stalinization and de-Maoization opened the door to correcting the flagrant lies and omissions that had distorted national identity. Even in an atmosphere of continued half-truths, accurate information kept sneaking through the cracks in the system, which grew wider in the information revolution. Truths about history are especially pernicious. Ideology had long required glorification of each twist and turn in the path to revolution and social- ism, matched by denunciation of whatever stood in the way of this dogma. Chinese and Russian leaders discovered that a more limited ideology cou- pled with a more subtle mixture of truths, half-truths, and omissions would serve to bolster national identity. The revival of ideology, often intentionally obscured, became unmistakable in the 2000s.

Ideology has a defensive element along with an offensive one. The latter presents an elaborate narrative of what must be repeated by all who write on sensitive topics. The former, by contrast, is concerned with what must not be mentioned, concealing, even after other ideo- logical themes have been downgraded, the horrendous crimes com- mitted in the name of communism. Although Gorbachev and Yeltsin divulged some secrets, the revival of ideology meant renewed secrecy, continuing to conceal many of the most damaging truths. For China's leaders there was more steadfastness in hiding the crimes in their party's history. Denial of information and censorship are methods for prevent- ing truth from subverting ideology.

A three-way combination applies to both Chinese and Russian ide- ology in recent years: holdover socialist core values, reconstructed tra- ditional values, and an influx of universal values. In both states, one observes a reaffirmation with new force of socialist values centered on state-party authority. If traditional socialist values of class struggle, egalitarian ideals, and anti-market obsessions were marginalized, those concerned with the vertical dimension of top-down control gained a new lease on life. Deng's "four fundamental principles" outdid Putin's "sovereign democracy" in explicitly validating socialism and the sanctified place of its founding fathers (Mao Zedong among them) as well as the Communist Party. The fact that Russia rejected these principles in 1991–92 should not obscure their revival, beginning in the Yeltsin era, in an ideology centered on the supremacy of the state, including many features from the old ideology.

Ideology was once considered a product of a few top leaders and a specialized wing of the Communist Party. It was assumed that other groups in the leadership pursued national interests and found that ideology got in their way. However, in the 1990s the security community rose to the fore, putting pressure on Yeltsin and taking satisfaction from one of their own replacing him at decade's end; and in China, its clout was growing, seen in the impact of the Persian Gulf War, Taiwan Strait crisis, and Kosovo war. Subsequently, its influence kept growing. The People's Liberation Army (PLA) emerged in 2009 as a supporter of an ideological approach to the history of the Korean War, seen as China's finest hour, when the Chinese people learned to love the PLA. The Russian army had not fared well for a time, given its bumbling efforts at reform and the fearsome image of conscription, but Putin championed it, and its history, as in World War II, served a similar ideological purpose. The nexus of political leadership and security establishment meant defending a civilization from what was seen as a dangerous ideological threat.

Both China and Russia faced growing momentum to place traditional values, however distorted their interpretation, above socialist ones. After long insisting in the era of orthodox communism that the two are fundamentally incompatible, the authorities made an about-face by arguing that in the new era, after class struggle is forgotten, these two types of values heavily overlap. Groping to clarify the meaning of the "Russian idea," Yeltsin invited public input, with a clear preference for *derzhavnost'* (putting state authority on a pedestal), as in traditional communism. China's leaders found merit in recognizing the benefits of blending Confucianism with socialism and seizing the theme of "harmonious society" to justify party-state control without checks or balances or room for civil society. Yet they were anxious to avert the real possibility that Confucian values would be seen as an alternative to socialism, privileging the state over the party. Rejuvenating the "liberal tradition" in either elite Confucianism or reform Confucianism, which had restrained imperial Confucianism, could endanger communism. Thus, claiming the mantle of traditional values is a double-edged sword for the survival of socialist ideology in the lead role, as shown in the caution exercised in narrowing coverage of this legacy.

Russia and China renewed ideological attacks on imperialism/hegemonism, countering the appeal of universal values. In Russia before 1917, the intelligentsia's acceptance of the Enlightenment was widespread. In the period 1987–93, even more than during the Khrushchev era's "thaw," humanism served as a rallying cry. Russians take pride in being part of European civilization. Yet the main thrust of ideology under Putin, as under Communist Party rule, is to insist on distinct values. Chinese spokesmen carry this differentiation further, disassociating Eastern values and substituting the term "Western" for "universal" when contrasting values in order to draw a sharp boundary between civilizations. As in Russia, recognition of the universal nature of values by many in the rising middle class puts pressure on ideological claims.

The three-way ideological amalgam of socialism, presocialist thought supportive of Sinocentrism or Russocentrism, and anti-imperialism is somewhat different in the two countries. Socialism has an explicit, leading role in China. Confucianism is under more pressure in China for its threatening impact than is the "Russian idea." Anti-imperialism or hegemonism is central to ideology, resonating more in China. Given Communist Party rule and China's powerful Central Propaganda Department, Chinese leaders put more stress on the ideological dimension, while Russian leaders struggle with ambivalence toward socialism and "Euro-American values," when they also see themselves as Europeans, presumably respectful of its cultural traditions.

Communism offered a full-fledged worldview to counter universal values, but China and Russia have nothing of the sort in reconstructing their national identities. After the October 2011 plenary session of its Central Committee called for reinforcing socialist core values, China was short on substance other than to oppose the West. The prospect of reconciling the Stalin-Mao legacy and Confucianism was too sensitive to discuss, just as Russia was in no position to clarify the confusion between the Stalin-Brezhnev legacy and the "Russian idea." Ideology is left in limbo, a force in national identity but not a foundation, as it had been in traditional communism.

THE TEMPORAL DIMENSION

Ideology has always been closely linked to history. Leaders demand that the past be interpreted to support the current version of ideology, including avoiding criticism of founders and officials considered sacrosanct. In turn, ideology is presented to salvage the past, rationalizing what might ordinarily be considered mistakes or crimes. Periodization is at the core of communist reasoning. It starts with dialectical logic about the replacement of one formation with its opposite. This requires strong contrasts between one's own country, which is building socialism and communism, and the rival capitalist states, which are mired in a broken system that could only be fixed by revolution. The entire course of world history figures into the didactic narrative on unilinear progress, but it changed as reform currents found pride in premodern history, lessons in capitalist development, and possibilities for coexistence and symbiosis in today's world. In the 1980s, the Chinese took the lead, followed by the Russians, in reconstructing history in the service of reform. This altered the identity narrative, but it did not dislodge some of its fundamental themes.

The temporal dimension refers to depictions in recent writings of three periods: (1) the premodern era and the transitional decades until the revolution; (2) the period after the revolution, including the Cold War era; and (3) the post–Cold War decades. If communists for a time saw premodern national identity as negative, its image, as reflected in foreign policy successes and state-building ambitions, had become largely positive in the 2010s. If memories of the Sino-Soviet split suggest a sharply divergent approach in the two cases toward the Cold War era, recent writings point to similar memories of the struggle against US imperialism in favor of building socialism at home and around the world. Especially in the post–Cold War era, we find evidence of identity overlap, refuting arguments that Sino-Russian ties are merely a convenience.

Temporal identity suffered a grievous blow from glasnost. After the end of demonization of the West in the Cold War and with the prospect of a new era of close cooperation, no period in history served to clearly bolster Soviet or Russian identity. The resulting confusion gave way to a backlash. The history of Russia until 1917 offered some solace. Efforts to venerate Russia's modernizing tsars, especially Peter I, and cultural heroes, such as Pushkin, persist. Merging pride in pre-1917 and post-1917 state building and foreign policy revives the temporal dimension.

Chinese leaders choose themes that resonate with Chinese history, but less often recall heroes from premodern times. Putin often does, citing names of previous Russian officials and military officers identified with a strong state. Although Putin usually does not mention Stalin by name, he presents a picture of courageous resistance to outside predators by forging a strong state identity. The premodern era looms larger in Russian than in Chinese national identity.

The focus on 1917 in Russia and on 1949 in China shifted to 1945, even as linkages were drawn between wartime success and the coming to power of the communists. In the 1990s, patriotic education in China centered on communist leadership in the war against Japan, while the revival of Russian historical pride focused on the war. For China, the meaning of the victory over Japan in 1945 and communist success in 1949 is jumbled together. For Russia, the victory over the Nazis in 1945 and the establishment of a strong state, which became a superpower, is also not easily differentiated. Memories of hard-fought success, framed in propaganda that distorts the truth, became more important for national identity. The Chinese campaign redirected attention from Maoism's dark side to the glory of victory after long years of humiliation. In Russia, memories of success counter revelations about Stalin's false claims or accusations from neighboring states, while focusing on unity in support of a strong Russia. The counterattack against the "falsification" of history to damage Russia began with the narrative on the war. As noted in

chapter 3, Vladislav Surkov in 2005 helped to found the youth organization Nashi, which harks back to Soviet organizations and takes as its most
important symbol the victory in the Great Patriotic War. Linkage of the
US threat of soft absorption (*miagkoe pogloshchenie*), in Surkov's words, to
invasions of the past follows from this thinking.[2] Russian innocence in
facing one hostile invader after another provides the backdrop for warnings that do not draw a clear boundary between military aggression and
cultural diffusion, as in recent "color revolutions."

To question past policies, even to the degree done in the late 1980s,
would threaten regime identity. The Korean War is a case in point. If
credence were given to the causes of the war, the edifice of support for
Cold War policies could crumble. Because demonization of current US
policy toward their country is attributed to a "Cold War mentality," it
is essential to trace this thinking back to the real Cold War as a mani-
festation of inherent anticommunism. China and Russia find common
ground in the past, leaving aside their earlier split and favoring memories rooted in communist rhetoric.

The identity overlap can be summarized as follows. In premodern
times, the national identity contrasts positively with identities in the
West and should be recalled with pride rather than disparaged, as persons
steeped in Western thinking presumably do. In the Cold War era, anticommunism in the West posed an existential threat, and pride is justified
in the way the Cold War was fought in resistance to this threat. Finally, in
the post–Cold War period the United States' pursuit of a single international civilization is just a continuation of its Cold War ideology, which
is justifiably countered by the thinking in the non-Western world. At its
core, this is a view of Stalin and Mao as saviors, whose mission remains
incomplete in a struggle for state building and cohesion and resistance to
hegemonism that is only intensifying in our times.

THE SECTORAL DIMENSION

By affirming that economic development follows a similar course in
both socialist and capitalist countries, leaders in the 1980s bridged what

had stood as a fundamental divide. Economic national identity would no longer be treated as a source of resistance to ideas from the capitalist world. This change also had ramifications for cultural identity. In order to overcome an economic divide, cultural issues would have to be addressed. After all, claims of cultural superiority over minority nationalities and other states had been tied to claims of economic superiority. Once culture entered the picture, political national identity could not be kept entirely separate. Reformers linked these themes, whereas conservatives feared spillover, forging their own linkages only as economic pride returned. At first, this dimension serves mainly a defensive purpose, blaming the intentions of the West. Later, it revives as a basis of claimed superiority.

If ideology was the overriding focus of identity under traditional communism, the focus turns to culture in the CGP (T1) NIS. In the 1980s, ideology was viewed with suspicion for blinding leaders to pragmatic reform, but it was also treated within the leadership as still necessary to prevent a complete loss of legitimacy. It could not be the foundation for a reinvigorated national identity. Culture attracted new interest, following its suppression in the name of ideology and the abrupt opening to global currents. It was essential to deflect "culture fever" that brought values at odds with existing ones and to shape a revival of traditional culture in ways favorable to a renewal of regime legitimacy based on national pride. Warning against an existential threat to national culture, leaders found a convenient hook for reviving identity.

China and Russia each had a strong cultural national identity that was challenged by the spread of Western culture in the nineteenth century. Russia had long confronted the apparent cultural superiority of the West, succumbing in obvious respects, such as its elites' preference for the French language, while also resisting through a fusion of state and religion, with enduring cultural consequences. During the nineteenth century, a vibrant cultural identity was closely tied to developments in circles across Europe, yet was also intensely preoccupied with the national distinctiveness of Russia. In China, there was no such challenge to assumptions of cultural superiority before the arrival of the West in the mid–nineteenth century. Yet by the early twentieth century, the popularity of Western culture in elite circles was posing a threat to tradition, arousing defensive reactions that at times were reinforced by state policies. The communist response was to poison minds against the intruding culture, varying in how it treated traditional culture while arousing a backlash from destructive actions taken against that culture.

Cultural national identity faced revulsion over the environmental destruction of Russia's landmarks and treasures, such as Lake Baikal. Such symbols could be used to attack Soviet national identity on behalf of Russian identity, as could the destruction of the peasantry and rural communities through collectivization. Given the prominent place of Eastern Orthodoxy in Russian culture, denunciation of the way in which the Soviet national identity excluded it dealt a further blow to cultural claims. Appeals for "humanism" drew on a global standard for cultural identity, which had strong roots in Russia's past. Chinese leaders worked hard to exclude similar appeals, even launching a campaign in 1984 that targeted *rendaozhuyi* (humanism), as they more gradually made space for the praising of Confucian culture.

One of the clearest statements about culture came in a 2008 Chinese journal article that pointed to cultural colonialism linked to US support for human rights and democracy as the driving force in the world moving to an era of anti-Americanism. Instead of the world rallying behind the United States after the September 11, 2001, terrorist attacks, stepped-up efforts to internationalize US culture are fomenting a backlash. US culture has marginalized local ones, leading to steps to boost one's own culture and to a need to borrow from other non-Western cultures. Although China is not yet a cultural great power, it is expanding its cultural influence. The Confucian cultural sphere is reemerging, beginning with a rising interest in Asian values. In this process, Confucianism is mixed with Marxism, emphasizing a harmonious world, including among diverse civilizations in Asia.[3] Russia is one of the objects of this appeal. Although Russians are less optimistic about harmony with Chinese civilization, they have agreed on rising resistance to US cultural imperialism and on a civilizational approach to this end.

China and Russia overlap in cultural pride in opposition to the threat of Western culture. Both nations' leaders and remnants of communist officialdom were determined to staunch the Western cultural invasion that accelerated with the post–Cold War borderless flow of information. In 2012, Chinese leaders showed no reticence in calling for "better ideological work" as well as greater cultural confidence.[4] At the same time, Russian leaders warned more loudly about the cultural danger from the West, accusing citizens demonstrating against Putin of being stooges of the West who were disloyal to Russian culture. What in the 1990s had been cautious critiques of Western culture had turned into a torrent of condemnation.

It has often been assumed that differences in political and economic identities were foremost in the divergence between the reform outcomes in China and the Soviet Union. Deng kept political identity off bounds, putting economic identity in the forefront, whereas Gorbachev allowed his country to become caught in the whirlwind of political identities that led to the unraveling of Communist Party rule and the Soviet Union, along with a long transition before Putin succeeded in establishing a clear sense of Russian political identity. To this mix, we should add cultural national identity, which, along with political identity, proved more problematic in Russia in the 1990s. As Japan and South Korea had done before it, China rode the waves of an "economic miracle" to cultural pride, climbing to new heights and, finally, seeing political identity take precedence, as all three types of sectoral identity intensified. Russia's economic national identity did not lead to similar confidence, as warnings kept being heard that reforms were needed to avoid a narrow reliance on natural resources. This dimension played a large role in reinvigorating national identity in both states, and it is in the forefront of Chinese arrogance while leaving Russians with greater ambivalence.

THE VERTICAL DIMENSION

Communism, as it developed in the Soviet Union and China, shifts identity away from independent collectives (e.g., religious, ethnic, community, kinship) and toward a single vertical state entity that is equated with the nation. Individualism has scant opportunity to develop, given the required "upbringing" and the dearth of outlets through which to express it. Atomizing society, Stalin and then Mao fostered a "cult of personality," in which the self-esteem of individuals depended on satisfying the supposed will of the leader. Extraordinary methods of reeducation left a powerful legacy, which was seen in the despair felt by many at the deaths of Stalin and Mao. After their departure, leaders sought to transfer the displacement of identity to the Communist Party, which was equated with the state. Despite greater skepticism about identifying with the party-state in a less coercive era, the legacy of weakened alternative outlets to vertical identity endured.

The vertical dimension remained unsettled in China starting in 1956, when Mao became obsessed with contradictions, leading to twenty years of peripatetic policy changes under the banner of "never forget the class struggle." Under Brezhnev, this dimension acquired a steadfast character, greatly influencing Russia after the fall of communism, although the social contract lost force and Communist Party control gave way to another highly bureaucratic system weighing heavily on small-scale entrepreneurship. Even as markets gained ground in both states, the number of officials with few checks on their authority remained huge. In the reform era the vertical dimension was long unsettled in Russia, but China made it a bulwark of identity.

Dictatorship is not inherently inimical to widespread acceptance of shared identity centered on the state or its leader. With time and the corrosive impact of social injustice, however, there is a growing sense of loss of morality, a spiritual vacuum. Officials think that they are immune from the law as they recklessly pursue private gains at the expense of public trust. Some go too far, posing a threat to other leaders or leaving institutions hobbled. Individuals feel a sense of helplessness. For the state to remain their focus of identity, superficial responses do not suffice. Sensing alienation, in the early 1980s Yuri Andropov tried to reestablish party and state authority through greater discipline, but the problems were too deep-seated to be resolved and revelations of shortcomings added to mistrust. Gorbachev went further by allowing honesty about Soviet and world history, contradicting the tower of myths that had been constructed over seven decades. Although he saw this as necessary for the normalization of daily life and Moscow's integration into the international community, its destabilizing impact was difficult to control. Soviet national identity was soon shaken.

Deng and Gorbachev took advantage of enormous power concentrated in the hands of one person to launch reforms. What they accomplished depended on this legacy of personalized authority; but ironically, their reform agenda diminished the authority required to persevere. The hierarchy in both countries in the early 1980s was extremely top-heavy, investing unchecked power from below in Communist Party officials who were hostile to most if not all of the reform ideas. Ending class struggle did not threaten their power. Indeed, it had given them more security. Giving a voice to local soviets, entrepreneurs, and critics of existing shortcomings could expose their corruption and other crimes or arbitrariness. The struggle over the vertical dimension proved to be the most intense and it remains so.

A major concern for national identity in the 1980s was how to deal with the secret legacy of communist terrorism. Gorbachev decided to allow the legacy to be disclosed in order to reconstruct national identity in a manner favorable to reform. Deng chose instead to conceal all but some minimal features of the legacy in order to preserve the foundation of national identity. The notion that the Communist Party is the nation's trustee rather than its nemesis is at the heart of legitimacy. Tampering with the vertical dimension could put acute pressure on party rule, opening the door at the intermediate level to diverse other identities, such as ethnic and civil society, with dangerous consequences for the party. Russia opened this Pandora's box and spent the better part of a decade trying to put all the "evils" back in it. China opened the box a crack in the 1980s, but after June 1989 shut it, keeping the lid tight.

China saw the responsibility system give rise to an entrepreneurial peasantry, to special economic zones that serve as breeding grounds for foreign firms arriving by the thousands, and to spreading market competition, with localities vying to gain an edge through enticements to firms. Russia witnessed the rise of oligarchs capable of influencing politics as monopolies predominated over competition. Yet, when one reflects on the privatization of the state-owned enterprises, the similarities are also striking. Transfers of ownership favored the managers as insiders and left firms dependent on state power. Voucher privatization was of scant consequence in Russia, as was the elimination of Communist Party cells in the workplace. Pride in economic growth restored hubris about the state as the engine of the economy. Market forces did not stop state predominance. If Russia's success is shakier and its economic system is more suspect, its claims rest more on being part of the global rejection of the Western framework than on its own superiority.

After state properties were transferred to oligarchs in Russia, many considered it a blow to national identity, which had been associated with state control over resources. China kept calling attention to state control, as property was disseminated to many with close connections to the leadership in ways that could have been seen as no less legitimate. Putin reestablished the appearance of order and changed the narrative, but he failed to rein in the corruption associated with state permits, taxation, and law enforcement. The two cases are parallel. However, China renewed market-oriented reforms in 1992 and 2013 beyond what Russia had accomplished.

The secret police remained unchallenged in both China and Russia. In Russia, their role was questioned and they lost ground, but they were not much reconstructed or exposed for the havoc they had earlier wreaked. By the 2000s, both countries were strengthening internal security, rebuilding not only state capacity but also state control over all entities that could pose an identity challenge. After some recognition of human rights, as reformers recalled prerevolutionary movements for Confucian liberalism or parliamentarianism, the security services made sure that freedoms would be exercised only in limited ways, mainly related to the economy. Terrorism via massive surveillance was never uprooted.

Communism breeds rampant crime. By perverting market principles, it invites individuals at all levels to break the law in order to survive or to gain an edge in an unjust system. A relaxation of controls without the rule of law leads to even more blatant ways of circumventing the limits set by leaders. This does not strengthen universal values. Rather, it feeds into suspicion of any challenge to the vertical dimension of national identity that could undercut the illicit networks contributing to social mobility. Criminality is behind authoritarian preferences among business interests, even after prior controls were relaxed.

It proved easy for China and Russia to control religious and business groups, which elsewhere became the nuclei of civil society. Historically, they evolved in both countries as appendages of the state, enjoying neither rights to autonomy nor claims to a separate identity. Communism decimated their ranks, killing any with the potential for an independent identity and then gingerly allowing a few to be representatives tightly beholden to the state. After some resurgence in the 1990s, they were brought under new control. Russia's oligarchs lost any right to speak against the political leadership, and China's state-owned enterprises regained their dominance. State identity regained a virtually monopoly status.

Ethnic minorities pose a different identity problem for Russia than for China. In China, members of the Han majority migrate to the western regions for economic opportunity and with strong government encouragement dilute native populations. Migrants to the boomtowns across the rest of the country are overwhelmingly Han, who offend local feelings. Those arriving in Moscow and other Russian cities are largely Muslims from areas that were once part of the Soviet Union, whose customs make them scapegoats for lingering frustrations. Insistence that Han Chinese and Russians (*Russkie*) express national identity without multiculturalism of any relevance serves to reduce signs of intermediate identities, which are driven underground, resisting the center. Whereas the mainstream view in Russia favors assimilation, Medvedev came out against ethnocentrism and even in favor of multiculturalism. This was in contrast to the approach of China, which was hostile to allowing ethnic groups to develop their own identities, and was also at odds with the prevalence of intolerance and ethnic hate crimes in Russia. Yet Medvedev's rhetoric was removed from reality. The idea of multiculturalism faded away.

When at the same time in the mid-2000s Putin trumpeted sovereign democracy and Hu Jintao promoted harmonious development, these moves were explained as steps toward greater stability more than as national identity challenges to the values of the United States and its allies. With US president George W. Bush exhilarated about the spread of universal values, the Chinese and Russian moves were not seen as arrogant in the face of arrogance on behalf of a skewed notion of Western civilization. Yet when the US message mellowed under Barack Obama, Hu and Putin intensified their challenge. After vertical identity had been put in jeopardy by attacks on state interference in myriad operations of society and exposés of privileges given to officials that had previously been concealed, it was restored through censorship and reinforcement of a privileged elite heavily dependent on the leadership. The process was quicker in China and brooked less opposition, but Putin's policies led to similar results, notably starting in 2012.

Wen Jiabao led in appealing for both economic and political reform, returning to the goal of modernization as a comprehensive program. He warned that what China had gained from economic reform could be lost if it did not pursue political liberalization. In contrast, Hu Jintao spoke for what was clearly the majority of the Political Standing Committee in firming up "beliefs in socialist ideals with Chinese characteristics as well as the socialist theoretical system with Chinese characteristics." Campaigns in the years 2009–10 warned against views that contradict "Sinicizing, popularizing, and modernizing Marxism." In 2007, Wen had even advocated "universal values," including democracy, freedom, and human rights. Such reasoning was soon refuted by accusations directed against those "failing to distinguish between socialist and capitalist democracies" and "arbitrarily imposing Western concepts on the reality of China's political development."[5]

The "people" or "masses" became an abstraction in the Soviet Union and China to justify unfettered state or party-centered identity, marginalizing any type of identity that could interfere. With claims that the center represented the people and other entities did not, no room was left for intermediate identities on the vertical dimension. Although the period from the 1980s to the 2000s brought many changes, this overarching identity continued to overwhelm any alternatives. Russia accepted identification with the Eastern Orthodox religion in the traditional spirit of complete church subservience to the state's identity. China refused to allow any independent religious authority, while co-opting the Confucian tradition with a narrow interpretation of its support for state identity. Absent the abstraction "the masses," an assumption remains that the state embodies the identity of entities within it, erasing the local, regional, ethnic, and other identities that would undermine its preeminence.

Mao and Stalin made vertical national identity totalitarian. In the backlash to the confusion of the 1980s (and the 1990s in Russia), a process of rebuilding vertical identity gained momentum that has not slowed to the present. This means a strong state (party) unchecked by civil society, a security apparatus penetrating society, and a propaganda barrage justifying centralization in opposition to democratization. China and Russia share both this identity and the conviction that it is endangered, largely by Western values. This is a unifying force in bilateral relations, which has been affecting relations with the United States as a threat. Changes in society have increased the resistance to such a hierarchical order, raising the possibility that challenges lie ahead, especially if the existing economic model flounders.

THE HORIZONTAL DIMENSION

The United States' efforts to narrowly define internationalism had an impact on China and Russia. For the first half of the 1990s, they centered on democratization and human rights, using the end of the Cold War and the collapse of the Soviet Union as proof. In the late 1990s, the Asian financial crisis fueled an obsession with financial globalization, pressuring Asian states where economic competition was greatest. After September 11, 2001, the Bush administration made the war on terrorism the test of international responsibility. During the second half of the 2000s, the prevention of the spread of nuclear weapons to "rogue states" and of other types of proliferation was most important. If China and Russia responded ambivalently to some of these tests of their support for internationalism, pressure to draw a firm line against the states regarded as pariahs or rogues found them resisting. Whether their resistance was based on charges that the United States was driven by a hegemonic ideology or that it failed to respect sovereignty, the fact that China and Russia could limit the UN Security Council's support for so-called internationalist thinking gave them some ability to shape the rhetoric. In the process, they also resisted efforts to make humanitarian intervention the basis for deciding whether to recognize internationalism, agreeing in 1999 to oppose a United Nations role in Kosovo; thereby, they denied that NATO's intervention was internationalism, a pattern that would be replayed many times with the charge that the West was using human rights as a smokescreen for its hegemonic ambitions, while concealing the fact that China and Russia were feigning realism to obscure their own obsession with clashing values as the basis of foreign policy decisionmaking.

Throughout the 1990s and into the 2000s, Chinese and Russian foreign policies were seen as prioritizing stability on their borders, cooperation with the United States, and a balanced world order resistant to domination by the West but still supportive of a gradual transition through cooperation with the West. In the 2010s, showdowns over Iran, Syria, and North Korea exposed a distinctly different outlook on horizontal identity. Instead of stability, the goal in nearby areas was to deny Western influence by forging regional spheres of influence and identity. Hostility to the United States proved to be much more intense than had often been revealed earlier. China's and Russia's joint mantra of multipolarization starting in the mid-1990s, when Evgenyi Primakov called for correcting Russia's imbalance between East and West, centered identity on preventing hegemonism, while blaming US leaders for sustaining a Cold War mentality through security "globalization," "universal rights" imposed on others, and demands for "responsibility" in meeting joint challenges. Under the guise of combating anticommunism, China and Russia revived Cold War thinking.[6]

The horizontal dimension was left vague for two decades, however, with no clear alternative to the international community. Both China and Russia appealed to the United Nations as the proper source of international legitimation, salvaging a semblance of internationalism, especially when in the period 2003–5 US unilateralism cast doubt on other notions of it. Joining the WTO, China increasingly insisted that it was defending internationalist norms against protectionist tendencies, winning approval after US globalization looked suspect in the world financial crisis. Yet the absence of any alternative for the world community cast a shadow on their identity claims. China had the edge on Russia, reviving its long-standing identification with the developing world, backed by much closer economic and political ties. China and Russia together welcomed regular meetings of the BRICS (Brazil, Russia, India, China, and South Africa) as the core of the new powers that are reshaping the international community. Also, as members of the new Group of Twenty, gaining precedence over the Group of Eight, they had another basis for leadership. Yet they faced vigorous moves by Obama to restore the international community and failed to articulate a credible, joint, or different vision.

China and Russia welcome international investment in sectors of their economies and often convey a tone of internationalism, accepting the global community. Yet this is contradicted in identity narratives that warn against the international community as it has been understood. Pragmatic diplomats and academics speak in a language reassuring to their counterparts around the world, but writings on identity take a different tone, which is often revealed to reflect the true sentiments of higher officials and many academics as well.

Both favor UN Security Council resistance to humanitarian intervention and pressure as the means to block nuclear proliferation. They seek a valueless global community that is respectful of a balance of power. Under the legacy of communism, both see Western aspirations for an international order to face diverse new threats as threatening to their national identity. The Arab Spring, especially after US and NATO policy seized upon the support of China and Russia for a no-fly zone over Libya to oust Qaddafi and topple his regime, brought clarity on the absolute priority of preventing international agreements on human rights or humanitarian assistance as a basis for armed intervention and regime change. At its core, this attitude is based on a dichotomy whereby ideas from the West pose such a threat that they must be demonized if one's regime or the civilization it serves is not to be put in jeopardy. Toppling other regimes might also cause a spiral effect.

In the first stage of the transition away from the Cold War, China and Russia kept the focus on narrow objectives to keep the international order from impinging, while not strongly challenging that order. Chinese leaders were more dismissive of the order, but they voiced concern especially about Taiwan and threats to China's territorial integrity. Russian leaders were attentive to Russians in the newly independent states of the former Soviet Union and also to purported threats to the new borders of the Russian Federation. Over time, the scope of the challenge to the international community widened. Regional issues gained salience, as infringement on spheres of influence, defined in civilizational terms and also for security, aroused responses. Eventually, the entire world became part of the clash of civilizations.

Concern about a United States–led international community ready to use sanctions or even force for "humanitarian" objectives that would tilt the global balance of power in its favor was used against NATO's intervention in Kosovo and was at the root of criticisms of US policies toward Iran and North Korea. Discounting assertions of security objectives to stop nuclear proliferation and civil war and assertions of human rights objectives to restore order and allow disenfranchised populations to overcome tyranny, leaders charged that the real aim of Western policies was to extend hegemony and contain states opposing the West—that is, China and Russia.

China and Russia groped in the 1990s and 2000s for regionalism that reinforced their national identities. The Association of Southeast Asian Nations plus China, Japan, and South Korea (known as ASEAN + 3) had potential for China, especially because in 2005 it was confirmed as the unit chosen to form the East Asian Community, but clashing views of the scope and nature of East Asian regionalism left China in a quandary, as leaders began to press for a more Sinocentric region. Although Russia had struggled in the 1990s to solidify the Commonwealth of Independent States to little avail, Putin set Eurasianism as the new goal for regionalism in 2011, hoping that Soviet nostalgia would counteract fear of Soviet revival. Whatever the prospects for these aspirations, they served to meet a need in each state's national identity for taking the lead over a community of nearby states. As Sinocentrism and

Russocentrism became more pronounced, the parallels were seen in the widening national identity gaps with the West much more than in a Sino-Russian gap.

Sinocentrism grew more intense, and Russocentrism morphed into Eurasianism, such that the possibility was growing that a rising focus of national identity would put China and Russia at loggerheads. Managing triangles became more complex, as discussed in a series of articles in *The Asan Forum* of November 2013. Most signs still pointed to the deepening of Transition 1, which was more than two decades old, but a shift to Transition 2 may be starting as a more confident China is less deferential in border areas and a more insistent Russia fears an identity gap anew.

THE INTENSITY DIMENSION

In the second half of the 1980s, reformers felt empowered, recognizing that the disasters that had befallen their countries, about which more accurate news was filtering out, were the result of a totalitarian system that needed to be exposed in order to enable them to move forward. Even if leaders made some reforms, they would be unlikely to alter the identity legacy weighing down their countries. Reformers sought to reinterpret identities in many ways, but after June 4, 1989, in China and after the mid-1990s in Russia, they were marginalized. Increasingly, the domestic constituencies that gained the ear of the leadership preferred the legacy of traditional communism to that of Western democracy. In this struggle, efforts were made not only to reconstruct identity but also to intensify it for an advantage.

The highly intense national identity of the Stalin and Mao eras had receded in the Deng and Gorbachev periods. Hu Yaobang and Gorbachev strove to refocus the identity narrative, but they could not control it and lost ground before they left office. A vacuum arose that Zhao Ziyang and Yeltsin found would not be filled by their early initiatives. A clearly reconstructed national identity backed by concerted top-down support gained in intensity under Jiang Zemin and Putin.

There was a conscious effort to rekindle identity, not as a short-term endeavor but in a crescendo building to a high, sustained pitch.

The Putin and Hu/Xi identity intensifications bear resemblance. Both combine hostility by elites fearing domestic instability and even delegitimation of the political system with public opinion aroused by symbols of national identity, as with NATO's expansion or arms sales to Taiwan. Voices of diplomatic pragmatism, academic cosmopolitanism, and the globalization of business were drowned out by outbursts of resentment at a failure to defend the dignity of the nation. In 1999, Chinese resentment rose to a feverish pitch as blame was heaped on the United States for actions that had been deemed disrespectful. In 2010, the response was also intense. Yet, with an eye to sustaining economic growth or restraining domestic volatility, leaders put some limits on national identity intensity. In 2013, such restraint toward Japan seemed to be fading, but it was still present in the initiative to forge a "new type of great power relations" with the United States.

Reform voices enjoyed about one decade of opportunities to steer thinking about national identity despite serious roadblocks. China silenced them more decisively after June 4, 1989, although on some themes that had been deemed less sensitive, it continued to offer moderate choices, even finding a way to persist after 2010. The tide against them had turned by the mid-1990s in Russia, gaining new force in the Putin era. In both cases, the vast security establishment, including the military-industrial complex, sought a more intense national identity. So, too, did the bureaucratic leadership, whose members were keen on a revival of centralization at the national and regional levels. In academia, there was also a large residue of personnel reared in traditional communist thinking hostile to the identity challenges aired in the 1980s. They were ready to embrace the surge in identity intensity of the 2010s without restraint.

Whereas in traditional communism, exporting ideology took priority, current thinking puts a premium on preventing the importation of civilization. Both approaches rely on a sharp differentiation from the West and assume a clash between civilizations. It proved to be an easy transition from ideological warfare to civilizational confrontation.

The Chinese and Russians have substituted the notion of opposing civilizations for ideological struggle and even rival systems, although the Chinese are reverting to these other concepts, with the emphasis that Western Cold War thinking reflects a civilizational failing. Criticizing US extremism in pushing its own values, one source calls this imperialist thinking, a product of Western civilization still embedded in a desire to force its culture on others. By contrast, Hu Jintao's notion of the "harmonious world" seeks a new type of international relations that is accepting of differences between states or regions organized along different lines.[7] Outrage is justified by offensive behavior, to which China cannot but respond heatedly. In Xi Jinping and a resurgent Putin, these states had leaders obsessed with rallying support behind the emotionalism related to each of the five dimensions of national identity delineated above.

THE SUSTAINABILITY OF THE CGP (T1) NIS

Communists have the audacity to think that they can wipe the slate clean with a vilification of the old national identity, the eradication and reeducation of its advocates or those who potentially would be so, and the socialization of others, especially new elites and generations, into an entirely new national identity, colored by social class rhetoric, overriding all other collective identities. Yet over time, other identities prove their resilience and the people show that they are not so gullible and not satisfied to rest their self-esteem exclusively with the regime. Society proves to be more complex, in accord with universal strictures. This does not mean, however, that communism does not leave behind an enduring legacy.

The CGP (T1) NIS, evolving over a quarter century, is transitional in the wake of traditional communist identity, but it is intensifying rather than yielding to an alternative. Although we cannot assume that it has a stable future, we also should not imagine that it is vulnerable to easy or rapid replacement. The first lesson of the transition is that signs of abrupt change were misleading, because continuities have been reasserted. Future steps toward change should be viewed cautiously; transitional thinking is becoming embedded despite indications of resistance from a portion of the populace, especially in Russia's big cities.

The syndrome observed in China and Russia in the 2010s shows continuity with both the traditional communist era and a version of the previous national identity, which appeared credible to large numbers. The alternative national identity advocated in the late 1980s by Gorbachev and the reformers who were silenced in China after June 4, 1989, fared poorly over time, losing support and being denigrated as an alien imposition. If these stand as the two alternatives each country has before it over the next decades, then it would take a leap of idealism to predict the collapse of the syndrome in favor of the alternative. Yet there is a third possibility in both countries of a transition away from the CGP (T1) NIS, leaving this as an interim stage in national identity as traditional communism recedes from memory. To envision this prospect, we should consider both how this could occur and what would be the contents of each dimension should there be a second phase of identity transition.

The growth of a sizable, middle-class society is not proving sufficient to dislodge the syndrome, but, as seen in the resistance centered in Moscow to Putin's return to power and to the falsified December 2011 State Duma election results, it is marked by an upsurge of discontent. Uncontrollable corruption in the leadership permeating the administration can acquire more ominous significance if economic growth slows substantially as grievances lead to more frequent and larger demonstrations. Efforts to make national identity more extreme in order to preserve regime legitimacy and also to resort to more blatant coercion may lead to a backlash, exposing contradictions or distortions in national identity claims.

Although class struggle is dead as an explicit theme in China and Russia, calls for a middle-class awakening that is supportive of civil society are for now being dismissed as contrary to a "harmonious" or "vertical" society. Individual materialism is being encouraged. Support for an agenda decided on by a secretive leadership is expected, not pursuit of citizenship by any grassroots organizations. The goal is authoritarianism on the basis of consent without transparency, checks and balances, or redress for grievances. However, as economic growth appears to be waning in Russia and slowing in China, the danger is growing that warnings against chaos will lose their credibility, especially among the enlarged middle class. Appeals to national identity are meant to divert consciousness of shared interests. Linking supposed US plots for "regime change," "separatism," and "color revolutions" to domestic dissent widens the national identity gap, putting domestic critics on the defensive, as if they are antipatriotic. Yet Russia's middle class is more able to use the remnants of democracy from the 1990s for demonstrations and even election campaigns, drawing on identity themes less hostile to the West. Chinese national identity also faces resistance to a vertical dimension that is seriously distorted. Economic growth is likely to recede as the glue of social compliance.

However far Russia has drifted toward authoritarianism under Putin, the norms of a democratic state still resonate. China, by contrast, denies these norms, crushing signs of any opposition. Although both countries strenuously manipulate public opinion, China is blunter in opposing democracy as a narrow Western cultural attribute, defensive of the Communist Party as well as national dignity, and less concerned for the consent of the governed. In 2013, Putin also demonstrated that he more openly dismisses Russia's democratic norms.

On the ideological dimension, the current narrative is especially vulnerable. For China, socialism is so contradictory in content and so artificially revived by ideologues that credibility may be problematic. For Russia, a refusal to claim the persistence of this doctrine leads to no less confusion. Sinocentrism is also exposed by the absence of any countries supporting this concept. Russocentrism, too, cannot be expected to win adherents among states that cling to their sovereignty, and Eurasianism is faulty as a cultural ideal. Finally, if anti-imperialism remains the most resilient element of ideology, it is also limited in an economic downturn by the two nations' need to cooperate more closely with the United States and its allies. Ideology is a weak reed for sustaining national identity in a period of declining trust in the wisdom of leaders. Steps to emphasize it more in both states in 2013 carried the potential of an eventual backlash.

On the temporal dimension, there are too many discrepancies in the narrative of a country's supposedly glorious past to withstand scrutiny. Russians grasp in vain to show the superiority of their precommunist past, and China's glorified harmonious history is likely to face the same fate as Japan's pride in Nihonjinron (Japanese cultural identity), which was linked to assumptions rooted in a bubble economy that burst. The Cold War narrative is especially vulnerable, because it flies in the face of historical evidence about Stalinism and Maoism and the exposés popular in the 1980s. Most meaningful is the narrative of the post–Cold War decades, blaming the United States for containment and designs on regime change. Increasingly, this argument is the basis for widening the identity gap, and its viability depends on how conflicts will be handled over hot spots and on whether demonization of the United States is credible.

Both China and Russia have some fragility in their national identities, owing to simplifications and distortions in how identities are constructed. Although these countries' current identities demonstrate continuities with their traditional communist ones, they increasingly do not suit their changing conditions. But finding an alternative may prove even harder in the next decade than replacing traditional communism was in the 1980s. No obvious choice is emerging, because opposition politics in Russia remains quite fragmented, and dissenting voices in China face too much censorship to present a coherent narrative.

China's leaders, who are planning succession for a decade ahead, and Putin, who is projecting the image of stability in contrast to Yeltsin's peripatetic stewardship, plan on managing talk of identity themes for the long run. They prevent political modernization, controlling the main media, electoral candidates, and the use of money in politics. Yet wars between the clans at the center continue, while cynicism has been growing among Russian educated elites. Many people are apathetic toward the rhetoric of the regime. The days of the new Soviet man and the Red Guards are over. Many subgroups today have found collective identities far more heterogeneous than those in the past. The national identity narratives chosen are inflexible in boosting soft power abroad or appealing to groups with self-esteem at home. As a result, efforts to increase identity intensity also threaten to leave the regime isolated. In China, regime control is firmer; a sharp setback is needed to change the momentum.

CONCLUSION

The case for concentrating on differences between Chinese and Russian national identity is easy to make. In the period from the 1960s to the 1980s, observers pointed to them in explaining the Sino-Soviet split. In the 1990s, they also stressed them in explaining the sharp divergence between China's reforms, leading to an "economic miracle" under firm leadership, and Russia's, leading to economic collapse amid political instability. The Chinese peasant of old is viewed as an enterprising farmer within a large kinship network, some of whose members aspired to upward mobility through the examination system. In contrast, the Russian serf is seen as illiterate within a small, closed community, with scant opportunity for entrepreneurship or social mobility. Further differentiation occurred in contrasts between the two nations' revolutions that led to communism and the response to the market reforms that dismantled it. It was Russia that led in modernization, advancing far ahead of China for over a century. Yet these contrasts should not deter us from an objective examination of the similarities in the national identities of the two states as they evolved following the end of the communist heyday.

Chinese writings for the most part constitute a guided narrative in support of an evolving, centrally determined set of goals. There are moments and topics that reveal divergence and, more often, variations in pursuing these goals. The narrative proceeds, however, expeditiously through priorities and guidelines signaled from above, censorship instructions to exclude sensitive topics and points of view, and specific language (*tifa*) that leads the way. Although the Soviet period saw similar, if less nuanced, devices, there is no comparable propaganda apparatus and organization department to orchestrate post-Soviet writings. Russia's tightening restrictions on the media and pressuring to narrow the range of ideas highlighted after the heyday of the 1990s fall short of the substantial Chinese control apparatus, which was further mobilized in 2013, for inculcating a particular national identity.

Russian liberals achieved more of their national identity objectives than did Chinese liberals. This is understandable. The educated community in Russia was much larger, it had long been more receptive to the West, and it was better positioned to influence officials, who over three decades since de-Stalinization had been exposed to more information about the outside world and more of the realities of social problems at home. Convergence also appeared more compatible with the needs of Soviet society, which was at what was seen as a middle stage of modernization with pretensions to belong to the advanced stage. Two priorities that reinforced the liberal agenda were conversion to a civilian economy and transformation from an industrial to a consumer economy. Also, absorption of high-technology knowledge, a gateway to the new information age, called for trusting intellectuals and experts. China's economic needs were more varied, allowing an emphasis on labor-intensive development, at least during a transitional period. These differences led to divergent identity priorities.

The weight of liberalism was greater in Russia, complicating the reconstruction of national identity. It was associated with privatization, dependence on foreign capital, and integration into the West. To reform the Soviet leviathan meant reducing the state's role, with implications for the state's identity. But no sustained path forward was in sight. The Putin phenomenon was more in keeping with Russia's transition, given its background. A natural resource boom, fueled in large part by China's insatiable appetite, allowed Russia to break free of the West while reasserting state primacy. Liberalism had no answer for this turnabout in Russian fortunes in the 2000s, but its residual presence was still felt.

Why did the CGP (T1) NIS prevail? It did so after the liberal position had been marginalized. This happened in China in 1989, when various groups coalesced around regime stability. Leaders counted on a preference for stability, regardless of the attitudes of those who demonstrated in 1989. Rapid economic success further marginalized the liberals, who were seen as putting politics before economics. In Russia, economic growth required Western assistance, limiting options in the

1990s. Only as people came to doubt the value of that assistance and then, a decade later than in China, gained confidence in economic growth were liberals much more dispensable. The mirage that an alternative identity had strong support at high levels was exposed in both states, although later in Russia.

The Chinese people never had much chance to give major input into the search for national identity. There was no parallel to the glasnost encouraged by Gorbachev and the democratization and relatively free press that followed, notably in the 1990s. Russian voting behavior revealed that increasing numbers starting early in the 1990s were susceptible to the narrow identity appeals favored by the majority of the leadership and, in the 2000s, increasingly subject to manipulation from above. In China, voting did not open a window on national identity thinking, but the Internet offered evidence of a similar susceptibility to identity appeals inimical to democratic values. Communism was not just an artificial imposition forced on the people, which would be abandoned with economic reforms and a surge of information. As long as the leadership manipulated the legacy and ordinary people focused on symbols that obscured their deeper interests, leaders stood a good chance of retaining support in a favorable economic environment.

An emboldened Russia in 2004–5 and an emboldened China in 2009–10, after previous moves along the same line, revived elements of communist national identity that had been missing in recent years. Without calls for an ideological campaign, as in the heyday of communism, they renewed charges that US policy is driven by an anticommunist, hegemonist ideology. This was even put into a framework of two blocs: the West, intent on forging a monolithic world civilization based on so-called universal values that constitute cultural imperialism; and the rising powers, representative of the rest of the world and determined to prevent this threat. After once acknowledging the excess of past communist leaders, including Stalin and Mao, the two states now were keen on minimizing any airing of dirty linen about the history of the movement and their country, while putting the spotlight on a narrative that resembles the long-standing communist critique of Western imperialism and Cold War responsibility for events that shattered the peace, such as the Korean War. Empowered by recent economic growth comparisons, China and even Russia also had rekindled claims about capitalism's inferiority and the advantages of their increasingly state-directed economic model, but this rang hollow in Russia as growth rates dropped, and it remained uncertain in China as new reforms were announced in late 2013.

Russia's and China's national identities have striking similarities and also notable differences, which can be explained in part by different transitional paths but also as a reflection of how the EANIS combines with the CGP (T1) NIS in ways distinct from Russia, widening the divide with the West. Looking back, we find powerful parallels. An indigenous communist revolution sets in motion changes that soon acquire a momentum of their own. Russia and China have been gripped by those forces, although each has attempted at times to break free of them. Utopian impatience is one force linked to bending the curve. Another is reform breakouts without dismantling the pillars of the old order. When these deviations run their course, the general pattern resumes. Stalinism followed a track typically about twenty-five years ahead of Maoism. Radical socialism proved difficult to sustain after these charismatic leaders died. Reform socialism took a course that favored China, vaulting it into the lead. China's success in the 1980s contrasted to the Soviet stagnation in the 1970s and 1980s. Even more, China's extraordinary advances in the 1990s gave it the edge over Russia's twisted path during the decade. By now the gap favors China, but both states face difficult transitions to the subsequent CGP (T2) NIS, in which "T2" refers to the second transition that awaits both countries as the forces that made T1 possible in the shadow of traditional communism lose their impact.

Whereas Stalin and Mao were driven by an overarching obsession with building socialism and communism, Putin and the heirs to Deng are guided by a long-term vision of forging a state with maximum comprehensive national power, which can accomplish similar objectives of unlimited top-down control and successful competition against the West. It is unlikely that they can be sidetracked, because they consider their objective to be the destiny of their country, much as building communism had been conceived. Sticking with this legacy, they are obsessed with the civilizational antagonism between the West and their country. Echoing traditional communism, they see no room for convergence. Any spread of universal values, which are deemed to represent Western civilization, is perceived as an existential threat to national identity. This logic regarding the identity gap between the West (and the United States as its leader) and their own country (along with their fellow former partner in communism) is at the nucleus of today's syndrome. Economic success serves to reinforce this thinking. Serious economic setbacks raise alarm, which also can be twisted to sustain this thinking. Divisions in the leadership of each state exist, raising the prospect that serious economic or other setbacks could lead to a toning down of the recent assertive national identity. Public discontent is likely to grow, producing pressure from below to change course. Yet diverting the public by national identity appeals linked to symbols of foreign victimization or past humiliation is more likely than accepting the desirability of narrowing identity gaps. After all, at stake is not one leadership group but the legitimacy of a path chosen long ago by the communist movement and passed along as the national destiny.

There is a contrast between China's sustained coordinated construction of the CGP (T1) NIS under the strict discipline of the Communist Party and Russia's filtering down of CGP (T1) NIS under Putin's personalized, if less systematic, leadership. With a schizophrenic identity pronounced in Russian elite circles, the syndrome's hold on public opinion and academic discourse shows its shakiness. Medvedev's hesitant embrace of it conflicted with Putin's push in 2012–13 to intensify it through dictates from above, even as big-city resentment was mounting. Putin's team seemed confused over how to respond with identity arguments that could overcome the widening domestic divide. In comparison with China, Russia's electoral system and weaker censorship leave the central message garbled. China's syndrome is better entrenched and more scrupulously imposed, but in 2012 the cracks were also widening there. Revelations about leadership misconduct and internal struggles in the political succession process undermined acceptance of the top-down national identity. China's rising assertiveness added to identity intensity, while exposing fallacies in identity claims. These developments suggest that the CGP (T1) NIS will be seriously tested, despite more pressure to keep it a bulwark of regime legitimacy.

In 2013, both Chinese and Russian leaders were driven by the goal of intensifying national identity and widening the gap with a rival. Mass arousal served as a desired tonic against growing cynicism. It was deemed effective in isolating those who advocated an identity based on the international community, as diversity was becoming less tolerated. Memories of the loss of control over national identity in the 1980s remained a powerful inducement to keep a tight grip on the reins of control and preempt any challenges to the public on television, the Internet, and academic outlets. Identity gap widening had to be tempered in comparison with the Cold War era, given the different economic strategy and the greater prospects of widening the divide between the United States and its allies. Yet the legacy of polarization retained a strong hold on the thinking of policymakers.

In China, the national identity message is more insistent. The scales have tipped more decisively against alternative approaches. Multipolarity was more a transitional convenience than a lasting focus. There is less ambiguity about the desirability of an international community and, even more, about the question of whether China belongs to the West. Although Russians fretted over Eurasianism as a regional identity, realizing that this does not get a lot of traction when Belarus and Kazakhstan are the primary partners, the Chinese only pretended that "Eastern civilization" is something more than Sinocentrism. The Chinese Communist Party is veering toward a renewal of the bipolar ideological struggle, employing civilizational themes to replace citations from communist luminaries. And Russia's leaders are soon likely to face a crossroads that will test their illusions about straddling East and West. The CGP (T1) NIS parallels provided a strong stimulus for closer Sino-Russian relations, but differences in assertive identity are bound to test relations more seriously in the coming years even, as they raise the possibility that these states are entering a new (T2) transition.

PART II

SINO-RUSSIAN BILATERAL RELATIONS, THEIR IDENTITY GAP, AND EAST VERSUS WEST

CHAPTER 6

THE PROLONGATION OF THE SINO-SOVIET
SPLIT IN THE 1970s AND 1980s

In the 1950s, Sino-Soviet relations were framed through fraternal communist identities, with ideology in the forefront. Then, for the next
quarter century, the schism between these two countries was explained
as an ideological dispute, again focusing on national identities. Even in
the struggle for normalization of Sino-Soviet relations at the end of
the 1980s, identity issues kept complicating the pragmatic pursuit of
national interests. This history is not peripheral to later times. To understand Sino-Russian relations over the past two decades, it is important
to look back to the prior decades, recalling the mutual perceptions and
identity gap between Moscow and Beijing. The record of identity consensus for one decade, identity schism for a quarter century, and identity
overlap for the past two decades is interrupted by a decade of identity
confusion slowing cooperation after a decade of delay in overcoming
the schism. It is this prolongation of the split and then the confusion in
overcoming it that draws our attention.

The Sino-Soviet schism in the international communist movement
proved to be a momentous force in changing the history of communism and transforming the course of the Cold War. It has been studied
for its causes and consequences, mainly in terms of ideological analysis and theories of international relations. Here I take a different perspective, still concerned with both causes and consequences while also
applying a long-term identity framework connecting the periods of

alliance, split, and normalization of relations as background for assessing the post–Cold War relations. This shifting relationship opens a window on identity-driven changes.

The causes of the Sino-Soviet dispute include divergent security interests—peaceful coexistence for the goal of post-Stalin modernization diverged from Mao's revolutionary sponsorship on behalf of the spread of communism across Asia—but these differences, in large degree, reflected a rapidly widening Sino-Soviet national identity gap. Mao was consumed with the totalitarianism that engulfed China in the Great Leap Forward and, after several years of hesitation, the Cultural Revolution. In contrast, Khrushchev was obsessed with overcoming the legacy of Stalin's rampage of totalitarianism while preparing for long-term competition with the United States in the nuclear age. Even Brezhnev, after jettisoning de-Stalinization, perpetuated an approach that failed to narrow the national identity gap with China, which, after all, had kept resorting to extreme rhetoric in widening it.

The vitriolic rhetoric spewing from both sides of the Sino-Soviet dispute for nearly a quarter century bears witness to the intensity of the national identity gap between China and the Soviet Union. Given the nature of their communist great power identities, the two claimants to leadership in the international movement were unrestrained in how they demonized each other. Viewed through the six dimensions of national identity, the rhetoric they used to attack one another appears in a fresh light and is amenable to comparisons with later thinking.

The chronological coverage of identity gaps in this chapter begins with brief sections on the periods before 1949, the 1950s, and the 1960s and 1970s. Detailed analyses of dimensions of identity follow for the 1980s. The identity gap changed abruptly—from two distant neighbors, to Russian intervention claiming a special status, to competing sponsorship of revolutionary forces. Then the time of greatest national identity overlap gave way to the era of the most single-minded mutual assaults. Intensive assessments are reserved for the decade when both the struggle to normalize ties and domestic reform initiatives elicited unprecedented, but temporary, ambivalence about their identity gap.

THE SINO-RUSSIAN NATIONAL IDENTITY GAP BEFORE 1949

Russian interactions with China from 1600 to 1800 brought two contrasting views of international relations to the fore. China relied on the
tribute system (a hierarchical order with China at the center, surrounded
by dependent, tributary states) while perceiving a split between civilization and barbarism. Russia at least paid lip service to the Western view
of discrete and equal states. The two sides reached a degree of accommodation through the Treaty of Nerchinsk in 1689 setting borders, the
Kyakhta Treaty of 1727 permitting commerce, and, at about the same
time, the establishment of an ecclesiastical mission in Beijing.[1] This did
not, however, mean that real progress was made in mutual understanding.

From the mid-1600s to the mid-1800s, the identity gap between
China and Russia lacked intensity, but it was growing. On the Chinese
side, Russia was the first of the European states to draw scrutiny by sta-
tioning troops near its borders and succeeding in establishing a mission
and border-trading outpost. This did not count for a lot, just another civilizational inferior on the northern frontier, even if it garnered
special notice. Accustomed to looking down on Asians and peering
through the prism of a few centuries of easy expansion to the east,
the Russian side also understood that the immensity of China and its
dominant place in Asia made it special. Links to China gave Russia a
distinct status as "Europe in Asia," a kind of representative of a superior
civilization claiming to reject the imperialist approach. In a sense, each
side acted as a bridge between civilizations, but neither country took
the other's civilization very seriously when contacts were meager and
failed to dent the narrowly Sinocentric thinking of the Chinese and the
Eurocentric worldview of the Russians.

The Sino-Russian identity gap was transformed after the Opium
War and the Crimean War. Russia grew anxious about its international
status, losing ground to the south as it realized that it was no longer militarily or economically competitive with the other European
powers, and fearing encroachment from the east as others gained a
foothold with the possibility of carving up the "Chinese melon" and
advancing to Japan and Korea. The door was open to conceptualizing

Sino-Russian relations in different ways that would raise confidence in Russian identity. More gradually, the Chinese came to see Russia differently in the hope of capitalizing on rivalries among the powers. Mostly on the Russian side, there were discussions about a special bond between the two nations—and thus a way to change Russia's horizontal identity.[2] Neither side had much interest in the other as a force for transforming other types of identity.

Relations were nurtured by pretense. Russia disguised "its ongoing strategy of stripping away China's northern frontiers" in the narrative of a "disinterested mediator and magnanimous benefactor of China."[3] It saw its mission as civilizing, as Russians fell prey to a belief that the Chinese were grateful for their special friendship. At the same time, the Chinese did not reflect on their own history of imperial expansion, as they began to construct myths of sovereignty, which would gain intensity, as well as to take the path of only blaming humiliation by outsiders instead of internal weakness. Associating Russia with the enlightened West, Westernizers expected to help China become civilized, while Slavophiles suggested ways for Russia to team with China in asserting a non-Western identity.[4] China became a factor in Russian identity discussions; and later, the Soviet Union became a much greater force in Chinese identity struggles.

Starting in 1917, communist identity entered the narrative of bilateral relations. The contrast between the Soviet Union and the capitalist countries raised the stakes in identity discourse. Similarly, sponsorship of the international communist movement refocused Soviet thinking about China, even making it the prime target in spreading the revolution. Despite contentious relations with the Guomindang regime, locked in struggle with the Chinese Communist Party, the Soviet Union drew attention as an organizational model and even as a possible model for modernization, as a latecomer. It pursued a policy of self-interest (e.g., in Mongolia), while establishing a reputation of supporting China, including renouncing extraterritoriality. Even if specific policies failed, the language of anti-imperialism had an effect.[5] Although the Soviet Union's policies were not consistently admired, its advisers earnestly opposed imperialism.[6] Its identity significance rose considerably as a model for China's vertical identity and as a growing factor in its horizontal identity, notably as Moscow opposed Tokyo's encroachments and, starting in 1945, when a victorious Moscow became deeply entwined in China's civil war on the side of Chinese communists anxious for a model to confirm their success.

John Garver explores the intersection of Soviet nationalism with that of the Guomindang and Chinese communists during the period 1937–45. First, Mao Zedong broke the bonds of Soviet control over his party, disagreeing mostly on the class makeup of the revolutionary movement that would achieve victory in China. Then, at a time of Soviet preoccupation with the war against Germany, Mao emancipated his party from Moscow, despite praising it and counting on its support. He "turned Stalinism against Stalin," starting the Sinification of Marxism and anticipating China's leadership role.[7]

With China's communists mounting a serious challenge for power, Stalin was faced with uncertainty about the impact on monolithic socialist identity, notably in Asia. Disregard for his puppets and success for Mao's forces called into question not only Stalin's formula for revolutionary movements but also Soviet claims for how the march to socialism must proceed, combining class struggle and anti-imperialist appeals. However, when Mao's party celebrated victory in 1949, the differences were muted.

THE SINO-SOVIET NATIONAL IDENTITY GAP IN THE 1950s

Although, at times, Mao put a Chinese gloss on the meaning of building socialism or changing the timetable from the Soviet model, he set China on a course from 1949 to 1957 of emulating the Soviet Union and greatly reducing the national identity gap with it. The path to communism was deemed scientific and unilinear, proven by the Soviet successes and available for the Chinese to study and follow closely. Dismissing the past as backward and irrelevant, the Chinese leaders heralded a rosy future, taking Stalin as its seer. If in the background disputes arose over assistance, infringement on Chinese sovereignty, and prioritizing Taiwan, they were not allowed to cloud the image of a single socialist bloc led by the Soviet Union with a unified ideology and set of goals.

Josef Stalin tested Mao on his acceptance of Soviet leadership and the socialist bloc. In the Korean War, the decisions to approve the North Korean attack and later to rescue it by entering the war proved China's loyalty and identity.[8] And when in great need during the first years of the People's Republic of China, Mao leaned one-sidedly toward the Soviet Union. But growing confidence and the change of leadership after Stalin's death gave him more leverage in pursuing equality.

Whatever the degree of personal distrust between leaders and restricted access to each other's society, a remarkable consensus was projected vis-à-vis all dimensions of identity. China was depicted as following in the footsteps of its "elder brother," forging the same class-less society through the same campaigns of transformation. The nation's past cultural identity was dismissed as just a relic, soon to disappear. Solidarity in opposition to states in the capitalist bloc meant a shared horizontal identity. The precommunist past no longer had identity significance except for rebellions, and Soviet assistance to the revolution in China was credited as the sole salient and positive aspect of shared temporal identity.

In the years 1956–57, there were stirrings of division. Nikita Khrushchev's de-Stalinization speech drew a veiled rebuke. When Mao visited Moscow in late 1957 and Khrushchev visited Beijing in the fall of 1959, differences over peaceful transition and peaceful coexistence were growing, as each side focused on how it would accelerate its march toward communism. China insisted that the East wind now prevails over the West wind, justifying assertive moves, including its own toward Taiwan, and its intensified struggle at home to overcome class differences. In contrast, the Soviet Union conceived of a more harmonious society advancing to the next stage and peaceful competition with the United States that would increasingly give it the edge while benefiting from trade as it normalized its society. As ideological claims diverged, differences were aired indirectly, with little acknowledgment of the phenomenon of a widening national identity gap. Each leadership reinterpreted ideology for initiatives at home as mutual suspicions deepened. Yet when the split came into the open, the pretense persisted of fraternal relations in accord with a shared ideological blueprint. In 1960, each nation claimed to be loyal to Leninism, even as the identity gap intensified.[9]

Mao was hesitant to raise identity concerns in light of Stalin's seniority, but after Stalin's death the horizontal dimension gained salience. A subordinate role in the world revolution and deference in managing ties to Moscow were problematic before the de-Stalinization speech that attacked the cult of personality, drawing the vertical and ideological dimensions into the picture. Mao's Great Leap Forward was a defiant response, and in the course of 1958 sovereignty was at stake following Soviet proposals for a listening post and submarine base on Chinese soil. Attacking Soviet revisionism put the spotlight on ideology and the vertical dimension, while later adding the charge of social imperialism invoked the horizontal dimension.[10] As the dispute started, claims to ideological superiority, including having the better and faster way to communism, were deemed the path to Mao's success domestically and in the struggle within the international communist movement.[11] A mixture of identity concerns figured into the relationship, but ideology had become the focus.

Ted Hopf explains the split in national identity as a more developed Soviet society shedding the outdated "new Soviet man" in order to address real problems and allow for the privatization of life, while greater Stalinization of Chinese society meant more repression and mobilization from above.[12] The two societies were out of phase, as repressed identity themes in the Soviet Union bubbled to the surface. Hopf adds that the Sino-Soviet compact reached in 1949 was premised on a hierarchical order, with Stalin accepting China as a subordinate vanguard championing colonial revolutions, while showing leniency to its underdevelopment as it followed in the evolutionary path blazed by his country. Khrushchev showed more sensitivity, agreeing to double billing with China in leadership of the socialist camp, but his tolerance was tested in 1956. The pretense of a narrow identity gap could not survive anger at the rejection by China when the Soviets pulled rank, and Soviet intolerance of China's response. It was not long before each country strove to outdo the other in proving its vanguard status in what was then called the Third World, as the Soviets no longer saw China filling a subordinate role.

In the heyday of traditional communism, sectoral identity reached a feverish pitch. First, the Soviet Union, and then China, claimed to be a beacon for the world—politically, on the path to communism; economically, in forging a system free of the waste of market competition with all of the advantages of state planning; and culturally, unburdened by the weight of social class divisions. Grandiose claims piled one on the other, as Mao shifted from advancing a distinct path in the Great Leap Forward to assailing Soviet revisionism as taking the wrong path. The indirect mutual criticism at the start of the 1960s gave way to scathing mutual assaults.

THE SINO-SOVIET NATIONAL IDENTITY GAP IN THE 1960s AND 1970s

The Sino-Soviet dispute in the period 1961–70 was high in invectives, notably mutual accusations in 1963–64, which fundamentally questioned each other's ideological credentials. During the Cultural Revolution, writings on both sides were rare. In China, excluding Mao's "Red Book," there were extremist slogans about Soviet revisionism with little evidence to support them, and in the early Brezhnev period Soviet accusations against China were perfunctory, suggesting hope for a turnabout in relations and uncertainty on how to deal with China's chaos and also the shift in Soviet identity after the confusion of the Khrushchev period. This was a period of real differences over the organization of society and foreign policy toward the United States and the Third World, but ideology overshadowed other types of discourse. Once national identity intensifies to the point where ideology is deemed to be scientific truth that only top leaders can decide, the race accelerates to prove one's greater purity.

Lorenz Lüthi has delved into the ideological causes of the Sino-Soviet split. In 1958, Mao chose an alternative model of socioeconomic development, challenging Moscow on the vertical dimension as well as in ideology. Adding anti-imperialism as a theme, Mao exacerbated the split over ideology. Because Mao was more fixated on national identity than Soviet leaders and was facing a greater divide among Chinese Communist Party leaders, he found more benefit in pressing ideological differences while widening the gap with the supposed leader of world socialism. He put other leaders in China on the defensive, winning a following in international movements inclined to extreme positions.[13] Having driven China into a wide-ranging crisis by 1961, Mao capitalized on the frustrations with simplistic answers linked to identity concerns that others found difficult to refute in public. Much more than the Soviet leadership, Mao saw a need to widen the national identity gap for his personal authority and national pride. The linkages were crucial: for conducting domestic purges, mobilizing the Chinese people, and congealing an uncompromising narrative of a national identity that put China fully in the forefront.[14]

Driven by identity, Mao gave little stock to national interests as he deepened the struggle against the Soviet Union and its model of socialism in the first half of the 1960s. Mikhail Suslov led an identity-ridden response on the Soviet side that left no room for compromise.[15] Although right after Khrushchev's fall there were signs of a more pragmatic Soviet outlook, those were not reciprocated, as Mao focused on domestic and international reasons to intensify identity themes, while Leonid Brezhnev perceived a threat to Soviet status in international communism, resuming polemics. The 1969 military battle on a border island led to intensified Soviet denunciations.

Chinese and Soviet national identities were being transformed in the 1950s. What was recognized as an ideological struggle starting at the end of the decade was not only about different interpretations of ideological doctrine; it was also assertiveness about Russian culture, regaining ground in a post–socialist realism atmosphere, and, on the Chinese side, about reclaiming distinctiveness after a backlash against the cavalier imposition of the Soviet model of socialism. Neither side characterized the struggle in this manner, but they began to blame the other side's culture for its deviation from socialism. Difficulty in resolving the split increased due to an emphasis on civilizational themes as if they were ideological ones.

China demanded equality in relations and in defining socialism. In 1960, Foreign Minister Chen Yi said, "Soviet Communism has bloomed a Soviet flower and Chinese Communism a Chinese one. Both are equally Communism."[16] After policies had deviated from the Soviet model, identity was more clearly declared to have a Chinese component.

The Sino-Soviet dispute reflected the Russification of the Soviet Union with de-Stalinization, and the Sinification of China as the initial borrowing of the Soviet model was concluding. It proved convenient to cite ideological differences, which mattered, and for China to highlight its grievances over the border. Yet these were secondary to Mao's confidence that "thought reform" following ideals long present in Chinese history about moral education would yield superior results. His trust in Chinese civilization and distrust of Russian civilization contributed to a breakdown in relations. Perceiving a loss of belief in Soviet communism, he was determined to boost political loyalty in China. Even if he failed in the antirightist campaign and again in the socialist education movement and Cultural Revolution, this imperative did not disappear. In the 1990s, Chinese leaders were again obsessed with this goal. Although, in the 1970s, Soviet leaders seemed to give priority to upbringing (*vospitanie*), China's leaders took this aim more seriously, adapting their methods from period to period.

For the Chinese, because Moscow was part of the West, they saw it as selling out communism, accepting Western humanist culture and retaining imperialist thinking, as in tsarist times. Even Stalin had not shed this thinking in how he dealt with China. Opposing peaceful coexistence was not just a strategic choice for China, which prioritized the recovery of Taiwan and the export of revolution. It was also a rejection of the cultural drift of Soviet reform thinking, as seen in the thaw literature and the criteria for de-Stalinization. Siding with the Third World might spark anti-imperialist revolutions beyond national liberation struggles and link Western civilization to imperialism.

Sergey Radchenko weighs international relations heavily in examining the course of the Sino-Soviet dispute throughout the 1960s.

Although the Chinese were no less guilty than the Soviets in widening the ideological gap, the Soviets were more at fault in failing to accept Chinese equality.[17] After a Chinese attack on the Soviet Embassy in the heat of the Cultural Revolution, and then the Soviet invasion of Czechoslovakia in August 1968 under what China saw as a theory of "limited sovereignty," China's critique of "social imperialism" intensified.[18] The Brezhnev Doctrine, articulated in the repression of Czech reform, deepened the divide over relations within the socialist bloc. Failure to coordinate in defining the strategic triangle with the United States and Asianism, covering from India to Japan, also complicated relations, as these issues were interpreted in identity terms—tacked on, respectively, to Soviet revisionism and Han chauvinism.

In the 1960s, China strove to seize the ideological mantle of anti-imperialism from the Soviet Union. Even after its rapprochement with the United States, it clung to this ambition, raising the profile of the Third World and putting itself at its center. When this was accompanied by attacks on the Soviet betrayal entailed by "peaceful coexistence," which meant cooperating with the United States, it had more credibility than after China's closer bond with the archimperialist country was forged starting in 1971. This handed the ideological advantage to the Soviet side, even as the Chinese redoubled their attacks on the legacy of tsarist imperialism. Yet when China sought to identify more closely with the developing world in the mid-1970s, it benefited from a narrower identity gap with the United States, Japan, and other countries, above all on the horizontal dimension.

China's rapprochement with the United States and Brezhnev's call, starting with the commemoration of Vladimir Lenin's 100th birthday in 1970, for a stronger identity message, intensified attacks on each other's heresy. Although Chinese writings on the Soviet Union remained sparse during the barren years through 1976, the role of foreign policy was growing in appeals to the United States, Japan, and others to be more vigilant in opposing the Soviet menace. Meanwhile, a spate of publications by Soviet authors cast China in a more damning role for its collusion with imperialism and its cultural legacy that had deformed the building of socialism. Despite a brief pause in Soviet invectives, Mao's death did not improve matters. It was not until the end of 1979 that Chinese sources dropped the label "revisionism," but the Soviet authorities pretended that Maoism still existed as late as mid-1982. The identity gap no longer depended as much on ideology, but it was slow to narrow. In the years 1978–79, Vietnam's invasion of Cambodia was followed by China's attack on Vietnam, and then the Soviet invasion of Afghanistan set back preparations for bilateral talks. As each side accused the other of seeking hegemony in Asia, they failed to build a basis for trust.

With ideology still coloring mutual perceptions, Moscow and Beijing stressed their differences over revisionism and imperialism, which proved to be short-lived. Their gap over the vertical dimension appeared serious until it was recognized as paling before the gap each side had with Washington and others in the West. Moreover, the gap over the horizontal dimension rested on China's perception of a Soviet threat and a containment strategy in Asia, which was reinterpreted as early as 1982 into three specific obstacles: the Soviets in Afghanistan; Soviet support for Vietnam's presence in Cambodia; and the Soviet military buildup in the north, including in Mongolia. Reforms made the notion of "revisionism" laughable. A shift in 1982 to an "equidistant" policy toward the two superpowers took the identity component from foreign policy. Above all, Deng Xiaoping claimed to eschew ideology in an appeal to pragmatism.

DIMENSIONS OF THE SINO-SOVIET NATIONAL IDENTITY GAP IN THE 1980s

The identity gap in the 1980s narrowed much faster than the normalization of relations occurred. There was a hangover effect from the extreme rhetoric in the prior period. Immediate national interests in China focusing on expanded economic ties with capitalist countries took priority over new national identity thinking. Most serious may have been the presence in the Soviet leadership of hard-liners obsessed with the demonization of China, who censored those who took a different stance and starting in 1982, when both states agreed to stop criticizing each other, prevented candid coverage of China's domestic and foreign policies. Even starting in 1986, after Mikhail Gorbachev had ousted the leader of this group and launched reforms that should have brought the two states much closer, closing the identity gap proved complicated. Now China grew cautious, fearing the thrust of these reforms, while the Soviets made the West the priority, given both immediate national interests and divisions on national identity.

The guardians of the wide identity gap with Beijing kept their influence until 1986, delaying initiatives that could have speeded the course of normalization at a time when its implications for identity would have been far different than they were in the years 1987–89.[19] Alexander Lukin describes the Rakhmanin group in charge of Soviet China policy as insistent that Maoist ideology was a type of anticommunism, impeding the development of relations as well as reinforcing narrow interests of the military–industrial complex. Yet he also points to the struggle by a nonconformist group of Chinese experts intent on changing Soviet identity and ready to demonize China to that end but also refocused on improving relations with China once they recognized the impact of Chinese reforms. The former group strove to keep the identity gap wide, while the latter group became vocal advocates after 1986 of narrowing the gap.[20] As Gorbachev's rhetoric and reforms alienated many in the political and academic elite, others went further in seeing an identity overlap with China as the best means to resist his embrace of the West. This complex struggle over China's place in the identity pantheon left policy directionless, as priority went to the West.

The Ideological Dimension

China was quicker to downplay ideology, in 1979–81 eschewing the term revisionism, while Soviet disappointment at Deng's early policies led to the new, pejorative label "Maoism without Mao." As Deng moved away from ideology in the forefront, Soviet critics argued that it was still there, serving their own gap-widening agenda. Yet they also gave considerable weight to the horizontal dimension, while warning that China was drawing closer to the United States and stressing China's failure to appreciate its historical bonds with the Soviet Union that had been useful to economic development in the 1950s and to the victory of the Chinese Communist Party.[21] Chinese writings on the Soviet Union had become more objective in the early 1980s, with reluctance to frame issues in identity terms, except for a tendency to find more positive images of the Soviet Union in an effort to salvage socialism in line with Deng's "four cardinal principles" and some residue of criticisms of foreign policy still linked to identity.

At the end of 1980, coverage of "Soviet social imperialism" called it "budding imperialism more desperate, adventurous, and deceptive than the imperialism of the old school," and Deng called foreign policy and the attempt to put China under Soviet control the main reason for the split two decades earlier.[22] Yet there was so much reversal of prior criticisms, including charges against "peaceful coexistence," that the identity gap was closing rapidly. Still, in 1981 charges of "militarism, hegemonism, and expansionism" negated the grudging recognition of socialism, which was accompanied by numerous denials that Soviet policies were effective, serving the goal of showing that China must also move away from them.[23] The tone changed, however, by the end of the year, proving that gap narrowing served multiple goals for China's vertical and horizontal identity, as the strategic triangle framework was gaining ground. With criticism of foreign policy being the main identity gap as China was shifting in the second half of 1982 to equidistance, the gap with the Soviet Union had narrowed to that with the United States, while on other dimensions tensions with the latter were expanding. In the years 1983–85, Chinese sources hinted that a narrow identity gap was within reach without receiving encouragement from the other side, where leadership instability made policy initiatives difficult before Gorbachev's ascent.[24]

After Mao's death in 1976, uncertainty about China's direction led to a reenergized campaign against the Soviet Union. Power holders who feared that their worldview would be challenged by reaffirmation of the Soviet model led the charge. Similarly, after Brezhnev's death in 1982, leadership flux in the Soviet Union gave those anxious about overtures to China as well as reform that could echo China's moves reason to resist positive coverage. Although the implications for domestic policy and power mattered, the thrust of criticism was turning to the other side's threat to world peace. Still, it was important when the Chinese started recognizing that no Soviet attack was being contemplated and when the Soviets could affirm that China's improved relations with the United States did not signify any interest in joining the imperialist camp. Both sides cleared up these mixed messages by 1985, giving Gorbachev a freer hand.

If anti-imperialism is the priority in national identity, then Mao and Stalin are treated as deserving of more praise than condemnation. If the most serious threat to the political elite is deemed to be reformers susceptible to sympathy for the West, then the external and internal identity challenges are closely linked. By 1980, China's leadership, despite sharp divisions, felt secure against the threat from the far left, as they agreed to protect Mao's mostly positive image. To do otherwise, as they agreed in 1956–57 when Stalin's image was in question, would sow confusion that could be used by the West. Indeed, given that Mao was in effect Lenin and Stalin combined, the damage to the Chinese Communist Party would be greater. This held potential to draw China and the Soviet Union closer, but the Soviets were slow to realize it and Gorbachev's shift in direction widened the gap, as China's leaders purged ideological reformers.

The Chinese strove to narrow the identity gap with the Soviet Union in the years 1982–88, getting mutual recognition that each country was socialist and that more flexible approaches to ideology and foreign policy were not a barrier to a shared identity. This meant strongly affirming that capitalism would not replace socialism in China, that anti-imperialism remained the main outlook on history, and that China still regarded Lenin as an oracle.[25] With Gorbachev's reforms, this effort intensified. On the Soviet side, Gorbachev's Vladivostok speech in 1986 accepted diversity in social systems and called for economic cooperation without regard to the split between socialism and capitalism, while downplaying the role of ideology in pursuit of the world community's common agenda. Defenders of past foreign policy were making room for new initiatives to China and blaming the United States for continuing its anti-Soviet policies while crediting China with

227

resisting "strategic collaboration" in favor of an independent foreign policy. If normalization still was proving complicated, the impression was spreading that Moscow and Beijing agreed on foreign policy issues such as North Korea, regarded each other as socialist, and were making progress on bilateral issues that would give a big boost to relations.[26] The identity gap was closing.

The ideological gap mattered greatly when Brezhnev and Mao were adamant on a single model of socialism and poised to pounce on any heretical interpretation. When Deng downgraded ideology, recognizing multiple types of socialism still at its early stage, and then Gorbachev renounced past ideology in more sweeping terms, there appeared to be no basis for a further ideological gap. Already at the start of the 1980s, Chinese sources had criticized the rigidity of Soviet ideology, praising every sign of more flexibility and no longer treating ideological differences as a basis for an identity gap. Yet this was deceptive, as was seen after Gorbachev took a much more critical stance toward ideology, renouncing so much of it that internally, at least, China's leaders resumed criticism of Soviet ideology. The trend line was as follows: During the period 1960–79, the ideological gap was huge; in 1980–85, the Chinese side downplayed this gap more; and in 1986–91, the Soviets downplayed the gap more. For a brief time in the mid-1980s, the two sides came close to relegating the dimension that had most troubled bilateral relations to insignificance. Indeed, there were even prospects of ideological overlap jump-starting relations, but they vacillated through 1991 with no breakthrough.

The Temporal, Sectoral, and Vertical Dimensions

China's narrowing identity gap with the Soviet Union in the first half of the 1980s contrasted with the meager attention given to China by the Soviets. An agreement to stop criticizing each other except on foreign policy did not lead to publications on China's merits or even a proper debate; the below-the-surface clash of opinions that had grown more heated and begun to come into the open was actually stifled, as China's own debate through internal circulation (*neibu*) sources intensified.[27]

Ideological differences narrowed as China pressed ahead with a controlled debate that until the mid-1980s denied reform interpretations regarding Khrushchev's positive role or Stalin's repressive purges, and then for a time seemed to parallel Gorbachev's early rethinking. The temporal dimension gap narrowed, too, as when the Chinese expressed gratitude toward the Soviet Union on the sixty-fifth anniversary of the 1917 Revolution and the endless spats over the history of party-to-party relations were stopped. In the Cold War, blame was shifting to the United States, unlike in the 1970s. As to the sectoral dimension, political identity as socialist states was closer, while cultural identity overlapped as the Chinese identified Marxism-Leninism as the core of "socialist spiritual civilization." Vertical identity depended on the balance of power in China between the conservatives, who pressed a campaign in late 1983 to early 1984, and the reformers, but the gap narrowed sharply and then even more so with Gorbachev's turn to decentralization in many of his reforms, echoing some reforms that Deng had launched.

Although Deng cautioned against open attacks on Gorbachev, China's leaders were alarmed starting in 1987, managed his visit in May 1989 to lessen the contagion of Soviet-style reforms, and stigmatized his moves from that fall as "ripping out the old tree by the roots and seeking to plant a new one in its place." [28] Despite the normalization of relations, the identity (and ideology) gap was widening again in the period 1987–92 after closing sharply.

The narrowing of the gap that had occurred on both sides was due to forces that would later be more consequential. *Pravda*'s growing enthusiasm for Deng Xiaoping was a sign that just as Gorbachev had gained the support of some Chinese reformers, who would soon be marginalized, Deng stood as the anti-Gorbachev by mid-1988 for some Russian conservatives, who would gain ground in the Yeltsin era. It was reported that Deng warned that socialism with poverty would be quiet about its merits, but in the middle of the next century, after modernization, it would be able to raise its full voice in speaking of the superiority of socialism over capitalism. Deng had opposed Mao's "barracks communism," as had the Soviet leaders. His reforms, after further consideration by many in Russia, were welcome news.

Another barrier between Beijing and Moscow is that as they turned sharply to the West to boost their economies, cultural national identity and the horizontal dimension figured very differently in their responses. Leaders in one case stressed the cultural identity that Mao had denigrated, albeit obliquely heralding "modernization with Chinese characteristics" and "socialist spiritual civilization" as they struggled to limit the penetration of Western culture into national identity. In the other case, they did not treat Western civilization as distant but built on Stalin's acceptance of Russian cultural traditions, taking pride in them as the embodiment of the Enlightenment. In the years 1987–89, when Chinese reform was at its apex, there was a further crackdown on the notion that early Marx was a humanist and that comparative communism shows the way to convergence with the West, at the very time Gorbachev was encouraging this line of thinking.[29] Looking back, the Soviets saw Khrushchev's "thaw" as a model in need of more vigorous support for jolting the country into this sort of convergence, while China's leaders saw Mao's "Cultural Revolution" as a negative lesson of how chaos can result from hasty tampering with ideology, making it easier to avoid the sort of convergence thinking espoused by Gorbachev. Above all, different views of the West and the ability to fall back on Chinese cultural and political identity divided the two nations.

In the 1960s and 1970s, communist identity obsessions fractured an alliance that in the 1950s had been steeped in identity collusion. In the 1980s, the two sides were slow to appreciate the potential for the resuscitation of their identity-driven partnership. The Soviet gerontocracy repulsed reform thinking that would have narrowed the identity gap rapidly before Gorbachev reimagined national identity in a manner that left China on the sidelines. In turn, China's revulsion at Gorbachev, and initially also at Boris Yeltsin, focused on the identity chaos that these two leaders wrought from 1986 to 1993. The inertia of the identity gap that was apparent from the mid-1950s survived until the mid-1990s. Yet a narrow gap was long within reach before the breakthrough in 1996, which Putin solidified in stages during his terms as president starting in 2000.

China and Russia were unable to agree on the stages of building socialism or transcending it with communism. Later, they struggled to agree on the character of dismantling communism, but that stopped being a national identity concern by the mid-1990s. Missing the chance to find a consensus on the nature of reform socialism, which both were striving to define by the mid-1980s, they recuperated after a decade by agreeing on the threat of Western ideology to states steeped in socialist thinking about the predominance of the state and the necessity to shape values that would be resistant to universal ones. In the period 1979–82, they overcame such ideological attacks as "Soviet revisionism" and "Maoism without Mao." By the 2000s, they had generally agreed on why the Soviet Union had collapsed, sharing ideas about how to avoid a repeat result for their regime. Whereas they had alternated in praising and vilifying each other up to the early 1990s, they now became convinced of the necessity of showing respect to one another without going to extremes again. The backlash from the split left a strong impetus.

The collapse of the Soviet Union prevented China and Russia from realizing the full fruits of their normalization. They had the potential for a closer partnership, which was not realized due to developments on the Soviet side and the impact of the United States. A review of Chinese explanations for the collapse of the Soviet Union is instructive on what might have been. Foreign enemies plotted against it, using the arms race, economic restrictions, and culture (peaceful evolution). Stalin's one-sided heavy industrialization, however much it succeeded in constructing a rich, strong socialist country that could serve as a base for world revolution, failed to address domestic imbalances—neglect of agriculture, for example. Khrushchev set the country on the wrong track with his handling of Stalin's legacy and his lack of vigilance, as in shifting toward the "whole people's party," which polluted the thinking of an entire generation. Failure to reform and the stultification of theory lasted for decades. Failure to rely on markets and to give firms the authority to respond to them proved harmful. The quest for hegemonism and overemphasis on military power were other causes. The mishandling of ethnic relations, denying "equality," was a critical problem, but what was decisive was Gorbachev's abandonment of Marxism and leadership of the Communist Party in favor of "humanistic, democratic socialism."[30] This grab bag of causes filled the vacuum in 1992 as the Chinese groped for a deeper analysis. Yet over the next twenty years, as varied studies appeared, the initial line of reasoning remained foremost.

Attempts to reassert socialism and also to rethink it proved sporadic and inconclusive in the 1980s. The Chinese leadership's stale invocation of struggle against "counterrevolutionaries" and between "socialism and capitalism" while internal sources were railing against Gorbachev's betrayal of socialism seemed out of touch. What was clear was that the drift of the 1980s as well as the Soviet transformation convinced the Chinese leaders to reaffirm the "centrality of the ideological question in Chinese politics," in line with Chinese tradition's "emphasis on the primacy of ideas."[31] While flailing away at the growing market economy as ideologically offensive offended Deng, leading him to close this line of narrative, a way arose to repackage ideology as a multidimensional affirmation of China's uniqueness. With Russia as a negative example, albeit not one to be criticized directly, by the time of the Fourteenth Party Congress in 1992 the Chinese leadership had settled on a broader strategy for combining political education, patriotism, anti-Westernization, and other ideas that were complementary to the evolving interpretation of the "socialism with Chinese characteristics" that they were still developing. This national identity would not be used to widen the gap with Russia; rather, it would narrow the gap, given the predisposition of much of the Russian elite to similar ways of thinking. At the time of the nadir in the two nations' relations, when the identity gap appeared to be the greatest, the potential arose for a far-reaching identity consensus.

If ideology failed to bind Moscow and Beijing from the 1960s to the 1980s, and no longer appeared to be a force after the collapse of the Soviet Union, shared reasoning about the vertical dimension of national identity filled much of the vacuum. In the 1980s, it was difficult to make this connection, and from the end of the decade this dimension served as a force for stunting normalization. China did not trust how Gorbachev and Yeltsin were treating the legacy of party and state power, and the Russian leaders distanced themselves from China's repression after June 4, 1989. However, as the Chinese began to perceive that Russia was rebuilding state authority and the crux of its Soviet legacy in opposition to Western pressure for democratization and human rights, and that many among Russia's elites admired China's social order and resistance to the Western model, the decisive role of the vertical dimension abruptly narrowed the identity gap and once again became a glue uniting the two countries.

The Horizontal Dimension

The view that the Soviet Union was more dangerous than the United States remained until the late 1970s, and then changed rapidly early in the 1980s. It was based on threat perceptions, but also on identity vulnerability. However, as ideology diminished and international relations rose in calculations of identity, the danger from the West surged to the center, while the urgency of preserving socialism put a positive spin on finding merit in Soviet achievements. For reformers and orthodox thinkers alike, Soviet superiority to China in the arts and living standards, among other fields, was proof that China could use socialism to gain ground. In a critical transitional era, this was a welcome message.[32] But as the Soviet image in foreign policy relative to that of the United States improved, ironically its image as a model was deteriorating. The comparative study of economic systems, education, and other practical concerns led to an emphasis on "reform socialism," which was in short supply in the Soviet Union in the first half of the 1980s.

Even the one source of a lingering serious gap, the horizontal dimension, was changing. Although the United States and Japan were vitally needed economically by China, their images elicited more criticism. The United States' Taiwan policy violated China's sovereignty, suggesting that it was the greater danger.[33] Japan's danger of turning into a "military great power" was linked to historical transgressions far more serious than those the Soviet Union had committed. Although Soviet ties were fragile, contrasts were a plus.

Breaking with the Soviet economic model and making this a test of socialist identity started the Sino-Soviet split. Three decades later, reconsidering economic national identity and accepting the legitimacy of divergent paths of development, including the Soviet socialist one, led toward normalization.[34] Because conservatives in China were alarmed at proposed reforms and started to equate the Soviet model with socialism, this could also have produced ideological convergence, but they were often rebuffed, and then Gorbachev's reforms reopened the divide. Given the new success of China's reforms, the old model was soon seen as Soviet, not socialist.

One reason Chinese leaders were slow to rebuild Soviet ties and recognize a shared socialist identity was concern throughout much of the 1980s that this would damage the ties to the West that were necessary for "peace and development." Having, under Mao, broken the barriers to relations with the United States and Japan, China could move ahead to Deng's "open door." Being more secure that it could preserve its cultural identity, China did not worry as much that economic openness and cultural openness would remove its barriers to the West. It had more confidence in its distinct civilization.

Deng and Gorbachev stressed pragmatism limiting the ideological dimension, widening cooperation with the United States and its allies in the horizontal dimension, and downplaying economic national identity with talk of the universal applicability of market mechanisms in the sectoral dimension. As to the temporal dimension, criticism of mistakes by past communist leaders lowered the intensity of divisions that had especially plagued Sino-Soviet relations. A shared appreciation of the identity needs of reform socialism—requiring peace, incentives, and development—would appear to have been all that was needed for mutual trust.

The national identity divide between China and the Soviet Union had become confused during the Gorbachev era. In the midst of energetic normalization marked by uncertainty over just how far that might go, national identities for a time seemed to give a boost to the process. Once the term "comrade" was revived in 1985 and the Soviets agreed that no party held a monopoly on how to define socialism, the national identity gap seemed to be fading, but it actually revived as a result of ideological struggles in each country.[35] In striving to break the hold of conservatives, Gorbachev ended up sustaining the divide with China; while in narrowing the scope of reforms, Deng widened the divide with the Soviet Union. The two never managed to invoke identity as a force for normalization of relations. If they had, the process would have been prone to rapid acceleration, as was demonstrated in the mid-1990s.

Gorbachev's impact, as Elizabeth Wishnick explains, included "distinguishing between the sphere of interstate relations and the global class struggle, emphasizing cooperation between states with different social systems, and allowing for diversity in the models of socialism adopted. . . . A common stake in the reform of socialism became a new ideological stance binding the two states together."[36] Yet this shared aspiration proved insufficient, given the necessity of Gorbachev and Deng to oppose hard-line opponents of reform by turning to the West, not to socialist camaraderie.

Having criticized the Soviet Union for interference in China's internal affairs and reinforced this theme even as other criticisms were being dropped, China made the horizontal dimension the focus of the identity divide with the Soviet Union in the 1980s as it refocused on it versus the United States, which was charged in its Taiwan policy and other matters with more serious interference. Modesty regarding economic national identity, in contrast to the Mao era, was not matched with caution about the threat to cultural identity and to China's sovereign rights. This turned China's leaders away from the United States, especially as the Soviets met China's foreign policy demands.

The Sino-Soviet split was rooted in the ideological dimension of identity. Although it reverberated through the other identity dimensions, they were not the driving force. Once two leaders—Deng and Gorbachev—emerged who challenged the primacy of ideology, there was little basis for a schism. Starting in 1985, foreign policy divergence remained without the old identity divide. Given the continued national identity gap with the United States in both countries, the potential existed for a dramatic reconciliation. This failed to occur along with normalization in 1989, but the conditions for it were building. In the critical period 1985–91, the potential for gap narrowing was not realized. Gorbachev bears some of the responsibility for not making China more of a priority. But turmoil in China's leadership also is a factor, arousing suspicions of Gorbachev when conservatives were ousting Hu Yaobang. For a time at the start of 1986, enthusiasm for Gorbachev and his early interest in glasnost and political reform held promise for overlap on reform socialism, but later in 1986 and early in 1987 China's appetite to rethink identity was stifled.[37] When some revival occurred under Zhao Ziyang later in 1987 until Zhao's ouster, the controversy over an increasingly reformist Gorbachev dampened talk of Sino-Russian convergence, which was seen as threatening not only due to a widening gap over vertical identity but also because Russia's" new thinking" favored ties to the West.

Just as in the Gorbachev era the Chinese found common ground with top Soviet officials who opposed the acceleration of reforms and the turn toward the United States, in the first half of the 1980s Soviets critical of Deng had found a common language with the more conservative leaders with whom he shared power.[38] Pro-Soviet attitudes in China were unable to gain dominance for a decade until Russia shifted course in the late 1990s, while pro-Chinese attitudes in Russia remained in the minority until the collapse of the Soviet Union. Forces inclined to draw the two sides closer kept being frustrated, but after June 4, 1989, contacts revealed growing mutual understanding.

Since 1949, Moscow and Beijing have coexisted under the spell of communist ideology and its legacy. In the first phase, they found common cause, as Stalin sought to forge a state at the head of worldwide communism uncompromising to the West and Mao sought to build a socialist state with a similar global agenda. Their identity goals heavily overlapped. In the second phase, however, the primary goal for Khrushchev was to normalize his socialist state, with mobilization greatly reduced and peaceful coexistence with the United States. In contrast, Mao set his sights on deeper mobilization of his socialist state and confrontation in Asia with the United States. Identity goals overlapped less, and Mao found reason to widen the gap. With his radical socialism during the Cultural Revolution clashing with the conservative socialism of Brezhnev, there was no identity impetus to reduce the gap. National identity in the Soviet Union had become too deeply entrenched to attempt a serious reconstruction without vigorous leadership. In turn, China's primary identity gap narrowing focused elsewhere. This accounted for a drift until Gorbachev took office, when the

four-year period before normalization saw a delay caused by miscalcu-
lations on both sides. The identity gap widened again in the years of
transition to Yeltsin and Jiang Zemin before it began to narrow in 1993.

Identity remained a problem in improving relations through
1992.[39] China was disturbed by Moscow's shift toward the West and
Eurocentrism, while Soviet leaders and then Yeltsin at the outset did
not give proper weight to the rise of Asia and China's centrality there,
fixating from 1989 on its communist core. These were conditions that
raised ideological divisions, which were overcome only by a series of
assurances on equality, mutual respect, and different mutual images
that were made starting in 1992. Even more important was a narrowing gap in vertical identity as well as in horizontal identity, as
the Chinese sobered to the Soviet collapse and the Russians awoke
to the state of their troubled country, taking a fresh look at China's
identity appeal. The Soviets had misjudged China's emerging place n
the world, failing to think seriously about the rise of Asia because they
were stuck in Atlanticism or Eurocentrism, and the Chinese leaders
were so viscerally opposed to Gorbachev for embracing the West that
it took until matters settled down in the mid-1990s for them to assess
identity challenges afresh.

The Soviet Union saw itself as a peer to the United States and considered its economic national identity to be far superior to China's. Thus,
reforms prioritizing the economy did not open the door to narrowing
the identity gap with China. But as the Soviet Union's economic case
weakened and its sense of superpower equality was dashed, the identity
gap with the United States widened, while it was narrowing with China.
The lesson of the Sino-Soviet dispute and the failure to resolve it until
1989 is that any distractions from confronting U.S. power are dangerous.
From Khrushchev's call for "peaceful coexistence" to Yeltsin's Atlanticism,
it was spared coordination between Moscow and Beijing in international
relations. Obsessed with the United States once more, the two countries
became determined to avoid a repeat of this misfortune.

There is a minority perspective on the Soviet collapse, which is
consistent with a different national identity of considerable appeal for
a time but was eventually marginalized in the mainstream narrative.

If Li Shenming, the vice president of the Chinese Academy of Social Sciences, saw the breakup of the Soviet Union as a disaster for the Soviet people and the world, Wu Jianmian, a diplomat, argued instead that the world had benefited due to the economic globalization that was now made possible without large-scale wars. Lu Nanquan, a prolific specialist, went further in arguing that the Soviet people benefited from steps toward democratization and the rule of law. For him, the Stalinist model was bad. Li Kaisheng, another specialist, was even bolder in warning that China still has not learned the lessons of the Soviet collapse; its history parallels that of the Soviet Union from the Stalin-Mao similarity to today. Without genuine reform, it is in danger of suffering the same fate.[40] The contrast is between blaming Gorbachev's political reforms under Western influence versus blaming the political stagnation extending from Stalin to Brezhnev without learning from world reforms. One side concludes that China has learned the lessons of the Soviet collapse, while the other side warns that it is in danger of following in the Soviet Union's footsteps. The first group prevails, expressing views consistent with today's confident national identity. Censorship has greatly reduced diversity in China on national identity themes, and I have treated them as a monolith, as in the other two books, aware that diversity later receded.

The Intensity Dimension

The rapid widening of the national identity gap in the late 1950s and early 1960s and the delayed narrowing of the gap in the 1980s are testimony to the intensity of the Communist Great Power National Identity Syndrome. A military-security-party tandem in authority was reticent to compromise and was inclined to widen identity gaps on all dimensions to the extreme. The legitimacy of their power was long tethered to an amalgam of ideas deemed to be infallible, excluding other ideas as antisocialist and thus unworthy of a hearing. The result is censorship that prevents timely debate to keep the gap from widening or to narrow it when opportunities arise. The two sides dug a deep hole from which they had great difficulty extricating themselves. Moreover, reformers in each country looked elsewhere and not at each other, in part because economic national identity was the priority. Hard-liners were prepared to pounce; so the Chinese and Soviet reformers were cautious in giving them new ammunition through a partnership with the other state. It was not possible to find common ground on reform socialism; opponents at home would misinterpret the partnership, while doubters abroad would mistrust it.[41]

As reforms gained momentum, there was much talk of pragmatism, as if the only concern of leaders was the national interest. Yet Gorbachev and Deng kept a close eye on identity matters, aware that moves related to bilateral relations would rebound in domestic identity struggles. The continued high stakes associated with intense identity concerns played a large role in shaping the course of these relations. A quieting of ideological identity permitted relations to be normalized. National interests rose to the fore, but they did not prevent national identity concerns from stirring responses on both sides. The misleading impression that identity was losing its importance should be rejected, because national identities shaped the process of normalization and lay in wait to again move to the forefront after a temporary interval.

Sino-Soviet relations stand as the extreme case of national identities trumping national interests, in the split that caused severe damage to both sides, in the delayed normalization of the 1980s that also had serious negative consequences for the two, and finally in the troubled aftermath of normalization for several years without new momentum. It was the high intensity of national identity in each of these periods that interfered with the pragmatic pursuit of national interests.

CONCLUSION

Searching for new answers regarding national identity, the Soviet Union and even more China could not escape rethinking views of the other center of socialism, with implications for bilateral relations. Having closely aligned their identities in the 1950s with each other and then sharply differentiated their identities in the 1960s and 1970s from each other, in the 1980s they struggled to adjust their identities in the face of comparisons with each other. The first identity question requiring a new answer was: What is socialism? For China, this demanded a reassessment of what is Soviet socialism; but even for the Soviet Union, turning to reform after China, clarification of how the other country's reforms related to socialism was not insignificant. Second was the need to reevaluate the history of socialism, entangling China in debates about the major turning points and leaders in Soviet history more than in its own history, which was more tightly censored. A third identity question was how do socialism and capitalism relate to each other, touching on convergence as well as coexistence. Looking over their shoulder at each other, the Chinese and the Russians were searching for answers in the midst of leadership struggles. Depending on the state of the struggle and on developments in the other country, some groups strove to narrow the gap in identities while others preferred to widen it. The response was not always the same for the separate dimensions of national identity, and it varied over the decade.

China had multiple identities available to it, more so than Russia had in 1992. The gap between socialism and presocialism was greater, allowing Confucianism to gain ground with ambivalent support that "Russian identity" based on the tsarist era struggled to achieve with full-scale support. Identity as a developing state gave more room for a post–Cold War alternative to socialism. East Asian identity proved helpful at a time of global fascination with the rise of this region. Russia found that Western identity was more complicated. Facing China at the start of the 1990s, the Russians tried to define their border as a junction of West and East, but this civilizational contrast failed when they lost the mantle of the West and treated China more as a socialist state useful for the struggle against the West than as part of the wider East Asian region.

Many dimensions of national identity stood in the way of narrowing the gap generated from the schism of communism, shifting to identity convergence tied to shared aspirations. China's serious reformers feared that renewed association with Soviet identity would stifle reform. They struggled to break taboos by separating China's political identity more fully from the Soviet model, which was associated with

Stalin. To serious Soviet reformers, who for a quarter century had considered China to be the heir to Stalinism, there was similar danger in being linked to that country politically as well as ideologically. Because fierce leadership struggles continued over ideology, it was not enough that Deng in the period 1979–86 had some appeal as a bolder reformer than did his Soviet counterparts and that Gorbachev in 1986–89 had a similar appeal. The overall image of the other country was a symbol of what would hold back dynamism. On the temporal dimension, this was especially true because reform meant rejecting the past, insisting that the level of development reached was much lower than previously stated, and focusing attention on how capitalist states had accomplished more in their past.

Widening or narrowing the national identity gap had powerful implications for bilateral relations. Because the gap widened precipitously and forces on both sides resisted steps to narrow it, bilateral relations had no prospect of improvement in the 1960s and 1970s. In the 1980s, first ideology, then horizontal identity, and finally vertical identity were the primary stumbling blocks in the fitful normalization process. The fact that it took two decades from the time of Mao's death to achieve the full thrust of normalization, boosted by a significant identity overlap, deserves attention similar to that given to the causes of the Sino-Soviet split for its international implications. Delayed awakening to a narrowing identity gap had a serious impact.

In 1960, the Sino-Soviet split burst into the limelight. The divide widened as the identity gap gave priority to ideology. In 1980, as both sides had reason to narrow the gap quickly, the horizontal identity gap delayed reconciliation and the Soviet side was slower to overcome the ideological divide. By the late 1980s, as the horizontal gap was diminishing rapidly, the vertical divide widened, linked to China's lingering ideological identity. Gorbachev flirted with an identity deemed by China's leaders as inimical to the Communist Party's monopoly on power and tight control of society. With multiple dimensions of identity in play, China and Russia had to wait until the mid-1990s before four decades of identity differences interfering with relations were past, and, unexpectedly, parallel identity changes became a force behind closer relations.

CHAPTER 7

THE NATIONAL IDENTITY GAP AND BILATERAL RELATIONS FROM THE 1990s TO THE 2010s

The gap between Chinese and Russian national identities was ostensibly at a peak in 1992. Not only had China's leaders regarded Mikhail Gorbachev as a traitor, possibly an agent of the US Central Intelligence Agency, but they also considered Boris Yeltsin an enemy of socialism, while blaming him for the geopolitical disaster of the Soviet Union's collapse and Russia's further swing toward the West. Russia was under the sway of leaders and media that treated China after June 4, 1989, as a pariah in the international community, a support to the retrograde communists within Russia who had attempted a putsch to revive the discredited old order, and a state with little to offer economically when Russia's needs were enormous. As the two states stumbled to prevent sensitive issues such as Taiwan and democracy from causing further damage to their relations, there appeared to be scant prospect that national identity would draw them close together. Indeed, it seemed poised to keep them far apart for an extended time.

Many observers assumed that the 1992 decision in China to build a "socialist market economy" meant acceptance of capitalism and the "free market" based on ever-wider integration into the global community. If leaders still spoke of socialism or patriotism linked to Communist Party leadership in the battle against Japan's invasion, it was presumed to be a doomed effort to sustain regime legitimacy in the face of an emerging middle-class society, which would reject this failed system and insist on a civil society. Russia was the discredited model, which showed the need to shed socialism, offering nothing to appeal to the Chinese public and little more than an embarrassing reminder to the leadership.[1] In turn, observers saw Russians nostalgically recalling their past within Europe and finding China a troubling reminder of the authoritarian yoke that had long stifled them. The gap in national identity had widened, nullifying any momentum gained from the normalization of the two countries' relations, and, presumably, would need to be handled with care to keep from widening further, because each country appeared to be inclined to narrow its national identity gap with the West.

These assumptions were based on a misunderstanding about the national identities of both countries. As early as Yeltsin's visit to Beijing in December 1992, two months after he abruptly canceled a trip to Tokyo, there were signs that relations not only were on the mend but that they also had potential to develop quickly. Earlier in the year, China had shifted to a positive tone on Yeltsin and prospects for bilateral relations, suggesting that Russian national identity would turn away from the West and find common cause with it.[2] Meanwhile, anti-Western forces had regrouped in Russia, many now calling for close ties to China and even treating it as a model.[3] With Russian arms sales developing, some interest groups as well as security officials were advocating closer ties. Most important, criticisms of China were muted, apart from a small number of Western-leaning liberals, who had few followers, and demagogues, who raised the threat of a "yellow peril" from stealth migration, which was sensationalized for the public but marginal in the prevailing identity narrative.[4] If one were not blinded by the paradigm popular in the West, signs of a narrowing national identity gap as early as 1993 would have been obvious.

Relations started to improve on the basis of national interests: the demilitarization of the border, which had been associated with great distrust and expense, in order for both sides to concentrate on urgent economic goals; and Russia's desire to secure China's support for its status at the UN Security Council as the replacement for the Soviet Union, in return for Russian support for the unity of China and no pressure as seen in "peaceful coexistence." After these security concerns, economic complementarity boosted ties, as Russia sought export markets, notably for arms, and China found a market for cheap consumer goods, linking its depressed Northeast to the needy Russian Far East. Stifling anger toward Yeltsin for destroying Soviet communism and the Soviet Union, Jiang Zemin welcomed him in an unusually personal manner in April 1996, helping him to defeat his opponent, Gennady Zyuganov, despite the latter's role as the head of the Communist Party of the Russian Federation. Looking to the East after the shock of NATO's expansion in the West, Yeltsin found China more convenient than India, Japan, or Iran as the focus, for reasons of national identity as well as national interest. China was clearly the emerging rival to the United States, and it gave heft to Russia's escape from overdependency.

Sino-Russian ties were strengthened on the basis of overlap on the vertical and horizontal dimensions, above all. This overlap sharply separated the two states from the United States. In foreign relations, neither state could accept a United States–centered international community or standards of civilization that judged their denial of civil society and international NGOs as derelict. Although they did not close their own identity gap on all nonideological dimensions, they overlooked it in the face of what many considered to be an existential threat to what they defined as a civilization. The smaller gap between them did not widen, while leaders were pressing to contrast their national identities more assertively with those of the United States and its allies.[5] When Vladimir Putin defied the West with his domestic agenda, Russia's need for China's support increased. Greater support from Russia helped to embolden China as well.

After Xi Jinping and Putin took presidential power, with both likely to hold it until the 2020s, the identity overlap intensified while its impact on bilateral relations became clearer. Despite the fact that Russia's mantra remained multipolarity while China edged toward bipolarity, Putin pretended that the two were essentially identical. Crackdowns on domestic critics grew harsher, driving the two closer together. Opposition to US policies in the Middle East brought the two closer. There was even talk of an alliance in mid-2013 on the pretense of converging national interests, but rooted more in national identities.[6] As identities grew more intense, bilateral relations improved, despite signs that national interests actually were increasingly diverging, as Chinese assertiveness left more Russians wary of marginalization in Asia, loss of predominance in Central Asia, or more condescension. National identities were trumping national interests, as shown in Putin's rhetoric playing into "old stereotypes about the Cold War," noted in US president Barack Obama's August 9, 2013, news conference, and in the secretive Document No. 9 of the Chinese leadership discussed in the *New York Times* on August 20, 2013.[7]

Signs were growing that the intensification of Sinocentrism under Xi and Russocentrism under Putin could lead to a crossroads. China was apparently newly insistent on Russia's acceptance of its agenda, as in the Silk Road Economic Belt announced in September 2013, and Russia was pressing more anxiously for its own Eurasian community and for closer ties to Asian states at odds with China's plans. One identity theme could cast a shadow on others if Xi and Putin did not find a way to control the currents gaining force in the horizontal dimension. If the momentum was still in the direction of even closer relations based on an identity overlap, the possibility of a turnabout in the not distant future was suddenly noticeably greater than before.

CHANGES IN THE NATIONAL IDENTITY GAP FROM 1992 TO 2013

Chinese fears in early 1992 centered on two prospects: that Russia's foreign policy would align with the West, abandoning balance-of-power logic and putting pressure as part of the international community on outliers, above all China; and that Russian values now would echo those of the West. Seeing China as militarily weak and stuck in a discredited socialist system, Russia might widen the identity gap with it, which would be a natural result of the long-standing view that the East is inferior to the West.[8] Conveying warnings that the United States was bent on weakening Russia, undermining both its cultural and political identity, Chinese urged Russians to be vigilant in foreign relations and preserve stability.[9] This was a call to strengthen the state, block NGOs, conceal truths about the history of the Communist Party, and showcase distrust toward the West in foreign policy. If a revival of the Communist Party was not on the agenda, China was hopeful that the vertical dimension would, in any case, be bolstered against external interference as the horizontal dimension made room for the Sino-Russian partnership.

Some Russians warned as early as 1993 that their nation had suffered a loss of national consciousness, leaving it vulnerable, especially to China. Charging that China was seeking to expand its territory to the Russian Far East while engaging in uncivilized commerce, they were drawing on old stereotypes of the West versus Asia, while appealing for more unity at home and an assertive expression of identity versus China.[10] Yet they were overshadowed by Russians critical of the West, who saw blaming China as a distraction. In turn, the Chinese responded to US president Bill Clinton's 1993 effort to take leadership of the "new Pacific community" and his call in 1994 for a three-pillared foreign policy focused on security, economic development, and the spread of democracy, as a serious challenge. They welcomed Russia's response to US policy, as it turned from one-sided dependence to great power politics, cooperating, at last, with China in a triangular orientation.[11] As ties improved, it proved useful to insist that this was only due to national interests; so economic reforms would not be set back by outside fear of a revival of the 1950s pairing.

Although, in the mid-1990s, China and Russia were heading in the same direction, China was making rapid progress in rebuilding its national identity but Russia was not. Desperate, Yeltsin grasped for a symbol to instill pride in the past (launching a broad search for the "Russian idea") and embraced great power politics.[12] Failure in the war he had started to subdue Chechnya made these endeavors more urgent. The search for normalcy that involved ridding Russia of Soviet-era lies and myths was losing steam. Soon, anti-Americanism became the cornerstone of a revived identity centered on victimization.[13] On the horizontal dimension, China saw its opening. Showcasing the notion of a two-headed eagle facing east and west, Russia depicted its relations with China and Asia as balanced or equidistant, but the thrust of its criticisms on what was damaging the international system fixated on US unilateral dictates.[14]

As late as 1995, the Yeltsin administration was still leaning to the West. Its Atlanticist identity complemented its democratic credentials, even as defensiveness over its own civilization, seen as endangered, led to growing interest in uncovering not only a Russian identity but also a Eurasian one.[15] The notion of the international community was treated cautiously, at the United Nations and on matters related to both culture and security. China lacked great appeal except as a counterweight to the United States, not only from a balance-of-power perspective but also a civilizational one. Stirred by the expansion of NATO, the economic crisis of 1998, and the frustrating impact of an infirm and unpopular Yeltsin, Russia was ripe for a backlash. At this time, anti-Americanism was also spreading rapidly in China, where it was associated with recent tensions over Taiwan.[16] The horizontal dimension rose to the forefront in criticisms of hegemonism, calls for multipolarity and noninterference in internal affairs, and a rejection of "universal values." The joint appeal to identity was becoming quite intense.

As the tide of anti-Western sentiment grew, Russians took solace in a multipolar order, assuming that China's rise would be delayed by problems and that Russia could serve as a bridge, avoiding falling prey to American civilization.[17] One challenge was to dispel the notion of a "China threat."[18] The message from China was that the West was changing from regarding China as a socialist state that is doomed to the same fate as the Soviet Union to seeing China as a threat to forging a global civilization, to which a weakened Russia will be vulnerable unless it turns to Asia and rejects Western civilization.[19] The Chinese extolled a legacy of Confucian harmony between civilizations.[20] Memories of the Sino-Soviet split were fading rapidly, as if it had only been caused by communist ideology.

The next stage in narrowing the identity gap occurred in the years 1999–2000. Both states regarded the NATO war over Kosovo as an identity threat. For Russians, the Serbs were seen as fellow Slavs; and for both countries, humanitarian intervention was regarded as a precedent for intervention in their countries and a subterfuge for power projection. Putin's priorities as president were welcome to China, because he hurried to rebuild a strong, centralized state unwilling to tolerate challenges to Russia's vertical identity. Despite some uncertainty about how far he would distance his country from the West, the Chinese took satisfaction that both vertical and horizontal identity kept drawing their states closer under the rule of Putin, who increasingly replaced Yeltsin's indecisiveness about identity vis-à-vis the West.[21]

In the first part of the 2000s, the Chinese were bemoaning Russia's lukewarm attitude toward their relationship, charging that Cold War thinking persisted, as certain Russians took a Western view of China as the "other"—that is, as socialist and totalitarian—and others accused it of plotting territorial expansion.[22] Repeated joint assertions that the two sides are almost in complete agreement on international issues naturally led the Chinese to question why many Russians were still raising doubts. Identity seemed to be getting in the way of interests. However, in the period 2004–7 a new wave of assertiveness in Russia raised the prospects for bilateral trust. The shock of the "color revolutions" on Russia's doorstep and in states long recognized as within its sphere, as part of the Soviet Union, alienated its leaders more deeply from the West while revealing the overlap in their values with China's. The balance between regionalism and international community in their outlooks was similar. On regional hotspots, such as North Korea and Iran, China and Russia were also cooperating more closely, depicting the threat from the United States similarly. Although in the period 2004–8 China tended to accentuate its positive ties with the United States as a "responsible stakeholder," and in 2009–11 Russia under Medvedev praised the "reset" with the United States, these merely delayed forces that were gathering steam. Putin's aggressive tone in 2007–8 (and even more so when he reclaimed power in 2011–13) and China's similar tone starting in 2009 fortified a strong identity foundation. An important impetus to improved trust was Putin's shift away from US ties and toward China by the years 2006–7. On December 20, 2006, he called for deeper bilateral relations and integration into regional processes, soon leading to dropping some barriers to China's active role in the

Russian Far East. He defined China as an opportunity, not a threat, even as he pushed to expand Russia's security presence in the area.[23] A firm rebuke was being given to Russians who spoke of a "yellow peril" and "Chinese expansion." In the name of balance and authority in facing the West, and on the premise that China shares in seeking a multipolar world, the Russians argued that Chinese ties are the only way to develop the Russian Far East and Siberia and even that they are based on a shared global vision.[24]

A cloud hung over Sino-Russian relations in the period 2008–11, when China hesitated to back the Russian war in Georgia and the sovereignty of two breakaway areas supported by Russia, Medvedev's rhetoric soft-pedaled the national identity themes China espoused, and China's growing assertiveness left some Russians concerned that their country would become a target. In acquiescing to NATO's intervention in Libya, Medvedev was seen as unreliable. Some Chinese saw the Russians as culturally unable to accept the rise of China, as some Russians saw the Chinese as still culturally alien. Yet, when Putin renewed his hard-line rhetoric in 2011, many Chinese at last felt reassured that the recent cloud had lifted.

If confidence had earlier allowed Putin to draw closer to China, that confidence was not the cause of his renewed turn in that direction. Seeing the European Union and United States in difficulty over their economies and blaming them for abusing the UN Security Council on Libya by ousting its leader, Russia shifted direction in 2011, which was signaled by its increased backing of North Korea, including food assistance and support for an unconditional revival of the Six-Party Talks. Asia had risen in Russia's identity, and China was the obvious channel for its claims in the region. When Medvedev met with Kim Jong-il in August, the signal grew louder. Putin's October visit to China brought more agreement. After a lull, it appeared that Russia was trumpeting its Asian identity, not only as a balance and bridge but also as a brake on the US identity impact for an emboldened Russian opposition. Sino-Russian identity overlap tightened.

In 2012, a combination of developments brought China and Russia closer, putting national identity convergence in the forefront: the intensification of national identity in China starting in 2009 that gained momentum with Xi Jinping's rise to the top position, a shift in Putin's strategy toward national identity in the course of his reelection, a hardening of positions on the horizontal dimension centered on the United States, and a reevaluation of civilizational discourse linked to vertical and sectoral identities. Claims do not need to be buttressed by warmth and confidence in each other. The Russians often find the Chinese to be arrogant, fearing the revival of charges of "tsarist imperialism" and "unequal treaties" from the time of the Sino-Soviet split once China is in a commanding position. The Chinese are, at times, concerned that as China's rise proceeds, the Russians will exaggerate a "China threat." A narrowing national identity gap should not be misunderstood as genuine trust. The final chapter of a 2013 Russian textbook on bilateral relations points to some Russians' nervousness about Russia losing prospects for multipolarity due to China, but this concern is overshadowed by insistence that current relations are extremely positive.[25]

In summit after summit, Chinese and Russian leaders trumpet improving relations. Writings in both countries, especially China, reinforce these claims. Public opinion has largely accepted the thrust of these claims. This relationship is depicted as embedded in similar views of important principles connected to each dimension of national identity: opposed to the threatening ideology driving the West; supportive of a broadly shared outlook on the Cold War and post–Cold War eras; opposed to the spread of Western civilization; committed to noninterference in internal affairs; and approving of multipolarity opposed to US unipolarity. These may sound like platitudes, but they are the core of identity gaps. Widening their gaps with the United States and its allies, each has found the other closer.

In the periods 2000–3 and 2009–11, the Chinese were surprised by the fickleness of Russia's leaders, who, after pressing for better relations, explored closer US ties. The Chinese said in early 2003 that they should not dramatize the setback, and in 2009–11 they were also cautious in criticizing Medvedev.[26] Some were frustrated by the self-centered nature of Russian identity. If Russia was using China against the United States, it was not drawing close to China, not only in the

251

Shanghai Cooperation Organization (SCO) but also on other matters of civilizational significance, such as in finding language to describe a shared community. Russia seemed to want to be the pivot in the triangle with the United States, while China sought two standing together versus one. Relations grew more stable starting in 2003, but only in 2012–13 did they deepen on the basis of major progress in narrowing the identity divide as both were widening it with the West.[27] Awakening to his need to oppose the West more vigorously, Putin in 2003–4 reassured China, and he did so again in 2012–13 as he reclaimed Russia's presidency with new stridency.[28]

Claims that relations are better than ever and indications of further narrowing of the identity gap should not blind us to an undercurrent of unease as Xi proclaimed the Silk Road Economic Belt, a type of regionalism with meaning beyond economics linked to historical identity, and Putin pressed other states to accept the Eurasian Union with nuances of Eurasianism. This divide was indicative of intense national identities, which, however little they opened direct gaps with each other, carried the potential to put these countries on a collision course in the reorganization of Asia.

THE IDEOLOGICAL DIMENSION IDENTITY GAP

The mantra in Sino-Russian relations as they have improved is that the age of allowing ideology to interfere with national interests is over. Both see the Sino-Soviet split as a costly error, insisting that now their relationship is only about the balance of power and maximization of economic and other interests. Yet the pace of cooperation is hard to explain on this basis, and the language justifying it is often couched in identity terms, feigning resistance to a pursuit of ideological goals by the United States. Some Russians concede this point by warning that no long-term strategy for modernization exists, and that overreliance on China fails to serve Russia's need for diversity in Northeast Asia.[29] Mostly, however, the criticism of shortsighted ideological thinking concentrates on the Yeltsin era for the crisis in Russian national identity it induced. Shock therapy, the weakening of the state, and the chaotic management of the national identity transition from communism are all noted in comparisons that refer to China's success in sustaining a monolithic ideology under firm leadership. Russia suffered from the loss of ideological and vertical identity, but also temporal identity, which was blamed on its treating its past in a way that shattered belief in identity. Alexander Lukin actually equates Russia's 1990s with China's Great Leap Forward in its disorienting impact.[30] Even many who were very critical of the prior ideology came to accept the determination that the way it had been so abruptly and fully discarded wreaked havoc. A new ideology is blamed for causing unnecessary deterioration in relations with China, but rejection of that faulty ideology leaning to the West opens the door to another ideology, still in the shadows, overlapping with China's.

Disclaiming any new ideological consensus, the Chinese and Russians conveniently insist that they are joining in a struggle against an ideologically driven opponent. The worldview of the United States and its allies—called anticommunism and a Cold War mentality—is deemed ideological. Yet this critique lumps neoconservative unilateralism for regime change with liberal humanitarian multilateralism, connecting talk of the "axis of evil" to the compulsion to make China into an enemy.[31] Moreover, it disguises an ideological orientation drawn from past anti-imperialism with more than a trace of the reassertion of socialism in views of the past, if not quotations from the founders.

The fact that China is socialist and is becoming more assertive in that identity matters little, given the sympathy shown by Putin and many close to him to the Soviet legacy. Fervent anti-imperialism centered, as of old, on the United States draws the two states together, although there is potential for discord over China's more outright anti-Western ideological drive. As China grows assertive about Sinocentrism and manifests it in Asia, where Russocentrism is expressed, the potential for a clash rising to ideological significance exists. So far, however, the Chinese have been deferential in Central Asia on identity issues, and the Russians have referred rather obliquely to signs of the upsurge in Sinocentrism that are alarming to other states. The ideology identity gap—defined as a scale of 0 at the narrowest to 5 at the widest—may have been as high as 4 briefly in Yeltsin's first year, but it is now as low as 1. For it to widen significantly would require flagrant Sinocentric disregard of Russian sensitivities or a sharp about-face in Russian thinking about US ideology.

THE TEMPORAL DIMENSION IDENTITY GAP

Communist periodization was long preoccupied with an unassailable narrative on the progression from feudalism to capitalism to socialism. Historical orthodoxy brooked no serious dissent, although reform voices at times managed to slip in deviant ideas. As China tightened control starting in 1989 over coverage of the history of socialism, it allowed a little debate on other sensitive topics, such as the Korean War, in narrow academic studies that normally did not find their way into mainstream identity discourse. Interpreting the past to support a virtuous China versus a flawed and often rapacious West and Japan, the Chinese have refocused temporal identity on nation rather than class. With the intensification in identity since 2009, the message has sharpened to establish a civilizational divide, where even the nations closest to China, such as North Korea, fail the test of respect for the benevolence of China's tributary system. Even more serious is the divide over the treatment of Chinese communist rule during and after the Cold War. Russia fares best in the post–Cold War period and has an improved image during the Cold War era, but the threat remains that tsarist imperialism will again become a target should Russia offend China, opening an identity gap.

The temporal dimension is linked to the horizontal one. Looking back to history before its revolution, each state seeks a boost to national identity. Already in Stalin's time there had been a shift from praising only the class struggle and rebellions to expressing pride in Russian culture and foreign policy. Conservative forces had found scope to make a strong appeal starting in the 1960s for strengthening Russian, as differentiated from Soviet, identity, with pride in pre-1917 history in the forefront. Reform forces also capitalized on this, associating Russian pride with Western civilization and pointing to capitalist success in development before 1917, which could be revitalized. These reform currents played a role when intellectuals seized the opportunity of glasnost and Yeltsin's early democratization. China's serious reformers were more prone to link "feudalism" with socialism; premodern history had been so denigrated and remained so censored in the 1980s that it was not widely invoked for reconstructing identity. Having separated Chinese history in 1949 far more fully than the Soviets had used 1917 as a divide, China's leaders made sure that when they did reclaim dynastic history as glorious for its "harmonious society" or "harmonious world," it would be a sanitized version that, contrary to what was said earlier, found continuity with today.

Russian coverage of history is more complicated, but the same overall trends are evident: glorification of precommunist history; reconsideration of earlier critiques of the dark side of socialism, but with more dissent and honesty than in China; a reemphasis on a Cold War divide in which the Soviet-led bloc was more virtuous than the United States–led bloc; and insistence that the post–Cold War decades formed a transitional era troubled by the triumphalism of the United States that is leading to balanced international relations and a lesser role for Western civilization. Although China and Russia have different ideals for the future, raising doubts in Russia, so far these have largely been brushed aside. The Sino-Soviet dispute is depicted somewhat differently by the two, but differences in assigning blame rapidly lost traction for identity in the 1990s. A shadow lingers from past disputes, because the Russians are distrustful of whether China has really dropped the belief that it deserves the territory lost in unequal treaties and the Chinese are suspicious that Russian preference for Europeans feeds into fears of a China threat. In settling their territorial dispute without either side allowing a debate on the results, they have quieted these concerns. The potential exists for a wider identity gap on this dimension, but it is unlikely to soon rise above 3 on the 0–5 scale. The two states have narrowed the earlier vast gap when the Chinese demonized tsarist imperialism and blamed the Soviet Union more than the United States in the Cold War after 1960, while the Soviets searched Chinese history for distortions of normalcy that served as the origins of Maoism. This legacy has not been erased, but it has mostly been eclipsed.

China's outlook on history poses a danger that is well understood in Russia. Aware that the Chinese see loss of territory as humiliating and unjust, the Russians fear that claims will be directed against their Far East. The struggle over Koguryo—an area which straddles the contemporary borders of North Korea, China, and Russia—indicates a secretive project in China starting in 1997 to reexamine the area, which, after the taboo was lifted in 2003–4, burst forth as a dispute over ancient history with powerful ramifications for disputes over territory and the cultural identity of those who dwelt there.[32] Such Sinocentrism is worrisome for Russia, but the demonization of Western history in all periods, if not as far-reaching as in China, is the basis for a narrower gap with China that contributes to positive bilateral relations.

THE SECTORAL DIMENSION IDENTITY GAP

The late 1950s saw an economic identity spat over which state was advancing rapidly toward communism, which soon was cast into the shadow of a cultural and political identity split over which state was entitled to lead the international communist movement. In the 1980s, divisions over sectoral identity faded, although China's lead in reform socialism was later contested by the Soviet Union's claims to the political identity of reform. Scoring bragging rights in this dimension had inherent meaning in the evolutionary outlook of socialist theory. In the 1990s, China gained an edge, as economic identity surged with an "economic miracle," while Russia's political, economic, and cultural identity all became newly problematic.

In the 2000s, Russian sectoral identity recovered ground, with political claims of its unity and cohesion, insistence on having a separate civilization, and economic pride as an energy superpower with expectations to rise to fifth place in the world in gross domestic product. This favored relations with China on more equal terms. When in 2008–9 Russia was hard hit by the global economic crisis as China surged ahead amid talk of a Group of Two (i.e., China and America), it seemed that the sectoral gap would widen. Putin changed the tone when announcing the decision that he would run for the presidency, shifting from "modernization" of the economy to pride in expanding the military budget and making enlarged claims about politics and culture.

After vitriolic accusations at the height of the Sino-Soviet split faulting the other side's cultural identity, the dearth of cultural animosity might be surprising. Both sides are fixated on cultural clashes with the West. Although they resort to artificial steps—such as the "Year of Russia," 2006, in China, and the "Year of China," 2007, in Russia—to arouse interest in each other's culture, which has been lagging in comparison with political and economic relations, such relative apathy is better than the antipathy directed elsewhere. In comparison with the bombast emanating from China from the time of the 2008 Beijing Olympics, Russian cultural and economic pride pale in intensity. The 2014 Sochi Winter Olympics appeared to be a similarly lavish effort to arouse such pride.

As long as the spotlight in both countries is kept on the existential threat from the West, today's pretenses may persist. Much has been written in defense of the great Russian, including Soviet, civilization under threat of annihilation by Western civilization. As an example laced with diatribes, H. G. Kozin's book *Russia: What Is It? In Search of the Essence of Identity* opens the door to joining forces with China while abjuring any interest in exporting its civilization.[33]

An economic identity gap exists. China's call for "one economic space" in the Russian Far East and Northeast China scares Russians, while Russia's appeal for a balance in industrial development based on Chinese commitments to buying more than natural resources from Russia falls on deaf ears. Rapid growth in trade gives confidence to China about its leverage, but ambivalence to Russia, as it prizes Asian markets while fretting about their lack of diversity and the tough negotiating tactics delaying projects. Yet both states view Western pressure for liberal economic reforms at the expense of the state's dominant role and corruption as the target of their anger about an economic gap. To the extent that they shift to reform, however, this criticism of the West has been lowered intermittently.

The sectoral gap was large in the early 1990s, given the residue of the split and the contrasting effect of recent policies. It narrowed to its minimal level by 2008, but the possibility of widening was growing. The economic gap grew again when China spurted ahead as Russia sputtered. The political gap increased when Medvedev shifted Russia's tone with more talk of democracy and relaxation of central control. Moreover, the cultural gap was poised to widen amid claims of resurgent Eastern civilization led by China. If the gap had narrowed to 2 on the 1–5 scale for a time, the level approached 3 before Putin downplayed the divide in 2012. With many Russians nervous about China's politics, culture, and economics, and many Chinese disdainful of Russia in these aspects, this gap would remain a potential problem if censorship were lifted.

The collapse of the Soviet Union and its communist system left many ideologues floundering. In a remarkable turnaround, many on both sides who had been among the most vociferous critics of the other side's heresy rediscovered the virtues of the other country. With the renewal of Sino-American tensions after June 4, 1989, although probably not because of this, and the sharp rise of Russian resentment of American-Russian relations, the other side looked appealing in opposition to the United States–led political, economic, and cultural global community. Blocking the spread of Western civilization became a shared value obsession. This has drawn attention away from the Sino-Russian sectoral dimension gap.

THE VERTICAL DIMENSION IDENTITY GAP

The vertical dimension identity gap in Sino-American relations was wide during the 1990s. Themes such as human rights, democratization, and noninterference in internal affairs drew the spotlight. At the same time, the problem it posed in Sino-Russian relations faded.[34] Both countries made it clear that they would respect the differences in their systems, and it was not long before the lack of such respect by the United States became a joint rallying cry. It is a perennial theme in summits and is reflected in the "Shanghai spirit," which guides the SCO, whose regular meetings repudiate universal values while serving as a "model for international organizations." Beneath the surface, doubts survive that China's system is alien, whether due to association with the memories held by many Russians of abuses in the communist era or recent experiences interacting with Chinese in ways that have not inspired trust. Many Chinese also appeared to look down on Russia's domestic order for its xenophobia, often directed against Asians, and disorder, making business arrangements more difficult than is the case in Chinese corruption. This lack of respect for each other's social and political orders is tempered by mutual reserve in not openly raising criticisms, as accusations spread against US interference in internal affairs.

Demagogues in Russia, especially the Russian Far East, raised the specter of a Chinese plot to use illegal migration and other means for reasserting control over parts of Russia. This image of a nefarious China capitalizing on a disorderly Russia in unbalanced cross-border relations quieted after Putin ousted or silenced local leaders and agreed with China both to expand trade and to maintain an atmosphere of mutual respect. By 2009, the two states had made long-term plans calling for much closer economic integration, but with China buying little of Russia's industrial production and with the Russians' concern about the huge imbalance between the two economies and populations and their distrust of China's secretive system, fears were kept alive. Irregularities in cross-border ties have left a lasting identity gap.[35]

As early as 1994, M. L. Titarenko argued that Russian and Chinese civilization are together forging a new world order, as they reject the old idea, present even in Marxism-Leninism, that the West is superior to the East. Calling this synthesis of East and West Eurasianism, and equating it with equality and noninterference in other states, Titarenko contends that Russia has elements of Eastern culture, and he asserts that whereas the United States seeks to force the East to bow down in all respects, China and Russia have ended their mutual antagonism and support each other's rise, following their own separate paths.[36] This thinking, repeated over two decades, links identity in their vertical and horizontal dimensions, downplaying Sino-Russian differences while stressing the gap with the West.

Reminding Russians of how during the period of the split, Moscow and Beijing aroused each other's ethnic minorities, the Chinese emphasize in Central Asia, Xinjiang, and elsewhere that good Sino-Russian relations serve ethnic harmony.[37] With Putin fully in charge in 2012 and the Arab Spring reinforcing mutual apprehension about movements that arouse disorder, the gap on the vertical dimension hovers around 2. The shadow of Western criticism of human rights policies and the post–Cold War claim of civilizational distance from the West turned the two away from doubts about each other's social order. China serves as a counterweight to possible cultural and political infiltration.

THE HORIZONTAL DIMENSION IDENTITY GAP

In viewing the United States and the international system, China and Russia found considerable common ground after Russia changed direction starting in the mid-1990s. In their outlook on regional issues, differences have been slower to be resolved and have the potential to flare up. Because sources of overlap have been more central to national identity, this dimension has played a large role in the improvement in bilateral relations. The significance of the final territorial agreement between Moscow and Beijing in late 2004 is that both sides were willing to compromise on a long-standing identity matter in order to achieve a narrowing in their identity gap. China proceeded from a position of strength as it recalled the Sinocentric tradition of benevolence. This agreement cleared the deck for a major boost to relations, as Russia grew bolder in resisting the United States.

Rex Li stresses great power identities as the glue in Sino-Russian ties. Developing a theme I raised in 1999, Li explains that this became a driving force in the 1990s, when a "discourse of danger" linked to "peaceful evolution" intensified in China as the Soviet Union collapsed.[38] He sees it reinforced starting in the mid-2000s, even as a stronger China would presumably have faced little threat. The importance of forging a powerful, united China able to defend its sovereignty and territorial integrity paralleled coverage of Russia, whose struggle to regain great power status is highly praised in China and placed against the backdrop of its awakening to the myth of belonging to Western civilization even though it was not welcomed into the Western family. Russians seeking to rejoin the great power club found China alone welcoming, as opposed to the Cold War mentality of the West.[39]

During the mid-1990s, the Russians were rattled by both the expansion of NATO and the apparent irrelevance of their country in Asia, as was seen in the first North Korean nuclear crisis and Russia's exclusion from the APEC forum. After the abrupt fall from the Soviet Union's superpower status, a need was felt to boost the deeply wounded self-esteem of the Russian people centered on the revived international status of their country. At the same time, China raised the stakes on Taiwan, responding to affronts from its president and from US actions, such as inviting President Lee Teng-hui to speak at Cornell University in 1995 and responding with a show of force to China's missile tests before the 1996 Taiwan elections. Having faced sanctions and international condemnation after June 4, 1989, China was also seeking to boost its citizens' pride in the state's international role. A meeting of the minds resulted, despite doubts that the two countries could find much consensus managing Central Asia or other regional issues.

The SCO tests the Sino-Russian national identity gap, which has advanced mainly due to three factors: (1) determination in both states to resist Western values, keeping the West at bay and showing disapproval for its system of international relations, especially as the threat of the "color revolutions" loomed large; (2) awareness in two culturally narrow states of the potential for a cultural clash leading to geopolitical distrust, notably in Central Asia with spillover to Xinjiang, where the Sino-Soviet split had led to mutual subversion; and (3) agreement that an image of shared values in support of sovereignty, noninterference in internal affairs, and respect for cultural diversity reinforces their main identity themes. However, China's appeal to the "Shanghai spirit" hints at its centrality, as its eagerness to gain soft power contradicts Russia's aspirations for "Eurasian" integration without China.[40] In the period 2002–7, China and Russia found common ground for the "Shanghai spirit," responding to the "freedom agenda" of US president George W. Bush and supporting state values over civil society while opposing the "color revolution" threat to the "authoritarian club." Yet when Putin pressed for a more overt anti-Western posture while blocking any economic community, China balked, and when China in 2009 sought a joint arrangement to counter the world financial crisis, Russia was opposed. Agreement in opposing values linked to the West sustains the SCO, but tensions are not easing on how to proceed further as a community. In 2013, a Sino-Russian divide became clearer.

Central Asia and the SCO test how much Sinocentrism and Russocentrism are reconciled. When the US challenge is the focus, China bolsters Russia more than challenging it.[41] China and Russia may eye each other suspiciously in Central Asia, but Russia's identity concerns are alleviated by the lack of identity closeness in Sino–Central Asian relations and the continued impact of Russian ethnics and Russian-educated elites in the region. The most important identity concerns lie elsewhere. Taiwan is the first priority for China. Although cross-strait ties are calmer under President Ma Ying-jeou than at any time since the early 1990s, an emboldened China may well not be content with the slow timetable for improved relations, let alone continued uncertainty about reunification. Troubled ties with Russia would not serve this priority. Other concerns are maritime, keeping China's focus on the South China and East China seas. North Korea is an additional identity concern, which Russia has approached in tandem with China. Both sides deny any serious clash of identities over key priorities, as they keep the focus on gaps with others.

Raising the banner of Eurasianism in his return to the presidency, Putin vainly sought to distinguish Russia's sphere of influence and civilization as inclusive of Central Asia from both China and the West. He feels that Russia is a world pole, economically and culturally, that is capable of fending off emerging polarization.[42] His dual approach of joining internationally and blocking China regionally is indicative of the contradictions posed by the horizontal identity in Russia.

China's concessions to the United States came largely as a result of pressure and fear that it would be targeted: in the early 1990s, as the next communist state to collapse; at the end of the 1990s, as the "China threat" argument spread; and in 2003 and 2006, as North Korea took a bellicose stance and the United States was considered capable of either launching a preemptive strike or shifting the blame to China for blocking UN Security Council sanctions. By 2009, an emboldened China was much less likely to succumb to pressure.

Only Japan and India have some potential in Asia to give Russia balance against its one-sided dependence on China. In the case of Japan, through 2011 Russia appeared to be widening the identity gap, reflecting repeated frustration in restarting negotiations over their territorial dispute. Medvedev's 2011 visit to the Southern Kuriles (Northern Territories) served this aim, as did agreement with China earlier in 2012 on mutual support in their territorial disputes as China was ratcheting up pressure over the Diaoyu/Senkaku Islands issue. However, by the time of the APEC summit in Vladivostok in September 2012—when plans were made for a summit between Putin and Japan's prime minister, Noda Yoshihiko—Russia's tune on the territorial dispute had changed. It switched to a position of neutrality on the Sino-Japanese dispute and took an upbeat position on reviving the momentum achieved at the Irkutsk summit of 2001. In 2013, there were further signs of Russian interest in Japan, which was bothersome to China but not really a balancing force. Only China stands as a partner in Asia capable of meeting Russia's national identity objectives.

One constant in Sino-Russian relations since the mid-1990s has been the strong desire of both countries to make this relationship appear stronger than it is. When Putin visited China in June 2012, he again raised the specter of an unprecedented type of interstate relations, with even hints of an alliance.[43] This imagery testifies to the shared obsession of the two countries with opposing the United States. This stance also holds for the ideal of an international community, which they see as a US plot to enlist them in an order that they regard as illegitimate and counter to their interests. This attitude has less to do with US policies or presidents than with the legacy of communism. Even a problem-solving approach to international hot spots raises hackles associated with doing the "dirty work" of the United States.

China and Russia define "regional identity" as an exclusive sphere in which US intrusions are illegitimate. During the Cold War, this definition appeared as defense of socialism, and afterward it was discussed in security terms, despite the presence of deep cultural assumptions. It proved convenient to blame US hegemonism for reaching too far without spelling out what was sought by Sinocentrism and Russocentrism. This allowed issues to be framed as a US strategy, provoking a just response by a state with no expansionary aims.

China conveys an image of trust that belies the real state of bilateral relations.[44] If earlier it had some foundation in the deference that China showed to Russia in Central Asia and a recognition of past mistakes that led to the Sino-Soviet split, the narrative increasingly was a product of censorship and wishful thinking. In its narrative, China presented an idealized view of a successful great power relationship. The two sides uphold each other's sovereignty, privileging that concept over the resolution of global problems or humanitarian concerns. Respecting each other's dignity is welcome to China as it grows bolder. Also, they agree in challenging US hegemony on behalf of pursuing equality in the international community and change in the international order. In the years 2008–9, the Chinese were debating changing the model of the international system, stressing more cooperation to confront the West, and the Russians in 2011–12 seemed to agree. If the Soviet Union could accept this reality at the end of the Cold War, the Chinese insisted that it was now the United States' turn to abandon Cold War thinking, accepting China's rise and its plans to establish an East Asian community rather than a community centered on the West.[45]

Events during the 2011–13 Arab Spring and the Syrian civil war echoed the "color revolutions" in focusing Russian attention on the threat of interventionism. For Putin, as for China's leaders, a multi-pronged threat was posed by the use of military power in Libya, the economic sanctions on both Syria and Iran beyond UN Security Council intentions, and "illegal soft power" under the guise of "humanitarianism." Commercial and political interests were at stake, but also in jeopardy were dimensions of national identity: the ideology of anti-hegemonism, the sectoral identity of cultural autonomy, and the link between the US factor and the international community on the horizontal dimension. China backed Russia on Syria at the UN Security Council, as Russia seconded China's approach to restarting the Six-Party Talks.

Stephen Blank aptly distinguishes between Russia's neoimperial objective of multipolarity and Russia's balancing China as well as the United States, leading to an illusion of "anchoring China" to Russia, with China's dismissive thinking about Eurasia as it presses for Russia to bandwagon with it.[46] The Chinese focus instead on a bipolar world, widening the notion of East as it extends to the South and also reaches Russia and targets the West.

In 2011, I wrote about the debate in China (visible in 2009) on national identity and regionalism, indicating that one school of thought fighting a rearguard action stuck to the centrism espoused by the Association of Southeast Asian Nations and multipolarity as the mainstream was pushing ahead toward a more polarized view, attacking US hegemonism fiercely.[47] In 2013, I published an article on the struggle to stick to multipolarity in Russia against pressures to conflate it with support for China in a revived Cold War atmosphere, noting three schools of thought: Cold War, multipolarity, and international community.[48] These articles show a contestation over both national identity and moves away from multipolarity in foreign policy. In China, the shift has been sharper, leading to more pressure on Russia to boost bilateral relations, even to the point of an alliance, while in Russia multipolarity stands as a more important symbol of national identity, as it is being assertively employed in opposition to such an alliance.

In the second half of 2013, debate about Sino-Russian relations grew much livelier. Major voices in China, such as academic Li Jingjie, insisted that all was on course. Skeptics, alert to new diplomacy in triangular contexts and even to growing bilateral concerns such as Chinese naval vessels in the Sea of Okhotsk and economic advances in Central Asia, argued that a downturn was approaching. Writers in China and especially in Russia were more candid about uncertainties in relations. The conclusion that relations were at a crossroads centered on the horizontal dimension was supported by articles in the journal *The Asan Forum*, especially the "Special Forum" in November 2013 and the "Country Report: Russia" as well as the "Country Report: China," each of which appears bimonthly.[49]

The Chinese and Russians are both accustomed to seeing the world in polarized terms. Not having been able to achieve their identity aspirations as part of the United States–led international community, they have joined together in a separate community. What was initially explained as essential to preserve a civilization under threat has turned into something more, as the Chinese aspire to the revival of what they call Eastern civilization and the Russians, who regard dependence on the West as the worst outcome, are enamored of the idea of a "double-headed eagle," as if the West gives them no choice or respect because it sees itself as the center of the world and rejects multipolarity or civilizational diversity.[50]

The gap on the horizontal dimension has been at 2 on the 1–5 scale, but it threatens to grow to 3. If the overall identity gap widens, this is likely to be the driving force. Different views on the future of regional identity in Asia may burst the bubble of identity overlap. Careful control over what each side says, requiring self-control on the Russian side, keeps the gap level down, but the potential is building for Eurasianism and Sinocentrism to eclipse East versus West and begin to widen not only policy differences across East, South, and Central Asia but also the horizontal identity gap as a whole.

THE OVERALL NATIONAL IDENTITY GAP IN THE 2010s

Adding the five estimates of gaps on separate dimensions of identity, I calculate that the composite identity gap between China and Russia is roughly 10 out of a possible 25, by adding the tally for each dimension, whose maximum could be 5. In comparison with China's gaps with the United States, Japan, and South Korea, this is a low tally. Russian concerns about China are stronger than Chinese concerns about Russia. Political elites in the two states are agreed in sustaining a narrow gap, sticking to an understanding reached in the 1990s. Through top-down control over the coverage of bilateral relations and events in the other country, they have shaped domestic opinion. Although there is some artificiality to this manipulated outcome, it has had staying power. This may be surprising to some because there is no warmth in bilateral relations. A narrow gap is an indicator of low consciousness of an identity divide, not of feelings of closeness. Continuity reflects the priorities of Xi and Putin and those around them, suggesting another decade of this situation if their overall thinking remains intact.

The similarities on each of the identity dimensions mean that the overall identity gap is not large, but the nature of the divide leaves relations unlikely to draw much closer and in a state of perpetual fragility. The primary source of volatility is Chinese impatience to affirm a close embrace in order to speed action against the United States and its allies in a dualistic view of the horizontal and sectoral dimensions, whereas Russia inclines toward a multipolar understanding of these dimensions. Despite the fact that both countries have territorial disputes with Japan, China's interest in making common cause and securing Russia's backing for its tougher posture was not supported. In August 2012, a visit by State Councillor Dai Bingguo to Russia saw deepening divisions over China's desire to secure clear backing for its new assertiveness on maritime issues. But instead of supporting China's "core interest" on the territorial dispute in the South China Sea, Russia has been strengthening its ties to Vietnam. Moreover, rather than joining the Chinese and Russian disputes with Japan over islands into a joint cause, Russia is encouraging talks with Japan that could lead to compromise on its dispute. The Chinese side showed impatience with Russia's failure to reciprocate its support on Syria. References to these and other tensions appear obliquely, as censorship remains strong.[51]

Sino-Russian relations may be warm on the outside, tepid on the inside, and chilly underneath. There is an understanding not only that dirty linen should not be displayed in public, but also that a shiny gloss covers any scuff marks in their relationship. China is especially known to bristle at critical public statements by Russian leaders. Moreover, Russia has appeared to need China more than China needs Russia; even as it has had increased cause to express concern, it is more obliged to stay mum. In bilateral meetings, however, the tone is understood to be contentious, with much less compensating trust than existed when US-Japanese tensions over trade in the 1980s and 1990s cast a shadow over some bilateral talks. These are more serious disputes. On both sides, internal assessments of the other side are more sober, underscoring distrust that the two sides are determined to conceal.

A sense of shared identity is strongest at the top, between high officials shaping both strategy and identity in the two countries. A sense of shared interests is strong at the lower level, where contacts occur, as economic self-interest operates, liberally sprinkled with side payments and boondoggle trips from the Chinese. The lower the level (apart from these interests), the weaker the sense of commonalities. Exacerbating this problem on the Russian side are diverse voices outside the official hierarchy that cast doubt on China. In contrast, on the Chinese side, more comprehensive censorship and effective propaganda have decreased distrust more among ordinary people. A decade of showcasing exchanges and cultural friendliness has had some impact in building a better foundation of trust in order for the identity gap to remain narrow in case of challenges to come, but it is easy to get the impression that China's patience comes with unstated warnings that if Russia crosses some red line, the national identity card would be played, and in Russia there is a fear that crossing China would be akin to a Sino-Soviet dispute.

China is in the driver's seat in this relationship, even more so after the global financial crisis of 2008–9 hit Russia harder. A breach with China would damage Russia more than it would damage China. We can expect China to keep handling Russia with care to avoid serious trouble and for Russia to keep stifling misgivings in order to seek an edge from its China ties available from no other state. This works if the focus stays on the US identity gap, but that may shift at some future time.

The two countries do not have a shared vision of their future partnership. For China, despite stress on relations between equals and separate spheres of influence, the aim is to increase integration on terms that give it a big edge. Aware that the Chinese see Russia through the prism of their country's imperialist past and are growing more assertive with increased power, the Russians are wary of becoming junior partners with little say. Despite these realities, Sino-Russian relations are closer now than they have been since the 1950s and more consequential for the international system.[52] Failing to notice the narrowing national identity gap between them, as if national interests and a lack of trust in business and personal interactions are determinative, leads to misleading conclusions.

National identity is a double-edged sword. On one hand, it has drawn China and Russia closer together since the mid-1990s. On the other hand, it keeps them from finding a sense of closeness, as cultural ties remain troubled. Neither side sees the other's identity as appealing, and awareness that cultural relations trail both political and economic relations is widespread. By avoiding discussions of the other side's domestic politics and other sensitive topics, national identity is kept in the shadows. Even cultural problems are raised gingerly, with no effort to assess their serious implications.

Relations between Moscow and Beijing have frequently been marked by stilted language and deliberate silence on critical points. Today is no exception. What is said or omitted in these relations is understood to be a function of constructing identity gaps. A palpable fear exists that once Pandora's box is open again, as it was more than fifty years ago, both sides have much to lose. It is better to avoid the slippery slope of letting a hidden identity gap come into the open than to even acknowledge the gap's existence.

All our dimensions of analysis point to a gap that is not very wide. Why, then, is there an unmistakable sense of fragility? Three factors are apparently operating. First, on the temporal dimension, the history of a strong Russia taking advantage of a humiliated China has explosive potential should China's leaders unleash these emotions, leaving the Russian Far East exposed. All other territorial disputes may seem minuscule if this one is let out of the bag. Second, as for the civilizational aspect of the sectoral dimension, which is in the forefront when these countries look to the West, not only is there no meeting of the minds; there is the prospect that the Russians epitomize the traditional "barbarians" from the North and that the Chinese epitomize the "horde" from the East. These images resurfaced during the Sino-Soviet dispute.

Third, insistence that the core national interests of the two countries are heavily overlapping obscures implicit awareness that the horizontal dimension of identity applied to vital locations where interests are supposedly shared, as in Central Asia, is not really in sync. Rhetoric on each side that conveys few clues about identity gaps matters in shaping public opinion, but it does not suffice to reveal the deep-seated presence of both troubling memories and a sense of fragility about how present arrangements can falter. On the Internet, the voices of discord in bilateral relations are more pronounced, showing that weak cultural ties and popular distrust pose a continued risk. Compounding the problems is the clash of Sinocentrism and Russocentrism.

PROSPECTS FOR FUTURE RELATIONS

The national identity gap between China and Russia is not large, but further narrowing is not likely. Driving much of China's thinking is the notion of a world bifurcated between East and West, a factor that contributed to the Sino-Soviet split. In contrast, driving Russia is a desire for Eurasianism as a third important civilization. In the 1960s, China could not accept a dichotomy with Moscow on top of the socialist camp; and in the 2010s, Russia is unlikely to accept one with Beijing on top of the Eastern camp. China is linking socialism and the East, but for Russia prospects are low of accepting a shift that subordinates it to China under either heading. In light of the existence of the East Asian National Identity Syndrome, discussed in the previous books in this series as a force that intensifies national identity and identity gaps with the West, the likelihood is a lack of restraint by China straining relations.

In the 1950s, Moscow sought to keep Beijing under control in its socialist bloc, but the terms proved unsatisfactory for Mao Zedong, especially after Nikita Khrushchev combined de-Stalinization with peaceful coexistence with the United States. In the 1980s, Beijing and Moscow groped for normalization, but Moscow was slow to abandon its military assertiveness near China's borders and Beijing waited in vain for a Soviet leader to balance the merits of "reform socialism" with an economic open door with firm central control over ideology. The coming decade may well see a third test of bilateral relations, in which a newly confident Beijing seeks to accelerate its rise as the world's second power by capitalizing on closer ties with Moscow, while Russia faces a crossroads of yielding or asserting itself in defiance of China.

A parallel exists between the Soviet Union in the late 1970s and China in the early 2010s. After encouraging cooperation with the United States amid reassurances to neighboring countries, both countries grew confident of their growing power and even contemptuous of others. Seeing the post-Watergate (in the 1970s) or post–global financial crisis (in the 2010s) US leadership as weak, they thought their time had come. When the United States appeared distracted during the Vietnam and Iraq wars, there was more talk of cooperation, but the turn in 1977 and 2009 to a more multilateral US approach seeking to build on this base was rebuked with accusations that anticommunism was making it more hostile. In its new assertiveness, Moscow not only alienated the West but also delayed what would have likely been a quick normalization of its relations with Beijing, whose three obstacles took a decade to resolve. Now, a third of a century later, China faces the danger of overreaching with Russia and undermining the narrowing gap achieved over two decades.

The debate on Sino-Russian relations intensified in 2013. In the span of one week, two well-placed academics, Zhao Huasheng and Yevgenyi Bazhanov, offered sobering advice in response to the debates in their country. Zhao's message is to avoid overconfidence in pressing for an alliance with Russia, arguing, among other reasons, that the Russia side is not so inclined and opposes being dragged into conflicts, such as with the United States and Japan. To those who insist that ties can be based on national interests, not emotions, Zhao responds that trust is essential and may be jeopardized by seeking to reach a new level in relations that are fragile to the degree that public suspicions on each side can be readily aroused against the other. What appears to be a convergence of thinking in most respects falls short when a closer look is taken.[53]

Bazhanov offers a mixed view of China, which seems to downplay concern for its rise, but actually is warning Russians about closer relations: "The instinct of greatness is again awakening in the Chinese and their self-confidence is growing." He sees this in cocky statements, such as that "no Russian politician will dare confront the People's Republic of China." Confident Chinese make assertions such as "in the twenty-first century the center of gravity in the world will shift to Asia, over which giant China will tower," Bazhanov argues, noting "discussion in China of Confucianism eventually sidelining all the other ideologies and becoming the guiding star of human development for the long-term future. It is asserted that only this ancient ideology is capable of saving humankind from 'technicalization' and moral degradation, from wars and religious and ethnic conflicts." "The growth of China's might and ambitions gives rise to fear in the world around it and, as a consequence, to calls for the Eastern dragon to be restrained. Such fears also exist in Russian society. Warnings are being heard about China gradually pushing Russia out of Central Asia, plundering our natural resources, surreptitiously carrying out a demographic expansion in the Russian Far East, and, after gaining enough strength, unleashing military aggression on Russia." Yet Bazhanov incongruously insists that to give vent to these concerns would irritate the Chinese, spoil relations, and prove harmful, because the "Chinese giant" is "our long-term reliable partner."[54] It is feeling mounting US pressure, it needs partners, and Russia is of like mind and is too weak to appear threatening. Given China's other frictions in Asia and domestic difficulties, it values a long, peaceful border. Moreover, in the face of US moves to slow China's rise, Russians will support it, he argues. The two economies are complementary, and Russia must cooperate with China to overcome its backwardness, especially in Siberia and the Russian Far East. Bazhanov notes that some Russians are calling for an alliance, as are some in China, especially military analysts, but China is not really prepared to face the United States in this manner, while Russia would be held hostage if, for example, China decides to start a war over Taiwan. An alliance, he adds, would lead to a third world war. Instead, Russia should work toward a multipolar world, he concludes, while it puts its own house in order to build a foundation for long-term cooperation and soft power to stop fearing the Chinese dragon. Left unsaid is why, if China's attitudes are those described early in the article, even this foundation will forestall an upsurge of alarm in Russia.

In earlier times, some in Moscow and Beijing had raised the specter of an alliance as a psychological buffer to counter perceived pressure from the United States. In 2013, this drive was more intense than before and was coming from both sides. Putin viewed Washington as the inspiration, if not the instigator, behind growing domestic opposition. He needed to widen the national identity gap to marginalize his critics, looking also to Beijing to strengthen his case. In turn, having stirred up security concerns along its maritime borders, Beijing decided to pretend that "unprovoked" Obama "rebalancing" to Asia posed a threat, which could be partially countered with stronger ties to Russia, including access to more advanced military technology and mutual support in case any of their territorial disputes with Japan should threaten to turn into war and US support for Japan was becoming a factor. Talk of an alliance reinforced extremists on both sides in the face of warnings from experts, and more moderate voices not caught up in the national identity fervor, that these problems were of the leaders' own doing and could be managed in a more pragmatic way.

CONCLUSION

In the second half of the 1990s, the case for a narrowing of the identity gap between China and Russia was controversial in light of the demagogic rhetoric of local leaders, such as Governor Evgeny Nazdratenko, and popular writers offering hyperbolic estimates of the number of Chinese illegally present in Russia.[55] Trade was stagnant, and trust was in short supply. In the mid-2000s, when Bobo Lo argued that relations were no more than an "axis of convenience," many in Russia still cast doubt on Russia's willingness to draw closer, while China's ties with the United States and neighboring states were taken as proof that it would not be inclined to demonize countries contributing the most to its goals of peace, stability, and prosperity.[56] Even in 2011, there were assessments that these states are only "pragmatic partners of convenience, but the foundation of the relationship is eroding."[57] Explaining this conclusion, Linda Jakobson and three coauthors argued that energy and security are the two bases of relations, but on both the foundation is eroding, while the worldviews of the two states are diverging. They added that mistrust is not diminishing. China perceives Russia as blinded by European civilization, and Russia sees China as an alien civilization. With this assessment, one gets the impression of antagonistic identities. Such doubts have persisted for two decades, even as relations have kept improving. They capture some misgivings, but they miss national identity forces.

Four developments gave new momentum to Sino–Russian relations over a twenty-year period. In the years 1994–96, the combination of Russia's frustrating war in Chechnya, which was marked in the West for its human rights abuses, and Taiwan's push for de jure independence, which received support in the United States that was offensive to China, led to a strategic partnership. In 1999, the United States–led NATO humanitarian war over Kosovo drove the two states closer together. Then the "color revolutions" in the years 2004–6, on the heels of the US invasion of Iraq, angered both states, fueling additional cooperation. In the years 2011–13, the Arab Spring added new impetus to the relationship. In each case, Russia soured on the West and was driven into China's arms. The principal dynamic has been China's appeal to Russia to show more solidarity, while Russia has been prone to anger at the West and to turn to China in order to express it. These developments showcase the horizontal dimension, on which there are also growing strains in the 2010s as China's assertiveness clashes with Russia's in areas of Asia.

To appreciate the force of national identity in bilateral relations, I have used the six-dimensional framework. On ideology, Putin and Xi are both vigorously boosting the legacy of socialism and anti-imperialism. This narrows the two nations' identity gap with each other. On history, criticism of past US behavior, especially in the Cold War, is intensifying even as mutual criticism is kept in check, driving the two states closer. On the sectoral dimension, civilizational arguments against the West only keep being strengthened, as the Arab Spring serves that end. On the vertical dimension, Putin and Xi are toughening their positions, widening the gap with the United States, not with each other. There has been no letup in demonizing US foreign policy, leaving little room to criticize the other country. Although national identity keeps intensifying, the case for Sino-Russian coordination is not being undermined.

The possibility of a wider identity gap may be seen most clearly through the lens of the horizontal dimension. Ultimately, however, the Communist Party's willingness to downplay its obsession with the ideological and temporal dimensions will provide proof of China's direction, and a renewed struggle in Russia over these two dimensions will offer evidence of its response. Multipolarity may loom as the next test for Russia, but it is only a stopgap in a deeper struggle over democracy, economic modernization, and multiculturalism—that is, vertical and sectoral dimension issues. Russian identity is likely to be tested by more signs of policies in distress.

The argument that Sino-Russian relations are driven by similar national interests has wide currency, but it is premised on a misleading interpretation of US policies and of international relations and mistaken views of what drives domestic and foreign policy in the two countries. It would be more accurate to conclude that there now exists strong correspondence in regime interests, which can be traced to fundamental similarities in the reconstruction of national identity in the two countries. The essence of the overlap is the existence of regimes fearful of values associated with the international community and beholden to the legacy of traditional communism, having the goal of changing the rules of the global system. They proceed to define "core national interests" in similar ways, scarcely obscuring the way these are skewed to serve one-sided national identities. In both cases, these are defined in opposition to US interests.

National interests matter. Russia's economic rise starting in 2000 depended heavily on China's demand for natural resources and a stable border. As the West floundered economically starting in 2008, China's economic value grew. In turn, China viewed Russia as an important economic partner and an essential force in gaining leverage over the United States. Yet, across subregions of Asia and in national security, national interests are clashing more and more. This is clearest of all in Central Asia, but it also applies to India, Japan, Vietnam, and other states in Asia.

While national interests increasingly diverge, the overlap in national identities keeps growing. As proof of its autonomy from Western civilization led by the United States and to give credibility to an identity linked within Asia, Russia needs to associate itself with China's identity. This also validates its vertical identity resistant to civil society and its Cold War memories of opposition to the West. For nearly two decades Russia has buttressed Chinese arguments of multipolarity and of the lack of universality of Western civilization—which was seen as Russia's undoing in the 1990s, but from which Russia extricated itself to China's great satisfaction.

National interests point to poles in search of a balance of power, while national identities prioritize civilizations, validating a country's past and present distinctiveness. The Chinese have made a stronger case for the latter, seeking confirmation as superior to others for recent achievements and in justifying Confucianism and Sinocentrism for their lasting merit. The Russian case rests, even more heavily, on the legacy of traditional communism, fueling the need to narrow the identity gap with China. Yet the more fragile Russian national identity raises the prospect that this overlap will not be sustained. Just as Soviet identity could not be reconciled with Mao's notion of China's identity despite the overlap in communism, Chinese and Russian identities in our times, however narrow the gap along many dimensions, cannot forge the kind of solid linkages that the United States achieves with most of its allies. There is an inherent limit to Sino-Russian identity ties. In recognizing this, however, one should be wary of concluding that in the coming period, as Putin and Xi strive to solidify the legitimacy of their ruling group, the narrow identity gap between their countries will not persist for a time as a force in world affairs.

Lest readers attribute to the post–Cold War trend in national identities and its links to the communist era some lasting destiny for China and Russia, I want to make it clear that the Communist Great Power (Transition 1) National Identity Syndrome, or CGP (T1) NIS, is a transitional phenomenon, predictable from the legacy present in the 1990s to the 2010s, but not beyond change in a later period. Whatever that change may be, it cannot ignore what exists. The next transition must wrestle with a new legacy. In turn, the national identity gap will depend on transitions in both states, even as it starts with the foundation that leaves Sino-Russian relations drawing closer in the 2010s in an international environment boosting overlapping narratives. If Sinocentrism and Russocentrism become ever more central to national identity, as appeared likely by 2013–14 and may be seen as a natural outgrowth of the T1 process, then the parallel trends in identity that caused a narrowing in the identity gap may have the adverse, secondary effect of driving the gap to widen in the coming T2 stage.

NOTES

INTRODUCTION

1. See issues 1, 2, 3, and 4 of *The Asan Forum* (www.theasanforum.org), the journal I am editing.
2. These volumes are Gilbert Rozman, ed., *East Asian National Identities: Common Roots and Chinese Exceptionalism* (Washington, DC, and Stanford, CA: Woodrow Wilson Center Press and Stanford University Press, 2012); and Gilbert Rozman, ed., *National Identities and Bilateral Relations: Widening Gaps in East Asia and Chinese Demonization of the United States* (Washington, DC, and Stanford, CA: Woodrow Wilson Center Press and Stanford University Press, 2013).
3. *New York Times*, January 4, 2012.
4. *New York Times*, January 19, 2012.
5. Sergei Karaganov, "Why Do We Need National Identity?," June 9, 2013, available at adminvaldaiclub.com.
6. Fyodor Lukyanov, "A Country for People," May 9, 2013, available at adminvaldaiclub.com.
7. "Brezhnev Beats Lenin as Russia's Favorite Twentieth-Century Ruler," *RIA Novosti*, May 22, 2013.
8. *New York Times*, May 15, 2013.
9. Gilbert Rozman, ed., *The East Asian Region: Confucian Heritage and Its Modern Adaptation* (Princeton, NJ: Princeton University Press, 1991).
10. "Move to Shore Up 'Cultural Security,'" *South China Morning Post*, October 19, 2011.
11. "President of Russia: Meeting with Public Representatives on Patriotic Education for Young People," Kremlin.ru Archive, Sept. 12, 2012.
12. Murong Xuecun, "Chinese Internet: 'A New Censorship Campaign Has Commenced,'" *Guardian*, May 15, 2013.
13. Yekaterina Kravtsova, "Debate Rages Over State History Textbooks," *Moscow Times*, April 26, 2013.
14. Song Lubang, "Zhi you chu Zhongguo zaineng kandao weilai: Zhongguo zheng yinglai zixin shidai," *Qiushi*, no. 9 (May 1, 2013).

15. Anne L. Clunan, *The Social Construction of Russia's Resurgence: Aspirations, Identity, and Security Interests* (Baltimore: Johns Hopkins University Press, 2009).

16. Gilbert Rozman, "Theories of Modernization and Theories of Revolution: China and Russia," in *Zhongguo xiandaihua lunwenji*, ed. Zhongyang yanjiuyuan jindaishi yanjiusuo (Taipei, 1991), 633–46.

17. A. Buznev, *What Is Capitalism?* (Moscow: Progress Publishers, 1987).

18. F. M. Burlatskii, *Lenin, gosudarstvo, politika* (Moscow, 1970).

19. Zheng Wang, *Never Forget National Humiliation: Historical Memory in Chinese Politics and Foreign Relations* (New York: Columbia University Press, 2012).

20. *New York Times*, August 20, 2013.

CHAPTER 1

1. John W. Dardess, *Confucianism and Autocracy: Professional Elites in the Founding of the Ming Dynasty* (Berkeley: University of California Press, 1983), 288–89; F. W. Mote, *Imperial China, 900–1800* (Cambridge, MA: Harvard University Press, 1999), 948.

2. Geoffrey Hosking, *The First Socialist Society: A History of the Soviet Union from Within* (Cambridge, MA: Harvard University Press, 1993), 17, 34.

3. Richard Pipes, *Russian Conservatism and Its Critics: A Study in Political Culture* (New Haven, CT: Yale University Press, 2005).

4. Charles O. Hucker, *The Traditional Chinese State in Ming Times (1368–1644)* (Tucson: University of Arizona Press, 1961), 62–66.

5. Gilbert Rozman, ed., *The East Asian Region: Confucian Heritage and Its Modern Adaptation* (Princeton, NJ: Princeton University Press, 1991).

6. Fung Yu-Lan, *A Short History of Chinese Philosophy* (New York: Macmillan, 1962).

7. Zheng Wang, *Never Forget National Humiliation: Historical Memory in Chinese Politics and Foreign Relations* (New York: Columbia University Press, 2012), 44, 72–73.

8. Robert Legvold, "Russian Foreign Policy during Periods of Great State Transformation," in *Russian Foreign Policy: The 21st Century and the Shadow of the Past*, ed. Robert Legvold (New York: Columbia University Press, 2007), 80–81, 86–87.

9. Ibid., 109.

10. James H. Billington, *The Icon and the Axe: An Interpretive History of Russian Culture* (New York: Vintage Books, 1970), 303.

11. James H. Billington, *Russia in Search of Itself* (Washington, DC, and Baltimore: Woodrow Wilson Center Press and Johns Hopkins University Press, 2004), 2–5.

12. Ibid., 19.

13. Ibid., 30–31.

14. Ibid., 33–34.

15. James P. Scanlan, "The Russian Idea from Dostoevskii to Ziuganov," *Problems of Post-Communism* (July–August 1996): 35–42.

16. Teodor Shanin, *Russia as a "Developing Society": The Roots of Otherness—Russia's Turn of Century, Vol. 1* (New Haven, CT: Yale University Press, 1985).

17. Nicholas Riasanovsky, *Nicholas I and Official Nationality in Russia, 1825–1855* (Berkeley: University of California Press, 1969), 103.

18. J. R. Levenson, "'History' and 'Value': The Tensions of Intellectual Choice in Modern China," in *Studies in Chinese Thought*, ed. Arthur F. Wright (Chicago: University of Chicago Press, 1953), 146–94.

19. Marie-Claire Bergère, *The Golden Age of the Chinese Bourgeoisie 1911–1937* (Cambridge: Cambridge University Press, 1989), 259–60, 268, 286.

20. Astrid S. Tuminez, *Russian Nationalism since 1856: Ideology and the Making of Foreign Policy* (Lanham, MD: Rowman & Littlefield, 2000), 6–7, 39–42, 99, 226.

21. Robert C. Tucker, *Political Culture and Leadership in Soviet Russia: From Lenin to Gorbachev* (New York: W. W. Norton, 1987).

22. Suisheng Zhao, *A Nation-State by Construction: Dynamics of Modern Chinese Nationalism* (Stanford, CA: Stanford University Press, 2004), 28, 239.

23. Tim McDaniel, *The Agony of the Russian Idea* (Princeton, NJ: Princeton University Press, 1996), 86–105.

24. David Brandenberger, *National Bolshevism: Stalinist Mass Culture and the Formation of Modern Russian National Identity, 1931–1956* (Cambridge, MA: Harvard University Press, 2002), 5–15, 183–225.

25. Frederick C. Teiwes, "The Establishment and Consolidation of the New Regime," in *The Politics of China*, 2nd ed., ed. Roderick MacFarquhar (Cambridge: Cambridge University Press, 1997), 16–18, 69–81.

26. Sheila Fitzpatrick, "The Problem of Class Identity in NEP Society," in *Russia in the Era of NEP: Explorations in Soviet Society and Culture*, ed. Sheila Fitzpatrick et al. (Bloomington: Indiana University Press, 1991), 12–33.

27. Benjamin I. Schwartz, *Communism and China: Ideology in Flux* (New York: Atheneum, 1970), 20.

28. Roy Medvedev, *Let History Judge: The Origins and Consequences of Stalinism* (New York: Columbia University Press, 1989), 808–15.

29. Franz Schurmann, *Ideology and Organization in Communist China* (Berkeley: University of California Press, 1968), 32–35.

30. Graeme Gill, *Symbols and Legitimacy in Soviet Politics* (Cambridge: Cambridge University Press, 2011), 4–5.

31. Stephen Kotkin, *Magnetic Mountain: Stalinism as a Civilization* (Berkeley: University of California Press, 1995), 11–14, 357.

32. *Workers, Peasants and Soldiers Criticize Lin Piao and Confucius* (Beijing: Foreign Languages Press, 1976), i; O. Borisov, "The 20th CPSU Congress and Some Problems of Studying the History of China," *Far Eastern Affairs*, no. 4 (1981): 1, 4.

33. Yuri Slezkine, "USSR as a Communal Apartment: USSR and Ethnic Particularism 1920s–30s," *Slavic Review* 53, no. 2 (1994): 414–52.

34. Dmitry Gorenburg, "Soviet Nationalities Policy and Assimilation," in *Rebounding Identities: The Politics of Identity in Russia and Ukraine*, ed. Dominique Arel and Blair A. Ruble (Washington, DC, and Baltimore: Woodrow Wilson Center Press and Johns Hopkins University Press, 2006), 273–303.

35. Hadley Cantril, *Soviet Leaders and Mastery over Man* (New Brunswick, NJ: Rutgers University Press, 1960).

36. Vera S. Dunham, *In Stalin's Time: Middleclass Values in Soviet Fiction* (Cambridge: Cambridge University Press 1976).

37. William Parish and Martin King Whyte, *Village and Family in Contemporary China* (Chicago: University of Chicago Press, 1978).

38. Gill, *Symbols*, 123.

39. Sheila Fitzpatrick, "Cultural Revolution as Class War," in *Cultural Revolution in Russia, 1928–1931*, ed. Sheila Fitzpatrick (Bloomington: Indiana University Press, 1978), 40.

40. Jeffrey Brooks, *Thank You, Comrade Stalin! Soviet Public Culture from Revolution to Cold War* (Princeton, NJ: Princeton University Press, 2000), 238, 246.

41. Shiping Hua, *Chinese Utopianism: A Comparative Study of Reformist Thought with Japan and Russia, 1898–1997* (Washington, DC, and Stanford, CA: Woodrow Wilson Center Press and Stanford University Press, 2009).

CHAPTER 2

1. Richard Baum, *Burying Mao: Chinese Policy in the Age of Deng Xiaoping* (Princeton, NJ: Princeton University Press, 1994), 374–75.

2. David Shambaugh, *China's Communist Party: Atrophy and Adaptation* (Washington, DC, and Berkeley: Woodrow Wilson Center Press and University of California Press, 2008), 42–63.

3. *Sovetskaia Rossia*, March 13, 1988.

4. *Izvestiia*, April 6, 1988.

5. Gilbert Rozman, *A Mirror for Socialism: Soviet Criticisms of China* (Princeton, NJ: Princeton University Press, 1985).

6. Nan Li, "From Revolutionary Internationalism to Conservative Nationalism: The Chinese Military's Discourse on National Security and Identity in the Post-Mao Era," *Peaceworks* (US Institute of Peace) 39 (2001).

7. H. Lyman Miller, *Science and Dissent in Post-Mao China: The Politics of Knowledge* (Seattle: University of Washington Press, 1996), 49–50, 166, 245–47, 275–83.

8. Archie Brown, *The Gorbachev Factor* (Oxford: Oxford University Press, 1997), 219–24.

9. Wu Yufeng, "Cong shijie jingji jiaodu kan woguo de duiwai kaifang zhengce," *Shijie jingji yu zhengzhi neican*, no. 5 (1985): 1–7.

10. Nina Tumarkin, *The Living and the Dead: The Rise and Fall of the Cult of World War II in Russia* (New York: Basic Books, 1994), 50, 196–209, 225.

11. Edward X. Gu, "Cult Intellects and the Politics of the Cult Public Space in Communist China (1979–1989): A Case Study of Three Intellectual Groups," *Journal of Asian Studies* 58, no. 2 (May 1999): 426–28.

12. *Literaturnaia gazeta*, July 2, 1986; *Sovetskaia kul'tura*, March 17, 1987.

13. Francis Fukuyama, "Varieties of Russian Nationalism," in *The Collapse of Marxism*, ed. John H. Moore (Fairfax, VA: George Mason University Press, 1994), 44–50.

14. Yin Shuhui, "Confucianism and Modern Societies in East Asia," *Social Sciences in China* (Summer 1992): 178–80.

15. Yitzhak M. Brudny, *Reinventing Russia: Russian Nationalism and the Soviet State* (Cambridge, MA: Harvard University Press, 1998), 9, 17, 70–73, 92–94, 110–28.

16. Xu Wenci, "Sulian de jieti yu rendao de minzhu de shehuizhuyi de pochan," *Sulian wenti yanjiu ciliao*, no. 4 (1992): 6–10.

17. *Heilongjiang ribao*, February 14, 1993.

18. George W. Breslauer, "In Defense of Sovietology," *Post-Soviet Affairs* 8, no. 3 (1992): 222–24.

19. James R. Millar, "The Little Deal: Brezhnev's Contribution to Acquisitive Socialism," in *Soviet Society and Culture: Essays in Honor of Vera S. Dunham*, ed. Terry L. Thompson and Richard Sheldon (Boulder, CO: Westview Press, 1988), 3–19.

20. Linda J. Cook, *The Soviet Social Contract and Why It Failed: Welfare Policy and Workers' Politics from Brezhnev to Yeltsin* (Cambridge, MA: Harvard University Press, 1993).

21. Fukuyama, "Varieties," 42–43.

22. Tim Oakes, "China's Provincial Identities: Reviving Regionalism and Reinventing 'Chineseness,'" *Journal of Asian Studies* 59, no. 3 (August 2000): 667–92.

23. *Heilongjiang ribao*, February 17, 1993.

24. *Argumenty i fakty*, March 21–27, 1987.

25. Matthew J. Ouimet, *The Rise and Fall of the Brezhnev Doctrine in Soviet Foreign Policy* (Chapel Hill: University of North Carolina Press, 2003), 60–72.

26. Harry Gelman, *The Brezhnev Politburo and the Decline of Détente* (Ithaca, NY: Cornell University Press, 1984), 160.

27. Robert Legvold, "Introduction," in *Russian Foreign Policy: The 21st Century and the Shadow of the Past*, ed. Robert Legvold (New York: Columbia University Press, 2007), 18.

28. Ronald Grigor Suny, "Living in the Hood: Russia, Empire, and Old and New Neighbors," in *Russian Foreign Policy*, ed. Legvold, 65.

29. Robert D. English, *Russia and the Idea of the West: Gorbachev, Intellectuals, and the End of the Cold War* (New York: Columbia University Press, 2000), 9–11.

30. Ibid., 210.

CHAPTER 3

1. Angela Stent, "Reluctant Europeans: Three Centuries of Russian Ambivalence toward the West," in *Russian Foreign Policy: The 21st Century and the Shadow of the Past*, ed. Robert Legvold (New York: Columbia University Press, 2007), 393–441.
2. *Moskovskie novosti*, June 24, 1990.
3. *Sovetskaia Rossiia*, June 21, 1990.
4. Roy D. Laird, *The Soviet Legacy* (Westport, CT: Praeger, 1993), 13, 16.
5. James H. Billington, *Russia in Search of Itself* (Washington, DC, and Baltimore: Woodrow Wilson Center Press and Johns Hopkins University Press, 2004), 44, 48.
6. Ibid., 51, 70, 74, 77.
7. Anders Åslund, "Russia Gets on Track to Be a Normal Country," *International Herald Tribune*, March 19, 1997.
8. Wayne Allensworth, "Derzhavnost: Aleksandr Lebed's Vision for Russia," *Problems of Post-Communism* 45, no. 2 (March–April 1998): 51-58.
9. Vladimir Brovkin, "The Emperor's New Clothes: Continuity of Soviet Political Culture in Contemporary Russia," *Problems of Post-Communism* 43, no. 2 (March–April 1996): 25.
10. V. A. Kolosov, "Traditsionnye geopoliticheskie kontseptsii i sovremennye vyzovy Rossii," in *Regional'naia struktura Rossii v geopoliticheskoi i tsivilizatsionnoi dinamike* (Ekaterinburg: Ural'skoe otedelenie Institut istorii i arkheologii, 1995), 86.
11. James Clay Moltz, "Commonwealth Economics in Perspective: Lessons from the East Asian Model," *Soviet Economy* 7, no. 4 (1991): 342–63.
12. Fiona Hill and Clifford G. Gaddy, "Putin and the Uses of History," *The National Interest*, January 4, 2012.
13. *Sankei shimbun*, August 25, 2007.
14. Thomas Sherlock, "Confronting the Stalinist Past: The Politics of Memory in Russia," *Washington Quarterly* (Spring 2011): 93–109.
15. Andrei P. Tsygankov, "The Irony of Western Ideas in a Multicultural World: Russians' Intellectual Engagement with the 'End of History' and 'Clash of Civilizations,'" *International Studies Review* (2003): 53–76.
16. Catherine Wanner and Mark D. Steinberg, "Introduction: Reclaiming the Sacred after Communism," in *Religion, Morality, and Community in Post-Soviet Societies*, ed. Mark D. Steinberg and Catherine Wanner (Washington, D.C., and Bloomington: Woodrow Wilson Center Press and Indiana University Press, 2008), 1–20.
17. V. N. Il'in, *Manifest Russkoi tsivilizatsii* (Moscow: Knizhnyi dom Librokom, 2013).
18. Olga Troitskaya, "Nationalism Debate Has Become More Civilized," *Moscow Times*, February 1, 2012.
19. Alexander Dugin, "Eurasian Union Proposal Key Aspect of Putin's Expected Presidency," *Stratfor.com*, October 6, 2011.
20. *RIA Novosti*, January 16, 2012.

21. Andrei Sinyavsky, *The Russian Intelligentsia* (New York: Columbia University Press, 1997), 3–6.

22. Grigorii Minenkov, "Politika identichnosti dlia postsovetskogo prostranstva: Vvedenie v problematiki," *Perekrestki*, nos. 1–2 (2009): 5–21.

23. Alan Wood, "Siberian Regionalism Resurgent?" *Sibirica* 1, no. 1 (1993–94): 71–86.

24. Elise Giuliano, "Theorizing Nationalist Separatism in Russia," in *Rebounding Identities: The Politics of Identity in Russia and Ukraine*, ed. Dominique Arel and Blair A. Ruble (Washington, DC, and Baltimore: Woodrow Wilson Center Press and Johns Hopkins University Press, 2006), 33–61.

25. Rolf H. W. Theen, "Quo Vadis, Russia? The Problem of National Identity," in *State-Building in Russia: The Yeltsin Legacy and the Challenge of the Future*, ed. Gordon B. Smith (Armonk, NY: M. E. Sharpe, 1999), 43–45.

26. Theen, "Quo Vadis, Russia?"

27. Donna Bahry, "Society Transformed? Rethinking the Social Roots of Perestroika," *Slavic Review* 52, no. 3 (Fall 1993): 512–54.

28. *RIA Novosti*, January 16, 2012.

29. "Prime Minister Vladimir Putin Takes Part in the Conference of the United Russia Party," *Pravitel'stvo Rossiiskoi Federatsii*, November 28, 2011.

30. "Medvedev Urges Russians to Back Ruling Party in Parliamentary Polls," *Rossiya 24*, BBC Monitoring, November 27, 2011.

31. "Establishment of Eurasian Union Will Be President Putin's First Geopolitical Priority," *Kommersant*, October 5, 2011.

32. Dmitry Trenin, "Revising the Concept of Eurasia," Valdai Discussion Club, February 5, 2013.

33. Marlene Laruelle, *Russian Eurasianism: An Ideology of Empire* (Washington, DC, and Baltimore: Woodrow Wilson Center Press and Johns Hopkins University Press, 2008).

34. B. P. Kozlovskii and P. V. Lukin, "Ot aktivnosti k effektivnosti," *Rossiia v global'noi politike*, June 30, 2012.

35. V. I. Franchuk, "O vozmozhnoi globaliziriushchei roli Rossii v mirovom razvitii," in *Tsentr problemnogo analiza i gosudarstvenno-upravlencheskogo proektirovaniia, National'naia identichnost' Rossii i demograficheskii krizis*, 349–52.

36. Dominique Arel, "Introduction: Theorizing the Politics of Cultural Identities in Russia and Ukraine," in *Rebounding Identities*, ed. Arel and Ruble, 1–30.

37. Mikhail A. Alekseev, *Immigration Phobia and the Security Dilemma: Russia, Europe, and the United States* (Cambridge: Cambridge University Press, 2006), 14–39.

38. "Transcript: [Putin] Visit to Russia Today Television Channel," *Johnson's Russia List*, June 11, 2013, http://russialist.org/transcript-putin-visit-to-russia-today -television-channel.

39. V. A. Avksen'tev and M. E. Popov, "Transformatsiia Rossiiskoi identichnosti v kontektse natsional'noi i regional'noi bezopastnosti," in *Tsentr problemnogo analiza i gosudarstvenno-upravlencheskogo proektirovaniia, National'naia identichnost' Rossii i demograficheskii krizis*, 360–63.

40. Marlene Laruelle, "Rethinking Russian Nationalism: Historical Continuity, Political Diversity, and Doctrinal Fragmentation," in *Russian Nationalism and the National Reassertion of Russia*, ed. Marlene Laruelle (Routledge, 2009).

41. Marlene Laruelle, *In the Name of the Nation: Nationalism and Politics in Contemporary Russia* (New York: Palgrave Macmillan, 2009), 2–17.

42. Aleksandr Lukin, "Russia's New Authoritarianism and the Post-Soviet Political Ideal" *Post-Soviet Affairs* 25, no. 1 (2009): 56–92.

43. Igor' Chubais, *Rossiiskaia ideia: Stanovlenie i istoriia, razryv i vozrozhdenie, Rossievedenie, ili teoriia Rossii* (Moscow: Izdatel'skii tsentr "Akva-Term," 2012).

44. A. V. Lukin and P. V. Lukin, "Mify o Rossiiskoi politicheskoi kul'ture i Rossiiskaia istoriia," *Polis: politicheskaia issledovaniia*, no. 1 (2009): 56–70.

45. K. G. Kholodkovskii, "Problemy i protivorechiia Rosssiiskoi identichnosti," in *Identichnost' i sotsial'no-politicheskie izmeneniia v XXI veke, Vol. 2*, ed. I. S. Semenenko (Moscow: Rosspen, 2012), 243.

46. V. A. Tishkov, *Rossiiskii narod: Istoriia i smysl national'nogo samosoznaniia* (Moscow: Nauka, 2013).

CHAPTER 4

1. Yan Xuetong, Yu Xiaoqiu, and Tao Jian, "Dangqian woguo mianlin de tiaozhan he renwu," *Shijie jingji yu zhengzhi* (April 1993): 20–26.

2. *Renmin ribao*, November 4, 1992.

3. Wang Haihan, "The Current Situation and Future Prospect of Sino-U.S. Relations," *International Studies*, nos. 12–13 (1998): 1–6.

4. Zhang Chengfu, "Shenfen rentong yu Zhongguo waijiao," *Changchun gongye daxue xuebao (shehui kexue ban)*, 21, no. 1 (January 2009): 40–42.

5. James Reilly, *Strong Society, Strong State: The Rise of Public Opinion in China's Japan Policy* (New York: Columbia University Press, 2012).

6. Hosaka Masayasu and Togo Kazuhiko, *Nihon no ryodo mondai: Hoppo yonto, Takeshima, Sentaku shoto* (Tokyo: Kadokawa, 2012), 138.

7. Gilbert Rozman, "Chinese National Identity and Its Implications for International Relations in East Asia," *Asia-Pacific Review* 18, no. 1 (2011): 84–97; Gilbert Rozman, "History as an Arena of Sino-Korean Conflict and the Role of the United States," *Asian Perspective* 36, no. 2 (Spring 2012): 287–308.

8. Wang Jisi, "China's Search for a Grand Strategy," *Foreign Affairs* 90, no. 2 (March–April 2011).

9. Gilbert Rozman, "East Asian Regionalism and Sinocentrism," *Japanese Journal of Political Science* 13, no. 1 (March 2012): 143–53.

10. Geremie R. Barme, ed., *China Yearbook 2012: Red Rising, Red Eclipse* (Canberra: College of Asia and the Pacific of Australian National University, 2012), 31, 65, 132.

11. Kato Yoichi, "Interview / Wang Jisi: China Deserves More Respect as a First-Class Power," *Asahi shimbun*, October 5, 2012.

12. Feng Chen, "Rebuilding the Party's Normative Authority: China's Socialist Spiritual Civilization Campaign," *Problems of Post-Communism* 45, no. 6 (November–December 1998): 33–41.

13. Zhu Qi, "Renzhi gongtong liyi shi Zhongmei guanxi fazhan de guanjian: Zhongmei jianjiao 30 zhounian huigu," *Shijie jingji yu zhengzhi*, no. 11 (2009).

14. Xu Hui, "Zhongmei junshi huxin weihe nanyi jianli?," *Waijiao pinglun*, no. 2 (2010): 22–29.

15. Anne-Marie Brady, "State Confucianism, Chineseness, and Tradition in CCP Propaganda," in *China's Thought Management*, ed. Anne-Marie Brady (New York: Routledge, 2012), 57–71.

16. Zhaohui Hong and Yi Sun, "In Search of Re-ideologization and Social Order," in *Dilemmas of Reform in Jiang Zemin's China*, ed. Andrew J. Nathan et al. (Boulder, CO: Lynne Rienner, 1999), 33–50.

17. "Sulian jingji tizhi gaige shilun," in *Eluosi Zhongya Dongou yanjiu*, ed. Xing Guangsheng (Hong Kong, 2008), 91–94.

18. "More Party Influence in Higher Education Institutions Urged," Xinhuanet, June 20, 2012.

19. Zheng Wang, *Never Forget National Humiliation: Historical Memory in Chinese Politics and Foreign Relations* (New York: Columbia University Press, 2012), 86–113.

20. Ibid., 240–41.

21. *Waiguo wenti yanjiu*, no. 2 (1992).

22. Jing Haifeng, "Guoxue yu dangdai Zhongguo wenhua," *Hebei xuekan* 3, no. 2 (March 2010): 132–37.

23. Nicolai Volland, "From Reform to Management: The CCP's Reforms of the Cultural Structure," in *China's Thought Management*, ed. Brady, 112–13.

24. Peter Mattis, "Shoring Up PLA Military Cultural Security to Ensure Stability," *China Brief* 12, no. 14 (July 19, 2012).

25. Endo Hamare, "Kokka no meiun o toketa Chugoku no 'bunka taisei kaikaku,'" *Chuo koron* (January 2012): 124–31.

26. "Netizen Voices: Blasting the People's Daily," *China Digital News*, August 10, 2012.

27. Barry Wellman, Wenhong Chen, and Dong Weizhen, "Networking Guanxi," in *Social Connections in China*, ed. Thomas Gold, Doug Guthries, and David Wank (Cambridge: Cambridge University Press, 2002), 238.

28. "2003 nian de Zhongguo waijiao," *Shijie xingshi yanjiu*, nos. 51 and 52 (December 24, 2003): 2–3.

29. William A. Callahan, "Introduction: Tradition, Modernity, and Foreign Policy in China," in *China Orders the World: Normative Soft Power and Foreign Policy*, ed. William A. Callahan and Elena Barabantseva (Washington, DC, and Baltimore: Woodrow Wilson Center Press and Johns Hopkins University Press, 2011), 2–7.

30. Gong Keyu, "Zhongguo zai Chaoxian wenti shang de guojia liyi, zuoyong he qianzhanxing sikao," *Guoji guancha*, no. 5 (2008): 59–65.

31. Zhu Tingchang, "Lun Zhongguo zai Yatai diqu de quyi zhongxin diwei," *Shijiie jingji yu zhengzhi*, no. 1 (2010): 76–82; Zhao Yan, "Hexie lilun yu Zhongguo heping jueqi," *Shehui congheng*, no. 4 (2009): 5–8.

32. Tang Shanlin, "Meiguo dui Zhongguo jueqi de renzhi, duice ji Zhongguo de yingdui" *Shijie jingji yu zhengzhi*, no. 3 (2010): 30–38.

33. William A. Callahan, "Conclusion: World Harmony or Harmonizing the World?," in *China Orders the World*, ed. Callahan and Barabantseva, 249–64.

34. Kenneth Lieberthal and Wang Jisi, *Assessing U.S.-China Strategic Distrust*, John L. Thornton China Center Monograph 4 (Washington, DC: Brookings Institution, 2012).

35. Zhou Ping, "Lun Zhongguo de guojia rentong jianshe," *Xueshu tansuo*, no. 6 (2009): 35–40.

36. David Shambaugh, *China's Communist Party: Atrophy and Adaptation* (Washington, DC, and Berkeley: Woodrow Wilson Center Press and University of California Press, 2008), 104–27.

37. Chen Jianjun, "Lun 'quanxu rentong' dui Zhongguo waijiao lilun yu shijian de yingxiang," *Shijie zhengzhi yu jingji*, no. 12 (2009): 47–57.

38. John Pomfret, "China's Strident Tone Raises Concerns among Western Governments, Analysts," *Washington Post*, January 31, 2010.

39. Hu Jintao, "Meiyou wenhua anquan jiu meiyou guojia anquan," *Qiushi*, January 4, 2012.

40. Wang Yi, "Exploring the Path of Major Country Diplomacy with Chinese Characteristics," Remarks at the Second World Peace Forum, June 27, 2013, www.fmprc.gov.cn/eng/zxxx/t1053908.shtml.

41. See news.xinhuanet.com/world/2013-08/01/c.

CHAPTER 5

1. Robert D. English, *Russia and the Idea of the West: Gorbachev, Intellectuals, and the End of the Cold War* (New York: Columbia University Press, 2000), 31–51.

2. Ivo Mijnssen, "The Victory Myth and Russia's Identity," *Russian Analytical Digest* 72, no. 10 (February 9, 2010).

3. Pan Zhongyi and Huang Renwei, "Zhongguo de diyuan wenhua zhanlue," *Xiandai guoji guanxi*, no. 1 (2008): 24–29.

4. Russell Leigh Moses, "Protests and China's Party Cadre Problem," *Wall Street Journal*, July 5, 2012.

5. Willy Lam, "Premier Wen's 'Southern Tour': Ideological Rifts in the CCP," *China Brief* 10, no. 18 (September 10, 2010).

6. "China Hails Ties with New Friend," *Asia Times*, December 30, 1996.
7. Duan Gang, "Diguo siwei yu hexie shijie goujian," *Jiangsu xingzheng xueyuan xuebao*, no. 4 (2008): 74–80.

CHAPTER 6

1. Mark Mancall, *Russia and China: Their Diplomatic Relations to 1728* (Cambridge, MA: Harvard University Press, 1971), 3.
2. Alexander Lukin, *The Bear Watches the Dragon: Russia's Perceptions of China and the Evolution of Russian-Chinese Relations since the Eighteenth Century* (Armonk, NY: M. E. Sharpe, 2003).
3. S. C. M. Paine, *Imperial Rivals: China, Russia, and Their Disputed Frontier* (Armonk, NY: M. E. Sharpe, 1996), 343–51.
4. Alexander Lukin, "Russia's Image of China and Russian-Chinese Relations," *East Asia*, Spring 1999, 6–7.
5. Allen S. Whiting, *Soviet Policies in China, 1917–1924* (Stanford, CA: Stanford University Press, 1968), 252–58.
6. C. Martin Wilbur and Julie Lien-ying How, *Missionaries of Revolution: Soviet Advisers and Nationalist China, 1920–1927* (Cambridge, MA: Harvard University Press, 1989), 12.
7. John W. Garver, *Chinese-Soviet Relations 1937–1945: The Diplomacy of Chinese Nationalism* (Oxford: Oxford University Press, 1988), 79, 245, 260, 273–74.
8. Yang Kuisong, "Sidalin weishenme zhichi Chaoxian zhanzheng—Du Shen Zhihua zhu 'Sidalin Mao Zedong yu Chaoxian zhanzheng," *Ershiyi shiji*, February 2004.
9. Roderick MacFarquhar, *The Origins of the Cultural Revolution, Volume 2: The Great Leap Forward 1958–1960* (New York: Columbia University Press, 1974), 8–18, 263–74.
10. Chen Jian, *Mao's China and the Cold War* (Chapel Hill: University of North Carolina Press, 2001), 63–67, 84.
11. R. K. I. Quested, *Sino-Russian Relations: A Short History* (Sydney: George Allen & Unwin, 1984), 122–31.
12. Ted Hopf, "Identity Relations and the Sino-Soviet Split," in *Measuring Identity: A Guide for Social Scientists*, ed. Rawi Abdelal, Yoshiko M. Herrera, Alastair Iain Johnston, and Rose McDermott (Cambridge: Cambridge University Press, 2009), 279–315.
13. Lorenz M. Lüthi, *The Sino-Soviet Split: Cold War in the Communist World* (Princeton, NJ: Princeton University Press, 2008), 46–64.
14. Chen Jian and Yang Kuisong, "Chinese Politics and the Collapse of the Sino-Soviet Alliance," in *Brothers in Arms: The Rise and Fall of the Sino-Soviet Alliance, 1945–1963*, ed. Odd Arne Westad (Washington, DC, and Stanford, CA: Woodrow Wilson Center Press and Stanford University Press, 1998), 277.

15. William E. Griffith, *Sino-Soviet Relations, 1964–1965* (Cambridge, MA: MIT Press, 1967).

16. Harry Schwartz, *Tsars, Mandarins, and Commissars: A History of Chinese-Russian Relations* (Garden City, NY: Anchor Press, 1973), 154.

17. Sergey Radchenko, *Two Suns in the Heavens: the Sino-Soviet Struggle for Supremacy, 1962–1967* (Washington, DC, and Stanford, CA: Woodrow Wilson Center Press and Stanford University Press, 2009).

18. Keesing's Research Report, *The Sino-Soviet Dispute* (New York: Scribner, 1969), 103–7.

19. Radchenko, *Two Suns*.

20. Lukin, *The Bear Watches the Dragon*, 144–53.

21. "A New Attempt to Canonize Maoism," *Far Eastern Affairs*, no. 4 (1981): 80–91.

22. Gilbert Rozman, *The Chinese Debate about Soviet Socialism, 1978–1985* (Princeton, NJ: Princeton University Press, 1987), 84–85.

23. Ibid., 88–97.

24. Ibid., 109–40.

25. Hu Sheng, "Why Cannot China Turn Capitalist?," *Far Eastern Affairs*, no. 6 (1987): 90–102.

26. M. Kapitsa, "Problems of Peace and Security in the Far East," *Far Eastern Affairs*, no. 6 (1987): 3–13.

27. Gilbert Rozman, *A Mirror for Socialism: Soviet Criticisms of China* (Princeton, NJ: Princeton University Press, 1985).

28. *Pravda*, August 12, 1988.

29. Yan Sun, *The Chinese Reassessment of Socialism, 1976–1992* (Princeton, NJ: Princeton University Press, 1995), 240–57.

30. Ge Linsheng, "Sulian pengkui yuanyin pouxi," *Shijie jingji qingkuang* (June 15, 1992): 8–13.

31. Yan Sun, *Chinese Reassessment*, 7, 18.

32. Rozman, *Chinese Debate*, 74–80.

33. Ibid., 104–17.

34. Yan Sun, *Chinese Reassessment*, 59-83.

35. Gilbert Rozman, "China's Concurrent Debate about the Gorbachev Era," in *China Learns from the Soviet Union, 1949–Present*, ed. Thomas P. Bernstein and Hua-Yu Li (Lanham, MD: Lexington Books, 2010), 453–65.

36. Elizabeth Wishnick, *Mending Fences: The Evolution of Moscow's China Policy from Brezhnev to Yeltsin* (Seattle: University of Washington Press, 2001), 1, 7.

37. David Shambaugh, *China's Communist Party: Atrophy and Adaptation* (Washington, DC, and Berkeley: Woodrow Wilson Center Press and University of California Press, 2008), 56.

38. Rozman, *Chinese Debate*, 99.

39. Li Jingjie, "Xin shiqi de Zhonge guanxi," *Dongou Zhongya yanjiu*, no. 1 (1994): 8–17.

40. "Analysis: Twenty Years On, Chinese Media Reflect on Soviet Collapse," BBC Monitoring, December 29, 2011.
41. Rozman, *Mirror for Socialism*, 265–68.

CHAPTER 7

1. Gilbert Rozman, "China, Japan, and the Post-Soviet Upheaval: Global Opportunities and Regional Risks," in *The International Dimension of Post-Communist Transitions in Russia and the New States of Eurasia*, ed. Karen Dawisha (Armonk, NY: M. E. Sharpe, 1997), 147–76.
2. Michael E. Marti, *China and the Legacy of Deng Xiaoping: From Communist Revolution to Capitalist Evolution* (Washington, DC: Brassey's, 2002).
3. Gilbert Rozman, "Sino-Russian Relations in the 1990s: A Balance Sheet," *Post-Soviet Affairs* 14, no. 2 (Spring 1998): 93n113.
4. Gilbert Rozman, "The Crisis of the Russian Far East: Who Is to Blame?," *Problems of Post-Communism* 44, no. 5 (September–October 1997): 3–12.
5. Gilbert Rozman, "Sino-Russian Mutual Assessments," in *Rapprochement or Rivalry? Russia-China Relations in a Changing Asia*, ed. Sherman Garnett (Armonk, NY: M. E. Sharpe, 2000), 147–74.
6. Zhao Huasheng, "'Zhonge jiemeng' weihe quefa," *Renmin luntan*, July 24, 2013; Yevgenyi Bazhanov, "Do Not Fear Chinese Dragon," *Nezavisimaia gazeta*, August 2, 2013.
7. See www.cbsnews.com/8301-250_162-5759783, August 9, 2013; *New York Times*, August 20, 2013.
8. Anne L. Clunan, *The Social Construction of Russia's Resurgence: Aspirations, Identity, and Security Interests* (Baltimore: Johns Hopkins University Press, 2009), 81.
9. Gilbert Rozman, "China's Quest for Great Power Identity," *Orbis* 43, no. 3 (Summer 1999): 383–402.
10. Valerii Sharov, "Kitaiskaia karta," *Literaturnaia gazeta*, October 27, 1993, 13.
11. Yang Yunzhong, "Zouxiang 21 shiji de Zhong, Mei, Ri, E, siguo zhanlue guanxi," *Taipingyang xuebao*, no. 2 (1997): 47–49.
12. Marlene Laruelle, *In the Name of the Nation: Nationalism and Politics in Contemporary Russia* (New York: Palgrave Macmillan, 2009), 122–30.
13. Vladislav Zubok and Erik Shiraev, *Anti-Americanism in Russia: From Stalin to Putin* (New York: Palgrave, 2000).
14. Alexander Lukin, "Russia's Image of China and Russian-China Relations," *East Asia*, Spring 1999, 34–35.
15. Alexei Bogaturov, "Russia's Strategic Thought toward Asia: The Early Yeltsin Years (1991–1995)," in *Russian Strategic Thought toward Asia*, ed. Gilbert Rozman, Kazuhiko Togo, and Joseph P. Ferguson (New York: Palgrave Macmillan, 2006), 57–74.

16. Shelley Rigger, "The Taiwan Issue and the Sino-Russian Strategic Partnership: The View from Beijing," in *The Future of China-Russian Relations*, ed. James Bellacqua (Lexington: University of Kentucky Press, 2010), 312–32.

17. Aleksei Voskresenskii, "Veter s zapada ili veter s Vostoka," *Svobodnaia mysl'*, no. 10 (1996): 89–100.

18. L. P. Deliusin, "Sindrom 'veroiatnogo protivnika': Kto i pochemu presdstavliaet Kitai kak ugrozu Rossii," *Literaturnaia gazeta*, May 1, 1996.

19. Chen Peiyao, "Lengzhanhou woguo guoji huanjing chuxi," *Shijie jingji yu zhengzhi*, no. 3 (1994): 1.

20. Cou Shengli, "Diyuan wenming shijiaoxia de Zhonge guanxi," *Xiboliya yanjiu*, no. 6 (2010): 92–93.

21. Gilbert Rozman, *Chinese Strategic Thought toward Asia* (New York: Palgrave Macmillan, 2010), 133–53.

22. "Materialy Rossiisko-Kitaiskoi nauchnoi konferentsii, posviashchennoi 55-letiu ustanovleniia diplomaticheskikh otnoshenii, Beijing, September 9–10, 2004," *Jinri Eluosi*, special edition, October 8, 2010.

23. A. V. Lukin, "Vvodnoe slovo," in *Rossiisko-Kitaiskoe sotrudnichestvo: Problemy i resheniia*, ed. A. V. Lukin (Moscow: MGIMO, 2006), 12–13.

24. M. L. Titarenko, "Moshchnyi Kitai: ugroza, vyzov ili shans dlia Rossii?" in *Rossiisko-Kitaiskoe sotrudnichestvo*, ed. Lukin, 21–25.

25. Gilbert Rozman, "Review Article: Russian Perceptions of Sino-Russian Relations," *Asan Forum*, issue 1 (July–August 2013).

26. "Zhonge zhanlue huoban guanxi shifou fasheng bianhua?" *Zhongguo guoqing diaocha neican: guoji*, no. 3 (2003): 4–6.

27. Qin Minggui, "Zhonge guanxi wending fazhan de yinian," *Ouya shehui fazhan yanjiu*, no. 2 (2004): 1–2.

28. Rex Li, *A Rising China and Security in East Asia: Identity Construction and Security Discourse* (London: Routledge, 2009), 153–59.

29. Andrew Kuchins, "Russian Perspectives on China: Strategic Ambivalence," in *Future of China-Russian Relations*, ed. Bellacqua, 33–55.

30. A. Lukin, *Kitaiskie reformy i Rossiia*, vol. 1 (Moscow: RAN, 2000), 59.

31. Lin Yongtao, "Jiangou anquan weixie: Meiguo zhanlue de zhengzhi xuanze," *Shijie jingji yu zhengzhi*, no. 6 (2010): 128–28.

32. Jiang Weigong, "Gaojuli yanjiu chubian," in *Jingji wenhua jiaoyu xueke jianshe congshu*, ed. Jiang Weigong (Changchun: Jilin daxue chubanshe, 2005), 1–2.

33. H. G. Kozin, *Rossiia chto eto? V poiskakh identifiktsinonnykh sushchnostei* (Moscow: Akademicheskii proekt, 2012), 134.

34. A. Lukin, *Kitaiskie reformy i Rossiia*, vol. 2 (Moscow: RAN, 2000), 345–53.

35. Mikhail A. Alekseev, "Migration, Hostility, and Ethnopolitical Mobilization: Russia's Anti-Chinese Legacies in Formation," in *Rebounding Identities: The Politics of Identity in Russia and Ukraine*, ed. Dominique Arel and Blair A. Ruble (Washington, DC, and Baltimore: Woodrow Wilson Center Press and Johns Hopkins University Press, 2006), 116–47.

36. M. L. Titarenko, *Rossiia i Vostochnaia Azii: Voprosy mezhdunarodnykh i mezhtsivilizatsionnykh otnoshenii* (Moscow: POO "Fabula" 'Kuchkovo pole, 1994), 29, 99, 154.

37. Chang Qing, "Yi Xinjiang he Zhongya weili kan guoqing bianhua dui kuajing minzu de yingxiang," *Guoji guancha*, no. 6 (1998): 50–52.

38. Rozman, "China's Quest."

39. Li, *Rising China*, 34–37, 146–53.

40. Stephen Aris, *Eurasian Regionalism: The Shanghai Cooperation Organization* (New York: Palgrave Macmillan, 2011), 27, 38–46, 60–62.

41. Yang Xiqian, "Eluosi zai Zhongya mianlin duofang tiaozhan," *Jinri Dongou Zhongya*, no. 5 (1997): 4.

42. Aleksandr Lukin, "Tsena voprosa," *Kommersant*, October 21, 2011.

43. "The Beijing Project," *Argumenti nedeli*, June 28, 2012.

44. Zhou Xiaopei, "China-Russia Relations: Retrospect and Prospect," *Foreign Affairs Journal* (Spring 2009): 39–48.

45. Tang Yanlin, "Meiguo dui Zhongguo jueqi de renzhi, duice, ji Zhongguo de yingdui," *Shijie jingji yu zhengzhi*, no. 3 (2010): 39–45.

46. Stephen Blank, "A (Multi) Polar Bear? Russia's Bid for Influence in Asia," *Global Asia* 7, no. 2 (Summer 2012): 23–27.

47. Gilbert Rozman, "Chinese Strategic Thinking on Multilateral Regional Security in Northeast Asia," *Orbis* 55, no. 2 (Spring 2011): 296–311; Gilbert Rozman, "Chinese National Identity and Its Implications for International Relations in East Asia," *Asia-Pacific Review* 18, no. 1 (2011): 84–97.

48. Gilbert Rozman, "Russian Perceptions of Sino-Russian Relations: A Review Article on A. V. Lukin, ed., *Rossiia i Kitaia: Chetyre veka vzaimodeistviia— istoriia, sovremennoe sostoianie i perspektivy razvitiia Rossiisko-Kitaiskikh otnosheniii* (Moscow, Ves' mir, 2013)," *Asan Forum*, http://www.theasanforum.org/russian -perceptions-of-sino-russian-relations/.

49. See *Asan Forum* (www.theasanforum.org), issues 1, 2, and 3, 2013.

50. V. P. Lukin and A. I. Utkin, *Rossiia i Zapad: Obshchnost' ili otchuzhdenie* (Moscow: Sampo, 1995).

51. Sun Ying, "Once Warm Sino-Soviet Relationship Can Be Revived," *Global Times*, August 22, 2012; M. K. Bhadrakumar, "Calling the China-Russia Split Isn't Heresy," *Asia Times*, September 5, 2012.

52. Gilbert Rozman, "The Sino-Russian Strategic Partnership: How Close? Where To?," in *Future of China-Russian Relations*, ed. Bellacqua, 13–32.

53. Zhao Huasheng, "'Zhonge jiemeng' weihe quefa xianshi kexingxing," *Renmin luntan*, July 24, 2013.

54. Yevgenyi Bazhanov, "Do Not Fear Chinese Dragon," *Nezavisimaia gazeta*, August 2, 2013.

55. Garnett, *Rapprochement or Rivalry?*

56. Bobo Lo, *Axis of Convenience: Moscow, Beijing, and the New Geopolitics* (Washington, DC: Brookings Institution Press, 2008).

57. Linda Jakobson, Paul Holtom, Dean Knox, and Jingchao Peng, *China's Energy and Security Relations with Russia: Hopes, Frustrations, and Uncertainties*, SIPRI Policy Paper 29 (Stockholm: Stockholm International Peace Research Institute, 2011).

INDEX